SECOND EDITION

CASE STUDIES IN HEALTH CARE SUPERVISION

Charles R. McConnell, MBA, CM
Human Resources and
Health Care Management Consultant
Ontario, New York

JONES AND BARTLETT PUBLISHERS
Sudbury, Massachusetts
BOSTON TORONTO LONDON SINGAPORE

World Headquarters
Jones and Bartlett Publishers
40 Tall Pine Drive
Sudbury, MA 01776
978-443-5000
info@jbpub.com
www.jbpub.com

Jones and Bartlett Publishers Canada
6339 Ormindale Way
Mississauga, Ontario L5V 1J2
Canada

Jones and Bartlett Publishers International
Barb House, Barb Mews
London W6 7PA
United Kingdom

Jones and Bartlett's books and products are available through most bookstores and online booksellers. To contact Jones and Bartlett Publishers directly, call 800-832-0034, fax 978-443-8000, or visit our website, www.jbpub.com.

Substantial discounts on bulk quantities of Jones and Bartlett's publications are available to corporations, professional associations, and other qualified organizations. For details and specific discount information, contact the special sales department at Jones and Bartlett via the above contact information or send an email to specialsales@jbpub.com.

Production Credits
Publisher: Michael Brown
Editorial Assistant: Catie Heverling
Editorial Assistant: Teresa Reilly
Senior Production Editor: Tracey Chapman
Senior Marketing Manager: Sophie Fleck
Manufacturing and Inventory Control Supervisor: Amy Bacus
Composition: DSCS/Absolute Service, Inc.
Cover Design: Kristin E. Parker
Cover Image: © Sebastian Kaulitzki/Dreamstime.com; © Terry Chan/ShutterStock, Inc.; © Daemys/ShutterStock, Inc.; © 3d_kot/ShutterStock, Inc.; © monarx3d/ShutterStock, Inc.
Printing and Binding: Malloy, Inc.
Cover Printing: Malloy, Inc.

Library of Congress Cataloging-in-Publication Data
McConnell, Charles R.
Case studies in health care supervision / by Charles R. McConnell. — 2nd ed.
p. ; cm.
Includes bibliographical references and index.
ISBN-13: 978-0-7637-6619-1 (pbk.)
ISBN-10: 0-7637-6619-4 (pbk.)
1. Health facilities—Personnel management—Case studies. I. Title.
[DNLM: 1. Health Facility Administrators—organization & administration. 2. Health Services Administration. 3. Personnel Management—methods. 4. Problems and Exercises. WX 18.2 M478c 2009]
RA971.35.M276 2009
362.1068'3—dc22

6048 2009026089

Printed in the United States of America
13 12 11 10 09 10 9 8 7 6 5 4 3 2 1

TABLE OF CONTENTS

PREFACE

This volume is a collection of case studies intended for use in both the initial training and continuing education of supervisors and middle managers in healthcare organizations.

This is a second edition, considerably expanded from the first edition, *Case Studies in Health Care Supervision* (Aspen Publishers, Inc., 1998). The number of case studies has been increased from 75 to 100, and every effort has been made to ensure that these cases are relevant to managers in today's healthcare organizations. Also incorporated are a few of the more useful and timeless elements presented in *The Health Care Supervisor's Casebook* (Aspen Systems Corporation, 1982).

This book, usable as a free-standing educational resource in its own right, can also readily serve as a supplement and companion volume to *The Effective Health Care Supervisor* and *Umiker's Management Skills for the New Health Care Supervisor*, as well as complementing other instructional and self-learning resources. Suitable for classroom use as well as for self-study, it is backed up with additional material and test questions for instructional use.

All of the case studies presented in this collection have been used in training situations, some of them many times over. Some, in fact, were developed with the active participation of session attendees who contributed stories of their own for class consideration. Time and again these case studies have proven their worth. More important, however, is the fact that all of these case studies were taken from real situations; these are not exercises in "what if this happens." Rather, these did indeed happen. For obvious reasons they have been thoroughly fictionalized as far as the names of people and organizations are concerned, and all other potentially identifying circumstances have been altered. However, in each instance the essence of what occurred has been preserved. In most instances these little problem tales have been simplified from the real circumstances, with extraneous detail peeled away to reveal a single issue or cohesive set of issues that can stand alone. The key to the value of these case studies lies in the appreciation of the fact that each of these situations actually happened to someone; these are all real problems experienced by working supervisors and managers.

We can go just so far in studying theories and absorbing rules and principles. It is true that we can never completely erase the boundary between the academic and the practical, can never entirely close the gap between theory and practice. However, the use of real-world situations in case-study fashion can go a long way toward helping to bridge that gap.

About the Author

Charles R. McConnell, MBA, CM is an independent healthcare management and human resources consultant and freelance writer specializing in business, management, human resources, and healthcare topics. For 11 years he was active as a management engineering consultant with the Management and Planning Services (MAPS) division of the Hospital Association of New York State (HANYS) and later spent 18 years as a hospital human resources officer. As author, coauthor, and anthology editor he has published 26 books and has contributed about 450 articles to various publications. He is in his 28th year as editor of the quarterly professional journal *The Health Care Manager*.

Cases numbered 1–75 are from the first edition of this book under the original title *Case Studies in Health Care Supervision* (Aspen Publishers, Inc., 1998).

The following cases first appeared in the journal *The Health Care Manager* (Lippincott Williams and Wilkins). Most of these have been partially altered for use herein. Used with permission of the publisher.

#76 "An Expensive Game" Issue 20:1, pp. 37–39

#77 "The Reclassification Request" Issue 21:2, pp. 17–19

#78 "Seeking the Limits" Issue 24:4, pp. 347–348

#79 "A Peer Problem" Issue 21:1, pp. 62–63

#87 "She's Having a Rough Time" Issue 22:2, 113–114

#88 "Discharge for Cause" Issue 22:4, pp. 331–333

#89 "The Demanding Manager" Issue 23:1, pp. 22–23

#90 "The Uncooperative Colleague" Issue 23:2, 128–129

#91 "The Informant" Issue 23:3, pp. 235–236

#92 "Managing the Drama Queen" Issue 23:4. pp. 318–319

#93 "The Holliday Switch" Issue 24:1, pp. 29–30

#94 "The Elusive Employee" Issue 24:2, pp. 129–130

#95 "This Place Owes Me" Issue 24:3, pp. 225–226

Case #85, "The Management Expert," first appeared in *Management Principles for Health Professionals, 5th Edition* (Joan G. Leibler and Charles R. McConnell), Jones & Bartlett Publishers, 2008, pp. 406–408.

Case #86, "No Longer Pulling Her Weight," first appeared in *Umiker's Management Skills for the New Health Care Supervisor, 5th Edition* (Charles R. McConnell), Jones & Bartlett Publishers, 2010, pp. 509–510.

Case #96, "He Didn't Work Out," first appeared in *Umiker's Management Skills for the New Health Care Supervisor, 5th Edition* (Charles R. McConnell), Jones & Bartlett Publishers, 2010, pp. 104–106.

Case #100, "Promotion," first appeared in *The Effective Health Care Supervisor, 6th Edition* (Charles R. McConnell), Jones & Bartlett Publishers, 2007, p. 185.

Remaining case studies are new with this edition.

C. R. McConnell

October 2009

Part I

Introduction

CHAPTER 1

THIS BOOK AND HOW TO USE IT

WHY THIS BOOK?

This volume is a collection of case studies intended for use in the training and continuing education of supervisors, managers, and professionals working in health care or preparing for careers in health care. It is intended to serve as a guide for supervisory and management development programs and as a useful resource for a number of other educational activities.

It may also serve as a companion volume to *The Effective Health Care Supervisor* in that it can be used to supplement the cases and other activities provided in that publication.

For the most part, the case studies, which comprise the largest part of the book's contents, were developed from the experiences of managers actively employed in healthcare settings. Numerous questions, problems, frustrations, suggestions, and experiences—both positive and negative—originating with working supervisors and middle managers became the material for the cases and other activities. In many instances real situations were simplified for the purpose of encouraging users of the book to focus on specific problems or practices, but most of the cases are based on one or more actual situations. In all instances, however, the names of people, places, and organizations are fictional.

USING THIS BOOK

Individual Study

This volume can be used for a variety of purposes, including self-study, individual continuing education, and instruction in classroom situations. All of the cases can be considered in their entirety by an individual working alone; one need only select a topic of interest and look up one or more related cases. Also, the cases provide plenty of material for productive discussion by groups.

Assume, for example, that you face a problem dealing with the management of change and that this problem raises some questions about resistance to change. Look up *change* in either the index, case listing, or both.

You need only select a topic, look up pertinent references, and consider the information at your own pace. You may not immediately locate specific answers; however, by considering the cases related to your topic you will broaden your perspective, and the process of doing so may well provide the thought starter you need to solve your problem. Or perhaps the cases will help to define your problem more clearly, thus assisting you in determining where you should seek a specific solution.

It is recommended that in most instances you refrain from going directly to the case responses. Rather, take some time to think your problem through to one or more potential solutions before accessing someone else's thoughts on the matter. Keep in mind that the response provided for any particular case is not the only one available, and that there may be a number of possible "correct" responses to many of the cases.

As compared with the straightforward textbook approach, this volume furnishes the "problems at the end of the chapter" without providing the chapter. Or, when used in conjunction with a book on the order of *The Effective Health Care Supervisor*, this volume provides extra end-of-chapter problems.

One approach you might want to consider is to first wrestle with a problem of interest and later analyze your solution. Again, assuming your interest is change management, you might look up a single case about change that appears to contain some of the elements in which you are interested. Study the chosen case and develop the best possible solution under the circumstances. Then turn to another source, perhaps a chapter dealing with employee resistance to change, and see how well your solution aligns with theory and principles. If your solution seems to fit—that is, if it seems consistent with theory and principle and a published solution—pat yourself on the back. If it seems as though you went astray of the fundamentals, try another case about change—and another, and another, if necessary—until you can see that the principles of change management are reflected in your solution.

Alternatively, simply use this volume as a topic reference. You will rarely find specific answers, but you will often find in the cases and their responses the seeds of the solution to your problem.

Small-Group Activity

A particular hospital department manager made it a practice of getting together once each week with four supervisors who reported to him. They met on the same day each week in a quiet conference room and considered, informally, a case study chosen the previous week. This had been the department head's idea, but participation was optional. Each supervisor took the case of the week, analyzed it, and developed a tentative solution expressed in a paragraph or two. Over lunch the group discussed five solutions—the department head participated as well—and developed a single solution agreeable to all five participants. The five managers took turns selecting the problem that would become case for the following week. More often than not, the cases came from problems encountered in their own departmental units.

This volume can be used in the same fashion, as material for small-group management development activity. The setting could be as simple as someone's office, and the time could perhaps be taken during a meeting of the department's management staff.

Many managers make it a practice to use a portion of each regularly scheduled staff meeting for continuing education purposes. A single case can be ideal material for such an educational session. For a group of people informally pursuing a case each time they get together, this book can stimulate productive discussions for many months.

Supervisory or Management Development Classes

Depending on how supervisory or management development classes are structured, this book may be used as either a primary reference or a supplement to other material. It would be most appropriately used to back up a basic healthcare management text or other instructor-provided material. Cases help bring a topic to life by moving it out of the realm of pure recitation of principles and putting it into a form in which the principles are seen in simulated action. Any topic presented in the classroom setting will be all the livelier for having its principles illustrated by one or two case studies. Use this volume, then, as a source of material to stimulate discussion after lectures or other straightforward informational presentation.

ONE MORE TRAINING TOOL

No single reference is going to provide everything you need for supervisory or management training. Similarly, no single approach to education, including the case-study approach, serves all purposes or fills all needs.

Any educational activity should employ a mix of available resources and materials. Even independent self-study is aided by the use of multiple viewpoints on the same topics and the presentation of the same principles in a variety of forms and guises. In addition to providing a range of perspectives on a topic, presentation variety also helps to sustain interest and involvement. Even a lone supervisor independently pursuing knowledge of, for example, delegation, might consider using:

- A chapter about delegation from a basic book about healthcare management
- Several journal articles about delegation
- Two or three delegation cases from this book
- A video or audio presentation about delegation

Independent study is always beneficial; as in any other educational activity, you get out of it what you put into it—and a truly motivated independent learner can accomplish a great deal. However, a group activity offers the special advantages of shared insight, shared opinion, more and broader perspectives, and new ideas that are generated as participants' comments stimulate the thoughts and further comments of others. The dynamics of the situation usually assure that the educational accomplishments of the group are greater than the direct sum of the contributions of its individual members.

In any group training activity, it is important to employ a considerable mix of training approaches and instructional media. We have long accepted lectures supported by information on chalkboards, flipcharts, slides, and transparencies. Although we remember only a small portion of what we simply hear, we are likely to recall a larger portion of what we see, and a still larger portion of what we both see and hear at the same time. Thus, a few simple visual aids to support a lecture increase the listeners' chances of retaining the material.

Likewise, training aids such as videos, audiotapes, exercises, games, and case studies are helpful when used with each other and with other forms of presentation in a healthy balance. However, no single form of instruction can be employed by itself for long periods of time. Who wants to sit through 2 hours of lecture without a single break in pace or manner of presentation? Who can get a great deal out of a class that consists entirely of a 1-hour video? (The problems associated with video or film presentations are pertinent to many who manage in health care. Management training usually takes place during or after working hours on at least normally hectic days, and for many folks the darkened room and prolonged drone of a narrator are invitations to dreamland.)

These days, many high-quality educational programs are available on video, but all such presentations have their limitations. Even the most carefully packaged material raises legitimate questions, but there is no opportunity to discuss anything with a digital video disk.

An intelligent approach to management and supervisory development suggests that a mix of media and methods may be used to best effect in approaching a topic from numerous angles and sustaining interest through variety of presentation. However, given the reality of many training budgets, it may not always be possible to acquire packaged presentations when they are wanted. But it is usually possible to support oral instruction with chalkboards, flipcharts, overhead transparencies, and PowerPoint slides while keeping straight lecture to a tolerable minimum by using group activities such as question-and-answer sessions, learning games, exercises, role plays, and case studies.

The case study method of learning is valuable. It is especially helpful in that it often stimulates further learning. However, it remains just one of the training tools available to be used in combination with others for maximum effect.

THE CASE STUDY APPROACH: USE AND VALUE

As you work your way through *The Health Care Manager's Casebook,* it will often seem to you that there are few absolute, specific solutions to the cases. In fact, the frequent presence of numerous implications and a variety of potential solutions is why group effort can be especially productive in working with cases.

It should be stressed that the case responses included in this volume are not the only valid responses that could be offered. In each instance the response is well considered, the product of the thinking of one or more persons who have given the matter serious consideration. However, with case studies of this nature, as with the actual day-to-day problems of management, we are at work in a realm in which few absolute answers are possible.

Many problems may be legitimately solved in different ways, depending on differences in the people involved and organizational policies, philosophies of operation, and the environments in which the situations occur. Most of the cases involve relations among people, and we should all be well aware than any so-called rules for dealing with people are riddled with exceptions.

In some of the cases, certain management fundamentals or basic principles, such as fair and equal treatment of employees, may be self-evident. Also, in some instances, what is "right" or "wrong" may be obvious. However, many supposed solutions to case studies develop along lines such as, "What might happen if I do this?" or, "I'll take this particular action," and "If this particular result occurs, I'll then try this other possible step." Or simply, "This might work; it seems fair and it makes sense."

It should be evident to most working managers that there are few fixed solutions to many management problems. Frustrating as it seems, the correct solution to a given problem involving one employee may not be correct if a different employee is involved. If you have a dozen employees in your group, you may find that on any given day there are as many as 12 "right" ways of addressing a particular issue. Conscientious managers strive to be consistent in their application of principles and their treatment of employees as individuals. However, the employees of a department are often anything but consistent in their responses to the manager's actions.

In management development activities, case studies can help bridge the ever present gap between theory and practice. Recognize, however, that in matters of actual practice a case is but a simulation because it does not involve real people; and in this dimension is found the case-study method's one significant weakness.

THE LONE SHORTCOMING

Compare a case study in which you must decide upon the extent of disciplinary action for an employee with a working situation in which you must actually discipline an employee. Compare also your preparation for a theoretical confrontation with an intimidating higher manager with an actual confrontation with a higher-up who comes across as stern and domineering. Or think about developing on paper the manner in which you would approach a critical performance evaluation with actually giving someone a critical face-to-face evaluation.

Chances are that in each of the foregoing comparisons you have few, if any, reservations about the first part: deciding how you might discipline a *hypothetical* employee, preparing for a confrontation with the boss that *will not really happen*, or writing a sample critical evaluation that *you will never deliver*. However, actually disciplining an employee, actually facing an intimidating boss, or doing a real-life critical evaluation all have in common a dimension that you can never experience with a case study. It is a dimension you sometimes even feel physically, perhaps in the pit of your stomach or in other physiological ways. This is, of course, a reference to the manager's emotional involvement, that which the manager experiences by having a personal stake in the problem. This shortcoming is common to a great deal of training of various kinds; learning is not the same as doing, and make-believe doing is nowhere near the same as really doing.

The single shortcoming of the case study method is that it lacks the actual emotional involvement that a manager experiences with a real problem. Nevertheless, the case study represents a giant step away from theory and toward matters of practice. A primary purpose of the case method is to encourage the development and exploration of alternatives. The primary benefits of the case study method lie not in the identification of specific answers, but in the development of insights and the simulated application of principles.

CHAPTER 2

THE MANAGER AND THE TASK

FITTING THE MANAGEMENT ROLE

Basic Qualifications

Not every person is likely to fit appropriately into every job. Many jobs cannot be considered because an individual may not possess its basic qualifications. However, even qualifying for a position provides no guarantee that a person is going to fit in and ultimately succeed. In addition to technical qualifications are the intangible qualifications not met by credentials or work experience, but rather by aspects of personality and temperament.

Technical qualifications are generally easy to identify and understand. They might include so many years of schooling of a certain kind, a required degree or certificate, a specific license or registration, or a specified number of years of experience doing a particular kind of work. By and large, technical qualifications are tangible and objectively measurable.

In addition to bringing technical qualifications to the job, every employee also brings a unique set of personality characteristics, inherent capabilities, and personal preferences. Everything that makes the individual unique merges with that person's technical qualifications to form the unique employee, the worker who is likely to be better suited for some kinds of work than others, and who is certain to enjoy certain kinds of tasks more than others.

The manager can be described as requiring three kinds of qualifications. Two are the technical and personal qualifications already described. The third, wedged between the other two, might be described as *management qualifications*, or the technical qualifications of management, as opposed to the technical qualifications of the manager's basic field. For example, a nursing manager would be expected to have a specified academic background, a nursing license, and a certain number of years of nursing experience (technical qualifications); some facility for managing people, whether through education or experience (management qualifications); and the temperament to function as a manager (personal qualifications).

Not all persons who work as managers are equally good at all parts of the job; and certainly not all managers enjoy all parts of the management job equally.

Education in the "Middle" Qualifications

Of course, it is the qualifications of management that are being addressed in this presentation of the case study method of education.

A manager is least likely to fail through the lack of straight technical qualifications. In fact, the normal process for acquiring managers usually ensures that no one enters a management role without having met the technical qualifications of the job.

A manager may succeed shiningly or fail miserably or any gradation between for reasons of temperament—that is, because of personal qualifications. Some people who possess natural leadership abilities and by nature deal effectively with people perform outstandingly right from the start. Some individuals are suited to management and some are not.

Many people who do not fit well into the management role either voluntarily abandon it or fail. Others who may not fit the role especially well nevertheless remain managers, with widely varying degrees of success. It is likely that perfect-fit managers are the minority of the management population of any organization, so it is up to each manager who sincerely wishes to remain one to be conscious of personal weaknesses and compensate for them or otherwise work around them.

The person who is temperamentally suited to management and has the requisite technical qualifications must then be continually concerned with obtaining—and retaining—management qualifications. Case studies developed from actual work situations represent one versatile and highly useful means of supporting continuing education in the qualifications of management.

A Few Pertinent Questions

If you are considering your own suitability for management within health care, you would do well to ponder the following questions and develop the most honest answers you can. Then use your answers, as necessary, to help determine the direction of your continuing education in management.

Can I cope with a pace that is often hectic, and can I accept problem after problem as a daily way of life? To a considerable extent, the manager, especially the supervisor or first-line manager, is a frustration fighter. Much energy is demanded by emergencies, unanticipated problems, and a sometimes steady stream of interruptions.

Do I have the ability to see each employee as a whole person and not simply as a producer of output? A manager's willingness and ability to adopt a people-centered focus in part determines how well that manager fits into the healthcare work force.

Am I willing to work in one of the most regulated industries in the country? Much of what is done in the management of a healthcare organization is done because federal, state, and local governments so dictate. It is essential that the manager be able to recognize the reality of regulation and decide to do the best possible job within the restrictions posed by countless rules.

Am I able to cope with rapid change? Our general base of knowledge is expanding at an alarming rate, and in few areas is the expansion more evident than in health care as medical technology advances and medical knowledge proliferates. Also, the environment in which the healthcare organization operates is changing at least as rapidly as medicine itself as new approaches to the provision of and payment for medical care emerge and organizations continue to be swept up in the growing wave of acquisitions, mergers, and other affiliations.

Do I have a genuine interest in the kind of work I will manage? If managers dislike their own work before becoming managers, chances are that they will not like it more when they must manage others in those activities. A manager's lack of interest in the work can readily show up in the quality of supervision he or she provides to others.

Do I have a genuine interest in working with people, as opposed to working alone? Health care is labor intensive, with many people working closely together on behalf of other people in an immediate, usually hands-on context. Health care is generally not for the loner, nor is management in any industry for the loner, as it always involves getting things done through people.

Do I have a desire to do something I consider important to people? To people who remain in health care by choice, there is little that is more important than helping to preserve life, restore health, and prevent illness.

Do I experience a strong desire to see the results of my labor? The opportunity for immediate feedback regarding one's work is more prevalent in health care than in many other lines of work.

Do I thrive on variety in my work? The management role, in health care and elsewhere, is full of variety. This takes us back to the initial question concerning the often-encountered hectic pace involved in addressing problem upon problem. The effective manager, and the manager who truly enjoys the role, usually prefers variety over predictability (within reason, of course; some days it will seem as though there were too much variety for *anyone*).

The Manager's Two Hats

The healthcare manager invariably wears two hats, that of the *specialist* and that of the *manager*. All managers of varying titles at all lower-to-middle management levels wear these same two hats. This is especially true of the first-line manager, or supervisor, who at the lowest of management's levels oversees the activities of the people who do the hands-on work. The first-line manager must not only understand the tasks performed by rank and file employees, but he or she must also often perform some of these tasks personally.

Think about the various paths that people have taken into their management positions and you will appreciate that most people have functional specialties in which they began work and for which they have had formal training. The head nurse is trained as a nurse; the accounting manager has a background in accounting; the laboratory manager has a laboratory background; the physical therapy manager is a physical therapist by education and experience. Most people who manage at all but the highest organizational levels possess education or experience or both in the functions they manage.

At higher levels, perhaps at the top or at one level below the top of most organizations, or over a sizeable division or a very large department, it is possible to find some true management generalists—people who have been educated in *management as their primary specialty*. In most instances, however, supervisors and managers have usually risen through the ranks and now manage functions in which they formerly labored as nonmanagers. These individuals, constituting the majority of people who bear management titles, must know a great deal about the work of the function and must know how to manage. They must wear the two hats as the job demands.

The significant problem encountered in trying to wear two hats is that most of us favor the hat that fits best. Most managers are well trained and appropriately experienced in their specialties, having been promoted at least in part for being good at what they did as workers. However, they are trained little, if at all, in this second career called management, so a great deal of the time the hat of the manager rests uneasily on the head of the person who wears it. Experiencing doubt and anxiety about some aspects of the job, perhaps shortcutting or altogether avoiding them (e.g., involvement in budgeting, performance appraisal, and disciplinary action), the first-line manager finds refuge in the technical aspects of the job. In brief, this manager thinks and behaves more as a worker than as a manager.

It behooves every first-line manager to recognize that he or she is ordinarily much better prepared to produce than to manage, and to make the conscious effort necessary to compensate for this imbalance.

One can learn how to improve as a manager through additional formal education. One can also learn through experience, although first-hand experience is often a costly and painful way of acquiring knowledge. Experience is often like destructive testing in that useful information is acquired but something of value is drastically altered.

Why not instead endeavor to learn from the experiences of others, in this instance, many of the individuals illustrated in the case studies? The manager who pays conscientious attention to his or her continuing education in management will be the manager who ultimately masters the balancing act.

Every Manager as a Professional Manager

It has already been suggested that many first-line managers (supervisors) do not identify with management nearly as strongly as they identify with their basic occupations. It follows that an equally significant number do not see themselves as full-fledged members of the entity known as "management." Nevertheless, the first-line manager, by whatever title he or she may be known, is indeed a manager, and management is indeed a profession, and the first-line manager can become a professional manager largely through personal effort.

Becoming a professional manager requires overcoming some longstanding misconceptions about management; it may also mean overcoming organizational barriers to the full development of the supervisor as a manager.

False Distinctions and the Labeling Trap

Some of the widespread misconceptions about management hold that the various levels in the organizational hierarchy are populated by different kinds of people who perform distinctly different functions. Although the word *management* is almost always used as the generic term that it truly is (even though often qualified as in *top management*, *middle management*, *first-line management*, etc.), the specific label of *manager* is frequently applied in describing only people in the middle and upper ranges of the hierarchy. Because of this fairly strong use of the term to denote a position title, we are led toward the impression that *manager* is different from and automatically greater than *supervisor*.

Within many written works on management we can find a glaring inconsistency that occurs over and over again: Most such works use *management* as a convenient generic term to describe the business of running the organization or any of its parts, but then proceed to use *manager* in a less-than-generic sense to describe a particular level of activity somewhere between *executive* and *supervisor*. Thus have so many fallen into the labeling trap.

Although duties and responsibilities vary at different levels, all managers exist for the same basic purpose: to get things done through people. Misconceptions arising from false distinctions between levels come largely from the inconsistent use of *management* as a generic term and *manager* as a strongly entrenched, position-specific label. The problem is compounded by the fluctuating application of the label among organizations.

In any particular healthcare organization the "supervisor" usually cannot correctly be called "manager" in a position-title sense. However, the supervisor is a manager in the generic sense of the term and is legitimately a member of the body of management. As an important first step toward professionalism, the supervisor must accept that he or she is indeed a manager. This person who might be the lowest member of the organization's hierarchy is nevertheless a manager.

Authority: A Critical Element

To the extent that a supervisor is provided with the environment, responsibilities, and accountability to pursue and achieve the organization's objectives, he or she is an integral part of the management team. This is true only as far as it goes. It is completely true only if we may assume that "environment" is the total organizational environment, and that this includes the supervisor's authority to act. It must always be made clear that every supervisor—first-line manager—requires a clearly delineated, thoroughly understood measure of authority.

Responsibility—or accountability, which is the state of being obligated to fulfill one's responsibilities—is the load that the individual must carry. Authority is the container or conveyance in which that load is carried.

It is fundamental to the appointment of duties and responsibilities that authority be apportioned consistently with responsibility. At all levels of the organization it is essential that everyone who is given a task must also be given the wherewithal to accomplish it. Authority is essentially the hard currency with which something may be bought or demanded.

In many work organizations, people are made responsible for accomplishing tasks but are not given appropriate authority to do so. For example, if a supervisor is made responsible for reducing employee absenteeism but is denied the authority to discipline employees, the supervisor is left with less than the complete wherewithal needed to do the job.

This matter of authority often marks the most profound difference between the true professional manager and the manager in title only who has neither sought nor been accorded professionalism.

The professional manager recognizes the long-run hopelessness of trying to fill a certain level of responsibility with an inadequate amount of authority. This manager will either strive through channels to obtain sufficient authority or will simply assume sufficient authority when the matter of the moment seems to warrant such action.

Behavior Versus Treatment

Professional behavior and professional treatment are equal but opposite sides of the same coin. The work organization has a responsibility to treat as professionals those workers who it wants to perform as professionals. The employee who wishes to be considered a professional should perform and behave as one.

The matter of behavior versus treatment is a problem in many organizations that do not treat their supervisors or first-line managers as though they were true members of management. In truth there are, in healthcare organizations, more first-line managers than any other kind of manager in the organization. Yet frequently managers in the middle to upper ranges of the hierarchy, often supported by the upper ranks of professional workers, do not regard these supervisors as managers.

Although managers who have come up through the ranks are to be found at all levels in nearly all organizations, it is becoming more common for middle and upper-middle managers to enter the organization at managerial levels with formal training in management. However, most supervisors—first-line managers—have almost exclusively come up through the ranks, directly out of their own work groups in most cases, into management. Most supervisors are still involved to some extent with hands-on work. These supervisors are seen as more associated with nonmanagerial than managerial work, and thus the upper levels of the management hierarchy tend to treat them as nonmanagers. A normal, understandable reaction to such treatment is, for many supervisors, to feel less than professional and thus act less than professionally.

Although a great many supervisors identify naturally with occupation or department rather than with management, notable exceptions can be found in organizations in which supervisors are treated as full-fledged members of management. The more an organization treats its supervisors as true members of management, the more these supervisors identify primarily with management.

The key to the behavior-versus-treatment aspect of professionalism in management lies largely in the supervisor's initiative. To passively wait to receive professional treatment before extending one's best in the way of professional behavior is to hold one's own potential hostage. Not only is such behavior unprofessional, it essentially establishes one as unpromotable for all practical purposes. The organization's hierarchy may never consciously consider professionalism a factor at all, but upper management is still likely to be turned off by an attitude of passivity on the part of a supervisor. In most organizational settings, people who sit back waiting for something good to happen are simply bypassed.

The professional manager consistently delivers his or her best professional behavior regardless of whether consistent treatment as a professional is extended in return.

Communication Initiative

One of the surest marks of the professional manager is the demonstrated willingness to take the initiative in matters of organizational communication. A supervisor communicates with employees, supervisors, and others within the organization and does so in ways that differ from one to another, often to a considerable extent.

At this juncture, a serious discussion about communicating with one's employees could be constructively pursued. However, for present purposes there is but one point of importance that must be made: The supervisor is the key communication link between the individual employee and the rest of the organization. It is through this first-line manager that instructions, procedures, policies, directions, corrections, and rewards all flow to the employee. The supervisor is the employee's primary source of information about the organization, and, more than that, the supervisor is often the personality or embodiment of the organization for the employee. Thus as the individual employee sees the supervisor, so is that employee likely to see the organization. When this consideration is multiplied by the number of employees reporting to an individual supervisor, it makes one realize that the supervisor wields a great deal of power in shaping the attitudes of employees toward the organization.

The true professional manager is one who recognizes that he or she is never completely finished when it comes to making organizational communication work better.

The truly effective communicator is one who always, mindless of so-called fairness and without weighing "my part" against "your part," goes more the halfway more than half of the time in communicating with others, fully realizing that not always will all of one's efforts be repaid in full. This may be a difficult posture to assume, recognizing that one is deliberately extending thoughtfulness to a number of others who will never reciprocate, so it pays to remember that the primary beneficiaries of improved communications are oneself and one's own department.

Some Indicators of Professionalism

As with many endeavors, management can correctly be described as a profession. However, not all of its practitioners are professionals. The first-line manager may be considered a true professional manager if he or she:

- Accepts *supervisor* as synonymous with *manager*, and holds a view of self as a full-fledged member of management
- Is able to achieve an appropriate balance between the vertically integrated technical specialist role and the horizontally integrated role of the supervisor
- Strives to acquire and retain an amount of organizational authority consistent with the assigned responsibilities of the position
- Accepts as the primary role the business of seeing that the work gets done through the efforts of the total work group (which includes the supervisor)
- Is willing to earn (or try to earn) treatment as a professional by extending conscientious professional behavior to the organization and constantly take the initiative to improve his or her own communications posture within the organization

THE SUPERVISOR'S ESSENTIAL QUALITIES: BOTH OF THEM

Just Two?

Yes, just two. Two particular human characteristics, and the balance between them, seem to have a major influence on whether the individual is effective as a manager of people.

We could, of course, develop a lengthy, impressive list of characteristics we believe to be desirable in a supervisor; however, having done so, we could then proceed to identify a considerable number of apparently effective supervisors who lack many of the so-called desirable characteristics.

We are not referring to job knowledge or decision-making ability, analytical ability, the ability to delegate, time management skill, or the application of any of the other so-called management skills. Rather, we are speaking of two human characteristics that might sometimes be thought of as facets of personality: courage and compassion.

Regardless of knowledge of a working specialty or management techniques, in the last analysis the effective supervisor will be the person who approaches the job with the appropriate blend of courage and compassion. More than any other personal characteristics, these two, and especially the balance between them, can determine success in managing the activities of other people. In short, the effective supervisor must possess the compassion to ascertain what is right under any circumstances and the courage to do what must be done.

Courage

Lack of courage is displayed in numerous supervisory weaknesses. It is shown, for example, when supervisors fail to deliver deserved criticism or so water it down that it is ineffective simply because they are afraid of causing hurt, anger, frustration, or disappointment. Some supervisors go to great lengths to convince themselves and others that they are not being soft but rather are humane and considerate. However, it is more likely that the soft supervisor is simply afraid—especially afraid of not being liked.

This same lack of courage often causes supervisors to dilute deserved disciplinary action or avoid it altogether. Others attempt to blame the bad stuff on somebody else. ("I want you to know this isn't my idea—*they* made me do it.") Problems are avoided or dealt with lightly and responsibilities are shirked because a soft supervisor is working hard—usually quite unconsciously—to maintain the nice-guy image.

Granted, it does not feel good to be put in a position of having to do something that someone else would rather you not do. It does not feel good to be the one who has to step on someone's toes (although few people get their toes stepped on unless they are standing still or sitting down on the job). Given the choice, most people would rather be liked than disliked.

The effective supervisor finds it necessary to step on some toes now and then. There are, however, right and wrong ways of stepping. An old bit of fortune-cookie wisdom suggests that a good supervisor is one who can step on toes without soiling the shine on the shoes. The supervisor needs the courage to step when stepping is necessary and the compassion to know just where, when, and how hard to do so.

Some managers seem not to care at all what people think of them. They seem absolutely fearless where other people's responses to their actions are concerned. However, true courage in a supervisor is not displayed by ranting and raving and pushing people around. This behavior is more indicative of plain nerve than courage; nerve coupled with a lack of sensitivity to the feelings and needs of other people. A supervisor operating on an oversupply of brass or an undersupply of compassion charges forward with a damn-the-torpedoes attitude far more typical of a pusher than of a true leader. Such behavior may represent authoritarian leadership, but not effective supervision. The supervisor with real courage does not back away from tasks because they are difficult or unpleasant, but neither does the courageous supervisor boldly charge in with little or no concern for people.

Compassion

Just as boldness and aggressiveness are often put forth as substitutes for courage, compassion also has its misapplications. Too often, compassion is used as a shield for ineffectiveness, an excuse for failing to take appropriate supervisory action when called for. "Sure, maybe I was a little soft on him," says the supervisor. "I know he's been a pain in the neck, but the guy really needs the job." Compassionate? Perhaps, perhaps not. It is just as likely that the supervisor's attitude stems not from compassion, but rather from cowardice.

Backing away from tough situations is sometimes the better part of valor. However, backing away gets to be a habit for some. The effective supervisor backs away as far as compassion dictates, but acts with courage when the real crunch comes. The supervisor using compassion as a shield for cowardice backs away beyond any reasonable point at which action should have been taken.

In the long run the supervisor who acts out of fear of being disliked is in for a great deal of grief. Too many supervisors have discovered that no matter what they do it is not possible to be liked by everyone. It is far better to strive to earn the respect of your employees. A person's respect can be earned through fair and impartial dealings, and held by maintaining the relationship on that same level. On the other hand, a person's affection must be earned all over again each time a hurdle is encountered in the relationship.

Compassion, of course, involves caring for patients, employees, visitors, and others. Compassion does not consist of timid behavior in the face of potential anger or displeasure. It involves treating all people with dignity and respect, and being polite, considerate, and generally humane with all persons, even those who have broken the rules. The compassionate supervisor knows that more may be accomplished with reason and understanding than with anger or forcefulness.

The Balancing Act

Part of the difficulty in striking—or even describing—the appropriate balance between courage and compassion lies in widespread differences in human understanding of these characteristics. Courage and compassion simply do not rate equally with everyone.

To most people courage is a good word; it has a bold, brave sound to it. It denotes a noble and desirable characteristic, and most people believe it is admirable to be considered courageous. Compassion, however, is another matter. Although compassion carries a positive connotation for most people, it nevertheless does not rate as high as courage.

The human relations movement in management was largely a product of the middle part of the twentieth century. Years earlier, compassion had little place in organized work activity. Many employees had no voice in how they did their work; they did as they were told or they sought work elsewhere.

Old, widespread notions change slowly and with great difficulty. For more than a few people the word *compassion* continues to suggest a degree of weakness, and few of us wish to be considered weak in any respect. True compassion, however, is not weakness any more than simple boldness is courage.

In addition to seeing shades of weakness in compassion, some supervisors also see certain of their employees as undeserving of compassion. A supervisor's perspective often becomes distorted by repeated dealings with the same people week in and week out. A large part of a supervisor's life consists of dealing with employees face to face and solving problems stemming from employee behavior. It is the chronic misbehavers, usually a small percentage of the work force, who the supervisor sees and becomes aware of most.

The capacity for compassion suffers as a negative attitude toward people grows. Some supervisors come to believe that management is less *getting things done through people* than it is *getting things done in spite of people*.

The supervisor has a job to do. That job consists largely of getting other jobs, perhaps a great many of them, done through the efforts of other people. Doing this effectively requires that the supervisor exercise compassion in recognizing and treating each employee as an individual and at the same time exercising sufficient courage to keep employees' efforts channeled toward fulfillment of organizational goals. Whether practicing management at the work place or attempting to further develop their supervisory skills, effective supervisors are those who exhibit the courage necessary to do what must be done and the compassion to get it done with every human consideration.

CHAPTER 3

THE TOPICS AND THE CASE STUDY METHOD

WHAT'S IMPORTANT TO THE MANAGER?

Everything—that is, everything that can possibly be identified as a topic related to supervising the work of others—is important to most managers at one time or another. Therein lies the difficulty in categorizing topics in management; what is of immediate importance to one manager is of little present consequence to another. Importance to the manager seems governed in large part by two conditions: what the individual manager perceives as his or her present need, and the manager's personal interests.

The personally perceived present need is exactly that. For example, the manager who is able to admit to experiencing difficulty with disciplinary issues may well seek out help in addressing such matters. Managers capable of a reasonable amount of self-honesty are able to recognize and concede some (although rarely all) of their weaknesses or shortcomings. This recognition may motivate behavior in one of two directions: The conscientious individual seeks knowledge that can help correct weaknesses or shortcomings, and the not-so-conscientious manager may behave in a way that involves minimizing exposure to certain kinds of issues or tasks. For example, the manager who feels uncertain and excessively uncomfortable when presented with disciplinary issues may simply ignore them or address them only superficially.

Personal interests may also govern managers' quests for further knowledge simply by taking them more often toward favored topics in which they have a personal interest. The effects of personal interest are likely to come into play when managers are surveyed as part of a *learning needs analysis*. In such analyses involving the people who will eventually participate in training based on the results, "desires" often overlap "needs."

Customarily, an organization's determination of what its managers need to learn arises from one or more of the following:

- In-house assessment of learning needs in which someone, frequently a staff development or a continuing education person, surveys the population of potential course attendees and subsequently recommends programs
- Management designation—that is, based on perceptions of current needs and managers' present capabilities, upper management decides on the topics to be presented
- Consultants' recommendations, resulting from the observations of external consultants involved in any number of organizational improvement activities

No one of these sources is better than the others in dictating the design of a management training program. The three perspectives can be quite different from each other. In one institution, for example, a learning needs analysis showed that in the managers' judgment the least needed topic out of 15 choices was labor relations. The prevailing attitude among these managers was, "We don't have unions, we don't need unions, so we don't have to learn about them." However, top management, aware, as were many other employees, of healthcare union organizing in the region, felt so strongly that labor relations was a primary need that an entire day-long program was devoted to just one aspect of the topic (specifically, how to behave during union organizing).

Regardless of the source of the "needs" designation—the determination of what is included, excluded, or emphasized when the contents of a program are spelled out—limiting factors usually constrain the presentation of all that may truly be needed. These constraints are often related to time and money. Formal supervisory or management training is ordinarily limited to so many hours per session spread over so many days, weeks, or months. Because training represents expenditures of both time and money, and also because training is frequently regarded as less than an absolute necessity, if not an out-and-out frill (how top managers verbally support training throughout the year and how they treat it at budget time reveals significant contradictions), the resources allotted to training often cover just fundamentals and areas of immediate need.

Therefore, any topic that can be associated in any way with the day-to-day practice of management, the business of getting things done through people, is important. No matter how seemingly obscure a topic or how remote its implications, there are first-line managers to whom it represents their foremost need at the moment.

For the sake of convenience, the cases presented in this book are arranged according to the topic headings explained in the following paragraphs.

THE TOPICS

Authority

As the name suggests, the cases in this category address issues of authority: the authority of the first-line manager; the role of authority versus responsibility in proper delegation; the use of authority by the first-line manager's superior; undermining of authority by certain practices; authority and the chain of command; and other considerations.

Change Management

Considered under this heading are all of the ramifications of the adoption or imposition of change involving various elements of the work force, but especially the employees reporting to the first-line manager. Included is consideration of resistance to change and how it is addressed.

Communication

For the purposes of this book, this topic includes all aspects of interpersonal communication in the work setting, primarily spoken (as opposed to written), with primary emphasis on the one-to-one relationship between manager and employee, but also considering relationships between the first-line manager and higher management.

Criticism and Discipline

This topic includes all aspects of critical or corrective measures, from informally delivering constructive (or otherwise) criticism or receiving same, to the application of formal, documented disciplinary action in all of its possible variants.

Decision Making

This topic considers the elements of the basic decision-making process, including the concepts of risk, uncertainty, and judgment, and with consideration of when to decide and, occasionally, when not to decide.

Delegation

Of primary consideration under this topic heading is the importance of the fundamental process of delegation in getting things done through people, and its place as one of the most basic and frequently used and misused keys to the manager's personal effectiveness. Also addressed is the term *empowerment*, which may be considered essentially identical to thorough, proper delegation.

Employee Problems and Problem Employees

This is a significant category in addressing many management concerns, and as such it necessarily includes dimensions of most of the other topics. The primary focus of this topic category is dealing with human relations problems that have their origins in employees' attitudes or behavior.

General Management Practice

This category is something of a catchall for the fundamentals of management (for instance, the basic concepts of planning, organizing, directing, coordinating, and controlling) and the dual role of the first-line manager as both worker and manager. As such it includes a variety of relevant activities.

Hiring and Placement

This topic addresses the one-on-one, face-to-face interview situation, especially as it applies to the employee selection process, and also deals with postinterview activities such as interview follow up and reference checking.

Labor Relations

This topic deals primarily with issues related to labor unions in health care, and especially with the first-line manager's role relative to union organizing activity.

Leadership

Although this is a category that could conceivably include degrees of all other topics, the cases so categorized have much to do with the exploration of reasons why some people follow the direction and guidance of some managers more or less willingly than they follow others.

Meeting Leadership

This category primarily addresses the issues that arise in scheduling, running, and following up on meetings, but includes as well the implications for the continuing functioning of entities requiring multiperson communication on an ongoing basis (such as quality teams and departmental staff groups that meet regularly).

Methods Improvement

This topic addresses the continuing need for improved departmental effectiveness through improved work methods, which is a perpetual necessity (although rarely a conscious priority) for the first-line manager.

Motivation

This category encompasses all considerations of what causes people to perform or fail to perform.

Rules and Policies

This topic includes cases that suggest the need for rules or guides that deal with weaknesses, limitations, or misinterpretation of policies.

Time Management and Personal Effectiveness

The thrust of the cases in this category is how managers utilize their time. Also considered are other dimensions of personal effectiveness, such as planning and scheduling, that invariably have time management implications.

CATEGORIZING THE CASES

There is no ideal order in which to arrange the cases; a topic that might be of first priority for one manager may not figure at all in another manager's consideration of what is important. Therefore, for the sake of convenience the cases are grouped under the foregoing 16 alphabetized headings.

It is said that there is no ideal order because every case in this compilation can be used to illustrate two or three or more of the topic categories. For example, every case that involves contact between people can legitimately be considered a case in *Communication*; most cases having anything to do with *Leadership* also have relevance for *Motivation* and vice versa; cases having to do with *Change Management* can hold implications for *Motivation*, *Employee Problems and Problem Employees*, *Leadership*, and others.

Each case is identified with a single primary topic, and each has also been assigned one, two, or more additional topics. However, these assignments are neither exclusive nor all-encompassing. Every case can be used for discussions and activities concerning a range of topics of relevance to managers well beyond the primary and additional topics listed. The topic assignments are simply a convenience, taking the first topic that is likely to jump out at one as the primary topic of a given case and listing a few of the more obvious connections.

The cases are sequentially numbered from 1 through 100. Table 3-1 summarizes the distribution of topics.

THE RESPONSES

There is only one qualification to keep in mind referring to any of the responses, and that was stressed in Chapter 1: The case responses provided in this book are not the only valid responses.

In some instances, the range of choices may be relatively narrow, such that a sensible response is very nearly self-evident, leaving little room for improvement. However, when real people are involved, as they surely are in essentially everything a first-line manager does, the answers are never guaranteed. People are different from one another, and even the same individuals may behave differently at different times or under different circumstances. What works for one may not work for another; what works today may not work tomorrow.

Take each response as simply one—although a well-considered one and in many instances one that has worked in a real situation—of a number of possible solutions. Additional solutions are up to you.

TABLE 3-1

CASE TOPICS

Topic	*Primary topic of*	*Additional topic of*
Authority	21, 62, 78, 82	2, 20, 17, 22, 26, 31, 35, 39, 44, 46, 49, 50–52, 55, 58, 60–61, 63, 66–67, 69, 70, 73, 76–77, 79, 83–85, 87–90, 96–97
Change Management	8, 11, 15, 27, 34, 37, 64, 67, 73, 89	3, 17, 38, 97, 100
Communication	14, 22, 35, 38, 47, 50, 77, 81, 90–91, 100	3–7, 9, 13, 17, 19, 20, 25–27, 30–31, 36–37, 39–43, 46, 48, 51–53, 56, 58–60, 62, 64–75, 79–80, 82–85, 89, 92–95, 98–99
Criticism and Discipline	4–5, 9–10, 12, 16, 32, 71–72, 74, 88	1, 7, 13–14, 18, 21, 25, 39, 45, 49, 52–53, 58, 62, 70, 78, 81–83, 86–87, 91–92, 95, 98
Decision Making	1	21, 27–29, 34, 53, 60, 65, 76–78, 80, 86, 96
Delegation	6, 19, 24–25, 30, 33, 36, 46, 58, 63, 84	4, 7–8, 11–12, 14–17, 23, 26–27, 34, 37, 43, 48, 57, 72, 85, 98
Employee Problems and Problem Employees	7, 13, 17, 26, 39, 41–42, 44–45, 48–49, 51–53, 55, 57, 59, 66, 79, 83, 86–87, 92, 94–95, 98	1, 4–6, 8–12, 14–16, 18, 31, 36–38, 68, 71, 74–75, 81–82, 85, 88, 91, 93
General Management Practice	53, 80, 85, 97	2, 10–12, 28–29, 35, 40, 44, 47 57, 59–61, 82, 87–90, 94, 96
Hiring and Placement	68–69, 76, 96	41, 77
Labor Relations	65	
Leadership	2, 60, 100	6–8, 11, 16, 21–26, 30–39, 43–44, 46, 50–53, 55–56, 61–65, 67, 72, 78–79, 82–84, 86–89, 94–96
Meeting Leadership	3, 56	10, 71, 73
Methods Improvement		1, 11, 15, 20
Motivation	43	3, 6, 8, 10, 19, 21, 23–27, 30, 32–33, 36, 38, 41, 46, 48–50, 53–55, 58, 60, 62–64, 74, 76, 77, 79, 95, 100
Rules and Policies	75, 93	5, 9, 21, 37, 43, 45, 62, 66, 68–69, 88
Time Management and Personal Effectiveness	20, 28–29, 40, 61, 99	18–19, 22, 24, 56, 97

MAKING THE CASE METHOD A HABIT

Not the Real World, but a Little Closer

Case studies provide practice in analyzing problems and making decisions. Although true decision-making pressures and emotional involvement in the decision-making process are missing, you can use these real-world examples to practice on without risking damage from a few less-than-appropriate decisions.

A real-world decision often includes personal involvement, potential consequences, and often the pressure of time, so a case study cannot simulate all of the moves required in making and implementing a decision. However, a case study allows you to go through some of the necessary moves and thus more closely parallels reality than does a simple recounting of rules or principles. In one important dimension decision making is like many other human endeavors—the more you practice, the more proficient you become.

A Healthy Problem-Solving Outlook

A case study can illustrate the complexity of the real decision-making environment. Dealing with a case requires one to retreat from theory and other abstractions and face the uncertainties of the real world. Through the case study method you can learn to make necessary simplifications and cut through a maze of apparent facts and information to create a working order that you can deal with in a practical way.

No single case ever supplies all of the facts. Just as in pondering many real-life situations, it is always possible to ask, "What if . . . ?" But rarely does the manager have all of the facts in any but the simplest of real situations.

Trying to decide without full knowledge of a situation is often frustrating, but addressing frustration is part of the manager's task. If there were fewer such frustrations there would likely be fewer difficult decisions to make and fewer managers required to make them.

In spite of the shortcomings of the case study method, however, working your way conscientiously through a number of cases can leave you with a new outlook on problem solving. This new outlook may well include your recognition of the need to:

- Thoroughly evaluate all available information and arrange bits of it in some logical order.
- Arrange information into meaningful patterns or decision alternatives.
- Evaluate each alternative according to the objectives to be served by the decision.
- Make a choice.

Rarely is there a single "right" solution to a given case—or, for that matter, to any real-world problem except the most elementary. Sometimes it is even difficult to say whether one particular answer is better than another. In this respect, the case method supports reality; in real situations what is "right" is usually dependent on the conditions of the moment and the needs of the people involved.

The use of the case study method also reminds us of the true role of rules, principles, and theories. We quickly discover that rules, principles, and theories are only tools to work with, not ends to be served. We learn to arrange information so we can use our tools as they are needed, rather than attempt to organize our case analyses around the tools. In other words, we learn that theory *serves* practice; it does not *dictate* practice.

To help decide whether or not you are learning from the case study method, try to assess your response to each case you go through according to the following questions:

- Do my recommendations show that I fully understand the issues involved in the case?
- Without unforeseen circumstances, could my recommendations realistically solve the problem? That is, are they workable under the circumstances?
- Do my recommendations appear to be as fair as possible to all parties involved in the problem?
- Do my recommendations support the goals of the organization, rather than the desires of some specific person or group?
- If this were a real problem instead of a case, could I live with my recommendations?

SUMMARY: USING CASE STUDIES AND WHY

The advantages of the case study method are never more apparent than when cases are considered by a group of people working together. The multiple inputs provided by group activity serve as a strong stimulus to creativity. Ideas lead to more ideas; someone may bring up an idea that had not occurred to you, and this in turn can lead you to think of something that neither of you had yet mentioned. Ideas—implications, possibilities, etc.—build upon ideas, and often the thought that leads to a sound solution springs from discussion of peripheral issues or of matters of yet-to-be-recognized importance. Indeed, on some occasions discussions leading to sensible, viable solutions have been triggered by passing mention of some utterly ridiculous possibility. Much of the time, group consideration of a case reveals more potentially productive alternatives than one person would have generated alone.

Different people considering the same case bring different viewpoints to bear. Each of us possesses a unique viewpoint, the sum of our own attitudes, experiences, and backgrounds. Therefore, we are inclined to view the same problem in different ways. We see some factors as more important than others because of the way we are put together.

Consider, for example, a problem concerning a request for more housekeeping personnel arising during a period of financial restraint. To the finance director, the dollar problems may loom as the most significant part of the overall problem. However, the housekeeping manager, struggling with an overworked and understaffed crew, may see understaffing as the leading critical issue. And even without direct involvement in the problem, any two managers from different disciplines may well view things differently. The same hypothetical problem—the housekeeping staffing situation—may be viewed in different ways by, say, a registered nurse and a laboratory technologist.

Differing viewpoints come from different orientations. You stand in a unique spot in the organization, no one else views all things quite the same way you do. No department exists in isolation from all others in the delivery of health care, and there are few kinds of problems that do not cross departmental lines, so the views of a number of people of varying backgrounds usually contribute to the development of more numerous and comprehensive alternatives.

In adopting the broader view fostered by the case study method of learning, we find that our need becomes not that of developing the "best" solution to a problem—that is, "best" logically and economically, although it may serve the needs and desires of only one interested party—but rather developing a solution that is fair and workable overall and that serves the objectives of the organization and the needs of its customers.

Overall look for the case study method of learning to provide the following:

- Practice in idea generation and creative problem solving
- Familiarity with logical problem-solving processes
- Broadened perspective, owing to the sharing of ideas and viewpoints with others
- Encouragement in developing the habit of approaching problems analytically
- Practice in solving problems and making decisions

No supervisor's continuing education should rely 100 percent on the case study method, or for that matter, on any single training approach. Many rules, principles, and techniques are best acquired by other means. However, the case study method has characteristics that make it always worth considering as part of one's continuing education in management. It calls for active involvement in the learning process, and it significantly narrows the gap between theory and practice.

PART II

CASES

CASE 1

MORE HELP NEEDED—NOW!

Primary Topic—*Decision Making*

Additional Topics—*Criticism and Discipline; Employee Problems and Problem Employees; Methods Improvement*

You are manager of the health information management department of Memorial Hospital. You have 20 people in your group. Three of your employees have the title supervisor, but all are usually more involved in doing the work of the department than in supervising others. One of these, your transcription supervisor, is expected to devote 60 percent of her time to transcription duties and the other 40 percent to supervision.

Several times in recent months the transcription supervisor has mentioned that the backlog of work was growing and that she needed more help. She has never been more specific than simply saying that "more help" was needed, and her complaints seemed to be no more than passing remarks offered without preparation or forethought. Since you have been under pressure from a number of directions and your transcription supervisor's complaints seemed to represent no more than chronic grumbling, you have not felt compelled to add the transcription backlog to your currently active worries.

However, today, Monday, the transcription supervisor sought you out and confronted you with: "I need one more full-time transcriptionist and I need her *now*. I'm tired of waiting and tired of being ignored, and I'm sick of being overworked and taken for granted. If something isn't done about it by Friday, you can find yourself a new transcription supervisor."

Instructions:

Propose at least three possible solutions to this problem and describe the potential advantages and disadvantages of each.

The case places you in a trap. Describe this trap, explain why it is a trap, and explain how you believe you should proceed toward a solution in view of the hazards you face.

Explain what you believe is the general condition that caused the specific problem described in the case. Who is responsible for the matter, and what can be done to address the cause?

CASE 2

UP FROM THE RANKS

Primary Topic—*Leadership*

Additional Topics—*Authority; General Management Practice; Time Management and Personal Effectiveness*

After 8 years as a staff nurse in a medical/surgical unit, Julie was appointed head nurse of that unit. After a meeting at which her promotion was announced, Julie found herself surrounded by three coworkers offering their congratulations and other comments.

"I'm really happy for you," said Sarah, "but I suppose this means our car pool is affected. Your hours are bound to be less predictable now."

Elaine said, "And the lunch bunch, too. Management commitments, you know." The emphasis on *management* was undeniable. Julie was not at all sure she was happy with what she was hearing.

Jane offered, "Well, maybe now we can get some action on a few age-old problems. Remember, Julie, you used to gripe as much as we did."

"We've all griped a lot," Sarah agreed. "That's been a way of life around here." Her tone changed and her customary smile faded as she added, "Now Julie's going to be in a position where she can do something, so let's hope she doesn't forget who her friends are."

Elaine and Jane looked quickly from Sarah to Julie. For an awkward 10 seconds or so, nobody spoke. At last, someone passing by spoke to Julie, and as Julie turned to respond, Elaine, Jane, and Sarah silently went their separate ways.

Questions:

1. What possible advantages does Julie have in becoming supervisor of the group of which she has long been a member?
2. What are the possible disadvantages that may present themselves to Julie?
3. If you were Julie, how do you believe your promotion would affect your relationships with your former coworkers?

CASE 3

THE SILENT GROUP

Primary Topic—*Meeting Leadership*

Additional Topics—*Change Management; Communication; Motivation*

As the admitting manager recently hired from outside, it took you very little time to discover that morale in the department had been poor for some time. As you worked to become acquainted with your employees by meeting with each of them alone, you soon became inundated with complaints and other evidences of discontent. Most of the complaints involved problems with administration and the business office and the loose admitting practices of physicians, but there were also complaints from the admitting staff about other members of the department and a couple of thinly veiled charges concerning admitting personnel who "carry tales to administration."

In listening to the problems, you detected a number of common themes. You decided that much misunderstanding could be cleared up if the gripes were aired openly with the entire group. You then planned a staff meeting and asked all employees to be prepared to air their complaints—except those involving specific staff members—at the meeting. Most of your employees seemed to think such a meeting was a good idea, and several assured you they would be ready to speak up. However, your first staff meeting was brief. When offered the opportunity to air their gripes, nobody spoke.

The results were the same at your next staff meeting 4 weeks later, although in the intervening period you were again bombarded with complaints from individuals. This experience left you frustrated because many of the complaints you heard were problems of the group rather than problems of individuals.

Questions:

1. What can you do to get this group of employees to open up about what is bothering them?
2. How might you approach the specific problem of one or more of your employees carrying complaints beyond the department; that is, "carrying tales to administration?"

CASE 4

THE REPEAT OFFENDER

Primary Topic—*Criticism and Discipline*

Additional Topics—*Communication; Delegation; Employee Problems and Problem Employees*

"So I slipped up and made a mistake," said chemistry technician Arnold Adams. "All that proves is that I'm human, that maybe I'm a little careless once in a while, like everybody else."

"I can't call your behavior carelessness," said laboratory manager Elsie Clark. She slid a piece of paper across her desk to Arnold and continued, "I have to call it negligence, and that's what this warning notice says."

Arnold scowled and said, "I don't deserve a warning and certainly not for negligence." He spread his hands and added, "What am I supposed to be—perfect? I can't make an honest mistake once in a while?"

"You can't make mistakes like this one. The test request was clearly marked stat but you logged it in as routine and it sat for several hours."

Arnold shrugged and said, "Nothing happened to the patient, did it?"

"No," Elsie answered, "but Dr. Baker ordered it stat because of this particular patient's history. Something could have happened—we're just lucky it didn't."

"So nothing happened," Arnold repeated, "but I get a warning in my file? If a warning's supposed to be a form of punishment, how come I'm punished for something that didn't cause any harm?"

Elsie said, "Arnold, you're all by yourself every night at the satellite. We must be able to depend on you to process all requests according to procedure and to perform all stat work as it's received."

Arnold simply scowled at the warning notice as Elsie added, "And this sort of thing has got to stop. This is the fourth conversation we've had like this, and the most serious yet."

"Fourth?" Arnold's eyebrows rose.

Elsie nodded. "In 3 years," she said.

"I can't believe you'd hold some thing against me that happened 3 years ago. A warning that old ought to be wiped out. You've got no business using that against me."

"I'm using it only to point out a pattern. You seem to go along fine for 8 or 9 months or so, then up comes a major problem again."

"Just bears out what I said before," Arnold said. "I'm human. I make mistakes. And 8 or 9 months since the last mistake entitles me to a clean slate."

"I can't agree," Elsie said. She handed Arnold a pen and added, "Please sign the form to show that we've discussed this. You can write out any objections or comments in the space at the bottom. And should we have such a conversation again, you may find that more than a written warning is involved."

Questions:

1. Consider Elsie's statement, "You can't make mistakes like this one." Is this a valid statement? If yes, why?
2. What is wrong with Arnold's description of a warning as "a form of punishment?"
3. How would you deal with the repeat offender if you were in Elsie's position?

CASE 5

A GOOD EMPLOYEE?

Primary Topic—*Criticism and Discipline*

Additional Topics—*Communication; Employee Problems and Problem Employees; Rules and Policies*

Housekeeping supervisor Ellie Richards was faced with a situation that left her feeling uncomfortable about the action she would have to consider taking. In discussing the matter with Stan Miller, the other housekeeping supervisor, she began: "I have no idea how I should deal with Judy Lawrence. I just don't recall ever facing one like this before. Her attendance has deteriorated and this once truly good employee is causing problems for the department as a whole."

Stan asked, "What's the problem?"

"Excessive absenteeism," Ellie answered. "Judy has rapidly used up all of her sick time, and most of her sick days have been before or after scheduled days off."

"What's unusual about that? Unfortunately, we have several people who use their sick time as fast as it's accrued. And most get 'sick' on very convenient days. I have a couple I can count on to do it regularly."

"What's unusual is the fact that it's Judy Lawrence. She's been here 7 years, but this apparent sick time abuse has all been within the past few months. She's used up her whole sick-time bank in 7 months. And most recently, she was out for 3 days without even calling in."

Stan said, "You can terminate her for that."

"I know," said Ellie.

"Especially when you take her other absences into account. You've warned her about them?"

After a moment's silence Ellie said, "No, not in writing. Just once, face to face. I really didn't want to put pressure on her."

"Any record of it? Fill out a disciplinary dialogue form for her to sign? Something you've filed—even in your own office?"

"No," said Ellie. "I really hated to. I know I should have taken some kind of action by now, but I can't seem to make myself do it."

Stan asked, "Why not?"

"Because she's always been such a good employee. She's always been pleasant, she's always done what she's been told to do, and she's always done quality work.

She's still that way, except for her attendance problems of the past 7 months. I'm really afraid there's something wrong that she's not telling anyone."

Ellie shrugged and continued, "I guess what I'm really hung up on is: How do I discipline someone who is usually a good employee, and do it in such a way that it doesn't destroy any of what is good about her?"

Stan shook his head and said, "Good performer or not, I'd say you ought to be going by the policy book. That's all I can suggest."

Questions:

1. How would you advise Ellie to proceed in the matter of Judy Lawrence?
2. Do you feel that Ellie's failure to take action thus far affects her ability to take action now? Why or why not?

Case 6

The Clinging Vine

Primary Topic—*Delegation*

Additional Topics—*Communication; Criticism and Discipline; Employee Problems and Problem Employees; Leadership; Motivation*

"I feel like I have an open line of communication with Brenda," said building services supervisor, May Carey, "and maybe that's part of the problem. She never hesitates to come to me about even the smallest matter that she ought to know she can take care of without me. She checks in with me so often that I feel I might as well be doing her work in addition to my own."

Jane Scott, a head nurse and May's carpool companion, said, "Maybe you ought to be glad that she keeps you informed. I wish some of my nurses were better about bringing things to my attention. I don't know if there's such a thing as too much communication."

"In this case there is too much," said May. "Half of what Brenda brings to me is simple stuff, regular parts of her job that she's expected to take care of. And she's always asking me what to do next—and if she can't find me right away, she doesn't do anything until I show up and give her new instructions."

Jane asked, "How did Brenda get along with your predecessor? Same problem?"

"I don't know. The last supervisor's style was a lot different from mine. She seemed very authoritarian in the way she ran the department."

"Do you suppose Brenda ever got in trouble for not checking in? That may be why she thinks she's expected to do what she's doing."

"I don't know that either," May answered. "There's been so much to do that I haven't really begun to uncover all of the major problems in the department. I've been stalled for 6 months just trying to get at our antiquated job descriptions."

"Well," said Jane, "I should think you'd be glad to have the open communication that you have with Brenda."

"I am," said May, "and I'd like to keep it. But how can I go about getting her to work more independently without damaging that open line of communication?"

Instructions:

Develop a recommended approach for May to follow in instilling more independence in Brenda while attempting to maintain open communication with her.

CASE 7

THE INHERITED PROBLEM

Primary Topic—*Employee Problems and Problem Employees*

Additional Topics—*Communication; Criticism and Discipline; Delegation; Leadership*

Shortly after she moved into the position of kitchen supervisor, Donna Wayne decided that a food service aide named Sandra Cleary was emerging as a problem employee. Sandra, nearing the end of her 6-month probationary period, was frequently idle. She would apparently do what she was told to do and then do nothing until specifically assigned to another task. Donna grew especially sensitive to the situation when she began to pick up grumblings from several other workers about Sandra not doing her fair share of the work.

Because she did not want to be unduly influenced by what others might have said, Donna did not look at Sandra's record when she drafted Sandra's 6-month review. She tried to avoid focusing on the employee's attitude, which at best seemed to be distant and disinterested, and instead attempted to focus strictly on Sandra's performance. Even this approach yielded a highly uncomplimentary review; Donna had already decided that Sandra was probably the department's worst performer.

Donna set up an appointment for Sandra. In opening her conversation with Sandra, Donna said, "I've deliberately avoided looking at your 3-month review, but I'll be surprised if it's much better than the one I have to give you now."

Sandra responded with, "What 3-month review? I didn't know I was supposed to have one."

Astonished at this response, Donna dropped her plans to discuss the 6-month evaluation. Instead, she turned the conversation to Sandra's experience over the preceding 6 months. In her discussion with Sandra, and through personal investigation and a review of Sandra's record, Donna learned that:

- Sandra indeed had never been given a 3-month review, and in all probability had never been told there was such a review.
- Sandra had never been told that she was performing unsatisfactorily.
- Sandra felt that she was expected to wait for instructions before beginning any new task.
- There were no warnings or other indications of trouble in Sandra's personnel file.

It was with dismay that Donna reviewed the problem: The employee's performance was below standard, apparently through no fault of her own, and yet the probation period had expired and the employee was expected to be fully functioning.

Questions:

1. What probably caused the problem with Sandra to develop?
2. What should Donna do to try to correct the problem?
3. What should Donna tell Sandra about the apparent happenings of the past 6 months?

CASE 8

THE WELL-ENTRENCHED EMPLOYEE

Primary Topic—*Change Management*

Additional Topics—*Delegation; Employee Problems and Problem Employees; Leadership; Motivation*

When Dave Farren was hired from outside to be manager of communications for University Hospital, he gave little initial thought to the one-person mail room operation that was part of his department. However, he was soon forced to focus on the mail room because of an alarming number of complaints he received about mail room service. Other departments and elements of his own department complained of slow service on outgoing mail, late and erratic service on incoming mail, and frequent losses of interdepartmental mail.

The mail room operator, Mary West, was a long-time employee who had been in the same job more than 20 years. Her title was actually mail room supervisor, although she had never directly supervised any other employees. However, she had always been left to function very much on her own.

Before Dave could begin to make sense of the complaints about the mail room, Mary West launched something of a complaint campaign of her own. She insisted that she needed a full-time helper in the mail room, claiming that "There's far too much work here for one person and there's nobody to help me." However, Dave quickly learned from others that Mary's "I need help" campaign was an approach that she had used on all of his predecessors over the years.

Dave's first visit to the cramped, out-of-the-way mail room left him appalled. The area was cluttered, with battered interoffice mailers piled everywhere and just plain junk accumulated in every available space. Although Dave was ready to concede that some physical improvements could aid the situation, he was also forced to conclude that the biggest problem area was Mary West's complete lack of an efficient approach to the job.

Dave offered some suggestions aimed at improving the operation of the mail room. However, for the most part his suggestions were met with icy silence and he later picked up secondhand complaints to the effect that Mary wanted "real help, not some new boss nosing around and trying to tell me how to do my job."

Dave proceeded to authorize a few hours of regular overtime apparently budgeted for that purpose to see if that would help Mary get caught up and become more organized. The overtime had no noticeable effect; rather, it seemed to Dave that Mary spent most of her time wandering about the hospital visiting with people. It also seemed that everyone Mary visited heard all about how "overworked" poor Mary was.

After several weeks of casually observing Mary and pondering the mail room situation, Dave concluded that Mary was the major problem. She was apparently still working the way she had worked when she started on the job back when the hospital was less than half its present size.

Instructions:

Putting yourself in Dave Farren's position, develop an approach to the problem that includes:

- Development of a rationale with which to try "selling" the need for change
- An honest effort to win the employee's cooperation
- Identification of alternative approaches to consider should "selling" fail

Case 9

The Sensitive Employee

Primary Topic—*Criticism and Discipline*

Additional Topics—*Communication; Employee Problems and Problem Employees; Rules and Policies*

May as well get it over with, thought business office manager Theresa Fallon as she summoned billing clerk Barbara Goodman to her office. It was with dread that Theresa arranged the papers on her desk and waited for Barbara to be seated. Theresa felt that she knew exactly what was coming and she was determined that this time she would address the continuing problem as well as the specific problem.

Theresa handed a warning form to Barbara and said, "Barb, we have to talk about your excessive absenteeism. This is your second warning. I'm sure you knew it was coming."

Barbara barely glanced at the warning and dropped it on Theresa's desk. "I knew nothing of the kind," she snapped. "There's nothing excessive or unusual about my few days off because I was sick. I'm not signing any warning."

Theresa sighed. "Barb," she said, "you can count the days yourself. Ten sick days in the last 6 months, and 7 of them on Mondays."

"I can't help it if I'm sick a lot."

"Even if you're legitimately ill on those days, and honestly, Barb, it's tough to accept all those Mondays as legitimate sick days, you make it difficult to staff the department reliably."

"Why me? Why don't you lean on Judy for a change? She's been out as much as I have."

Theresa said, "No, she hasn't. Not nearly as much. At any rate, that's strictly between Judy and me. Just like this is strictly between you and me."

Theresa continued, "You know that you've used up all of your sick time."

"I know. This place made me use vacation the last two times." There was accusation in Barbara's voice.

"You wanted to get a full paycheck, didn't you?"

Barbara glared at her supervisor. "I think it stinks to make me use vacation when I'm sick."

Theresa looked at Barbara. Barbara's face was stony, her eyes cold, and her mouth a thin line. Theresa thought, *Any time now—the next thing I say will do it.*

Theresa, fighting against the knot in her throat, said, "Barbara, you haven't been reliable. I just can't count on you to be here when I need you. Your first warning was deserved, and this one is deserved. You can appeal, if you want, through proper channels, but the warning stands."

Theresa watched Barbara's face. Barbara's eyes grew round and quickly filled with tears. Her mouth turned down and she began to sob.

If any other employee had been involved, Theresa might have felt sympathy. However, she had been through this a number of times, in fact every time she had occasion to reprimand Barbara. The pattern was always the same: anger and defensiveness, even belligerence, followed by tears and charges of persecution and injustice. And as always, Theresa wondered what to do next.

Questions:

1. Although Theresa was well prepared with the facts concerning Barbara's absenteeism, she might have considered a different opening for the disciplinary dialogue. What opening would you consider suggesting? Why?
2. How did knowing "exactly what was coming" bias Theresa in her approach to Barbara?
3. What would you suggest as a possible way of dealing with this apparently resentful and emotional employee?

Case 10

The Enemy Camps

Primary Topic—*Criticism and Discipline*

Additional Topics—*Authority; Employee Problems and Problem Employees; General Management Practice; Meeting Leadership; Motivation*

Helen Williams was hired from outside of the hospital to fill the position of business office manager. She accepted the job suspecting that it was something of a "hot seat"; she was to be the fifth person in that position in just 3 years.

Although Helen did not know the specific reasons behind the short stays of her predecessors, after a month she decided that the atmosphere in the department was definitely unhealthy. Her staff appeared to be divided into two distinct rival camps. There was so much animosity between these groups that Helen began to think of them as "Enemy Camp A" and "Enemy Camp B." (Helen kept the "enemy" designation to herself, but she often referred in conversations with her superior to "Camp A and Camp B.")

From her first day on the job, it was apparent to Helen that many of the problems in the department stemmed from poor intradepartmental communications. She was surprised to learn, for instance, that her immediate predecessor never held department staff meetings. Instead, the previous supervisor met sporadically with groups of two or three people to deal with specific problems.

Helen instituted the practice of holding a weekly 30-minute staff meeting for all of her employees. She made it plain that everyone was expected to attend.

After 4 months of staff meetings it seemed to Helen that the atmosphere of rivalry between the "camps" had diminished substantially. However, it was still evident that the group was divided on many matters. It also seemed to Helen that "Camp A" was becoming her group in the sense that these people were steadily becoming more supportive of her and her approach to managing the department. Unfortunately, this condition seemed to ensure that "Camp B" would often be opposed to Helen herself on matters in which full staff cooperation was vital.

Early in Helen's seventh month on the job she received a quiet visit from Jeanette Woods, a longstanding member of "Camp A." Jeanette informed Helen that she had heard Sandy Davis, an acknowledged informal leader within "Camp B," admit to snooping in Helen's office and reading a number of confidential documents. When

Helen reminded Jeanette that most if not all of her confidential records were kept in a locked drawer, Jeanette responded with some reluctance, "I think Sandy has a key to your desk."

Helen's first reaction to Jeanette's revelation was to consider how she could successfully discipline Sandy without compromising Jeanette.

Instructions:

Consider the problem in terms of the following questions:

1. What hazards is Helen likely to face in taking direct action against Sandy based on what she heard from Jeanette? Why should she—or why should she not—take such action?
2. What would you do if you were in Helen's position?

Case 11

The Turnaround Challenge

Primary Topic—*Change Management*

Additional Topics—*Delegation; Employee Problems and Problem Employees; General Management Practice; Leadership; Methods Improvement*

In February, Fred Jarvis took over as manager of laundry operations. He came from outside the hospital, but he brought with him several years of experience in institutional laundry operations. He was told bluntly that he was following a weak (or perhaps unmotivated) manager who had allowed the department to become quite lax over a period of several years. Fred quickly recognized that his employees' apparent practice of doing just enough to get by fell far short of his own standards of acceptable performance.

Fred inherited an assistant supervisor who was, in that employee's own words, "Just a gopher with a title—the old boss never really gave me any responsibility."

For his first few weeks on the job, most of Fred's crew struck him as being friendly, reasonable people. However, in March, when Fred announced some new and carefully determined productivity targets, many of the smiles turned to scowls, and the crew's friendly chatter dropped off markedly. He was seeking improvement in output per personnel hour of 18 percent over a year, to be achieved at a rate of 3 percent for each 2-month period.

In spite of the turn in attitude, Fred's crew easily boosted productivity by 3 percent during March and April. However, during the May–June period output rose by only 2 percent, and over July and August productivity dropped by 1 percent.

Fred did his best to maintain a friendly but businesslike attitude. However, by the end of August none of his employees would initiate conversation with him, except for his assistant supervisor, who by then seemed to be getting the same treatment Fred was receiving.

Most of the laundry employees would respond when spoken to, accept Fred's instructions without question, and then go about their business at a pace that Fred could only describe as foot-dragging. Although few were openly resistant, Fred felt that most of his employees were passively but stubbornly fighting all of his efforts to improve output.

At the end of August, Fred was told by his manager, the vice president for general services: "I don't see much happening in the laundry. You know that you were put there to correct the problems that your predecessor allowed to develop, especially the intolerably poor level of output. For a while you seemed to be making progress, but now things seem to be sagging again. Tell me—just how long is it going to take you to turn the department around?"

Questions:

1. How long should it take Fred to turn the department around? Should the 7 months he has already been there have been enough?
2. Describe a tentative approach and timetable for Fred to consider in correcting the productivity problem, and explain how Fred should go about selling this approach to the assistant administrator.
3. Consider the kind of department—a laundry—and identify one or more seemingly drastic options that would probably take care of the productivity problem.
4. Would it assist your analysis to know about the age and condition of the equipment in the laundry? How?

CASE 12

ONE PERSON'S WORD AGAINST ANOTHER'S

Primary Topic—*Criticism and Discipline*

Additional Topics—*Delegation; Employee Problems and Problem Employees; General Management Practice*

You are second-shift supervisor in the food preparation area of the dietary department. Your normal hours are from 3:30 PM to midnight. However, about half of the people who report to you are finished for the day at 7:30 PM; for the sake of having maximum help available over the lunch and dinner hours, a number of food preparation workers are assigned to a shift that begins at 11:00 AM and ends at 7:30 PM. Because of these differences in work schedules, the persons who report to you from 3:30 to 7:30 have a different supervisor—the day shift supervisor—before 3:30.

You have felt that a problem was developing with Janet Mills, a kitchen helper assigned to the 11:00 AM to 7:30 PM shift. Janet frequently asked to leave early, as much as an hour or more before 7:30. It seemed to you that the more readily you accommodated her requests—you usually let her go unless you were short of help for the work remaining to be done—the more frequent her requests became. When you finally realized that Janet managed to punch out early at least twice a week, and when some grumbling about special treatment came to you from other employees, you decided it was time to start discouraging Janet's early departures.

After you had refused permission twice in the same week, Janet did not ask again to leave early for several days. You thought that perhaps the problem had been easily corrected. However, on Monday of this week the problem resurfaced in a somewhat different manner.

At about 6:00 PM Janet came to you and said, "Mrs. Carter said I could leave at 6:30 today. I'm supposed to tell you."

You could not imagine why Mrs. Carter, the day supervisor, would grant such permission on a day like this when all shifts were short of help. However, you did not want to contradict another supervisor so you simply let Janet leave at 6:30.

The next day you asked Mrs. Carter about Janet's early departure. When you told her what Janet had said, Mrs. Carter responded, "That isn't everything that was said. I did say, 'You can leave at 6:30,' but I also said, 'if the work is under control and the evening supervisor agrees.' I also told her that we were short of help and it was a bad day to leave early, but she said there was something very important that she had to take care of."

That day you spoke twice with Mrs. Carter and twice with Janet Mills. Their stories remained the same: Janet claimed that she had clear, unmistakable permission to leave early; Mrs. Carter claimed that Janet had distorted what was said to her and had in effect left without permission.

One day later, Mrs. Carter advised you that she was issuing a written warning to Janet Mills for her "distortion or misrepresentation" of what she had been told. She asked you to cosign the warning with her.

Instructions:

Consider the problem in terms of the following questions:

1. What is your immediate reaction to Mrs. Carter's request for you to participate in the warning?
2. What course of action would you follow if you are convinced that the employee is actively playing one supervisor off against the other?
3. How would you suggest attempting to minimize the communications problems that are bound to develop when an employee reports to more than one supervisor at different times?

Case 13

The Grouchy Receptionist

Primary Topic—*Employee Problems and Problem Employees*
Additional Topics—*Communication; Criticism and Discipline*

"As your assistant, I'm certainly not trying to tell you what to do," said Marie Stark. "You're the boss and I'm only pointing out—again—a problem that's leading us into lots of grief."

"I know," laboratory administrator Morris Craig said with more than a trace of annoyance. "I'm trying to take it the way you mean it. I've heard it from several people and I know we've got a problem with Jennifer. I just don't know how to deal with it, that's all."

"It has to be dealt with," Marie said. "As lab receptionist Jennifer is in a position to leave a first and lasting impression on a lot of people, and she's generating an endless trail of complaints. I've heard from patients, staff, and physicians alike—just about anyone you care to name—about her curt, rude treatment of them. It's been going on for months, and it's getting worse. And now she's starting to mix up appointment times as well."

Morris said, "I know. I had hoped that whatever was bugging her would pass. But it hasn't. She's gone from bad to worse. And it's too bad—she's been here a long time, and this is only relatively recent."

"One of us needs to talk with her. Or at least make some attempt to find out what's wrong."

Morris spread his hands, palms up, and said, "I've tried to talk with her. Just a week ago I gave her a chance to talk in private. I even asked if I could help out in any way, but. . . ." He shrugged helplessly.

"But what?"

"She told me nothing was wrong, or something like that. I got the impression that she was telling me—kind of roundabout—to mind my own business."

"Well, something's wrong," Marie said, "and we need to do something about it. Our receptionist is coming across as a first-class grouch and the department is suffering."

Instructions:

Develop a tentative approach for dealing with the apparent attitude problem presented by the laboratory receptionist. Make certain you provide for reasonable opportunity for correction of behavior and that you account for:

- Possible ways of assisting the employee with "the problem"
- The necessarily progressive nature of any disciplinary action considered
- The needs of the department

CASE 14

WHAT'S THE TRUTH?

Primary Topic—*Communication*

Additional Topics—*Criticism and Discipline; Delegation; Employee Problems and Problem Employees*

"I've really had it with that Stan Thomas," said maintenance supervisor Tom Davis to his boss, Harry Willis, director of building services.

"What's wrong?" Willis asked.

"You mean what's wrong *this time*," said Davis. "It's been one thing after another longer than I care to think about. This time I'd call it insubordination. He refused to clean up the scraps and leftover construction material behind the new business office when I told him to."

"A direct refusal of your direct order?"

"Not right away," said Davis. "First I put it in the form of a request, but he started making excuses about how much he had to do. I told him it had to be cleaned up today and he simply told me he had so much important work that he didn't know if he could get at it today. When I told him he had to do it today he simply glared at me for a moment and said, 'No way.'"

"No way?" Willis asked. "Those were his exact words?"

"Yes. His exact words."

"We'll see about that," said Willis.

Some time later, just before the end of the shift, Tom Davis located Stan Thomas. Thomas was performing the task that had been the focus of the earlier difficulty. When he saw Davis, Thomas stopped working, glared at him, and said, "I would have gotten this done as soon as I got a few things caught up. You didn't have to sic your boss on me. And you especially didn't have to tell him what you told him."

"What are you talking about?"

Thomas said coolly, "You lied to Willis about what I said to you. I don't forget things like that."

Davis tried to get Thomas to explain further what he meant by that remark. However, Thomas would say nothing else.

Tom Davis went looking for Harry Willis.

Questions:

Assess the foregoing incident and its possible causes, implications, and ramifications, from: (a) Tom Davis's point of view; (b) Harry Willis's point of view.

1. Considering the present state of affairs, what—if anything—would you recommend doing?

Case 15

In a Rut

Primary Topic—*Change Management*

Additional Topics—*Delegation; Employee Problems and Problem Employees; Methods Improvement*

"Sometimes I'm not sure you did me a favor by promoting me," said Sue Allen, the human resource department's newest employee and the newly appointed employment manager. "Maybe it's because I'm so new—to the rest of the folks in the office I'm still an outsider—that I don't seem to have any effect on the people in my little group."

"What do you mean?" asked human resource director Andy Miller.

"Well, I was under the impression that you put me in charge of the employment office so I could streamline things and bring a lot of our practices up to date."

"That's right."

"It doesn't seem to be working at all," said Sue. "I have all sorts of ideas about what we ought to be doing, and you seem to agree with everything I suggest. But I can't get this bunch to go along with anything. I took a great deal of time—my own time, I might add—to work out a plan of short-range and long-range goals and objectives for them, but I can't get them to do anything differently."

"Remember," said Miller, "most of them have been here lots longer than you and I. You've been here just a few months, and I came here barely a year ago."

"They act like they've been here forever," said Sue. "And I guess they have. They range from 7 to 15 years of service, with the average just over 10 years." She shook her head sharply and said, "Talk about people being set in their ways!"

Miller asked, "What do they seem to think about the changes you've wanted to make?"

"I don't know," said Sue. "They just listen quietly and then go about their business in the same old way as though I weren't here. It's really a frustrating situation, and I guess what I really want you to tell me is: How can I possibly go about setting new goals for a bunch of disinterested and inflexible people who've been doing the same thing in the same old way for years?"

Instructions:

1. Identify an apparent major error in Sue Allen's approach to the situation in her group and suggest how she might have proceeded differently.
2. Outline the kind of approach you believe human resource director Andy Miller should be advising the employment manager to follow.

CASE 16

THE UP-AND-DOWN PERFORMER

Primary Topic—*Criticism and Discipline*

Additional Topics—*Delegation; Employee Problems and Problem Employees; Leadership*

"I've come to the end of my patience with Roberta Weston," said accounting manager Sam Best. "The position she's in is so important to us that we simply can't afford any more of her omissions or mistakes. For the sake of the hospital and the department, I believe she's got to go."

"What's the problem?" asked human resource director Charlene Harrison.

"Problems, plural," Best answered. "She's so late in posting the receipts on rentals in the medical arts center that we wind up double billing a number of physicians every month. Actually, it's the same with just about all miscellaneous income—since she's responsible for all receipts except third-party reimbursement. We're losing control of income, and I get three or four complaints a week from people who claim they've been billed again for charges they've already paid."

Best shook his head and added, "I've really tried to give her every chance to turn around, but nothing seems to work. At least not for very long."

Harrison said, "I've reviewed Roberta's file. The only evidence of a problem I found was your rather detailed performance improvement review of 2 months ago. In that process, you're supposed to give the employee detailed direction aimed at correcting the problem—which you did—along with a warning that task performance will be monitored closely for 30 days and that she could be let go by the end of that period if her work hasn't come up to satisfactory levels. You did the review, but I didn't see anything about any follow-up."

Best said, "That's because she had shaped up by the end of the 30 days."

"But now she isn't working up to the requirements of the job?"

"Right. Her work was just marginally okay at the end of the 30 days, but within 2 weeks of that the bottom dropped out again, and the mistakes started rolling in."

Harrison asked, "What do you mean by 'again'?"

"This is the third time I've been through this with her. I go over the areas in which she's not working up to standard, she puts on a burst of effort and does better, and a month or so later she falls back into her old ways." Best frowned and added, "I can't put up with it any longer. Three strikes—she's out."

Harrison said, "According to her file it's just one strike. The only documentation is your single performance improvement review. What about the other two times?"

"Strictly verbal."

"You didn't write anything? You're supposed to cover oral warnings with a disciplinary dialogue form for the record."

Best said, "If I wrote up one of those every time I had to warn an employee, I'd never get done writing. It's a lot of work."

"I know it is," responded Harrison, "but you've got to have your documentation. As it stands right now, if you terminate her she could probably give us a real hard time with the state."

"So what should I do?" Best asked.

Questions:

1. Why could the employee give the institution "a real hard time" if she is terminated now?
2. What plan of action would you recommend to Sam Best for dealing with the up-and-down performer?

CASE 17

I'LL GET AROUND TO IT

Primary Topic—*Employee Problems and Problem Employees*

Additional Topics—*Authority; Change Management; Communication; Delegation*

Housekeeping supervisor Mabel Wilson felt she had little control over the activities of housekeeper Ellie Masters. It seemed Ellie was generally nonresponsive to special requests and instructions to perform unexpected tasks. Regarding her routine, regularly assigned work, Ellie usually did what was expected of her in a reasonable amount of time and with acceptable results; however, Mabel could count on Ellie's resistance to unanticipated assignments. Also, it seemed to Mabel that Ellie was unable to adjust her activities to account for anything that occurred unexpectedly.

For instance, this morning Mabel received a call regarding the sorry state of the hospital's emergency room entrance. It seemed that prolonged bad weather had created widespread mud and much had been tracked in. Because that was Ellie's area, Mabel sought her out and said, "The ER entrance is muddy and needs going over again. Please take care of it; it's bound to be slippery, and we don't want anyone to fall."

Ellie simply nodded and said, "When I get around to it."

She continued with what she had been doing when Mabel found her. It was not the first time Mabel had gotten that response from Ellie. One pace, one order of activities, one level of concern whether or not something was urgent, that was Ellie.

Instructions:

Develop a recommended approach for Mabel to apply in dealing with Ellie. Make certain your approach deals with the overall problem as well as with the immediate need expressed in Mabel's recent instruction to Ellie.

Case 18

The Alternate Day Off

Primary Topic—*Employee Problems and Problem Employees*
Additional Topics—*Criticism and Discipline; Rules and Policies*

Early in June licensed practical nurse Susan Butler approached her supervisor, nurse manager Mabel Wesley, and volunteered to work on the upcoming Fourth of July holiday. Although Mabel was well aware that Susan was volunteering to work a day for which she would be paid time-and-a-half, she accepted Susan's offer because a number of people had asked to have the holiday off and staffing would be tight, as it usually was on holidays.

Thus scheduled to work the holiday, Susan was entitled, by staffing policy, to take off an alternate day as her holiday. The policy simply said that the alternate day must be taken within 2 weeks of the legal holiday.

Susan Butler took her alternate day off 1 full week before the actual Fourth of July holiday. She said that she especially needed this day; getting this particular day off was the reason she volunteered to work on the Fourth of July. She pointed out that the policy that said the alternate day must be taken "within 2 weeks" of the holiday could be interpreted as meaning before or after the holiday. Mabel, however, could not recall a case in which the employee had not taken the alternate day within 2 weeks after the holiday.

Susan Butler, having already taken her alternate day off, came to work on the Fourth of July. However, she stayed less than half of the shift; shortly before 11:00 AM she said she did not feel well and punched out and went home. Mabel's unit had to function for the balance of the shift with less than its required staff.

Questions:

1. Do you believe Mabel Wesley should take any action regarding Susan? If so, what action might she consider taking?
2. What—if anything—could Mabel do regarding the alternate-day-off policy?

Case 19

If You Want Things Done Well . . .

Primary Topic—*Delegation*

Additional Topics—*Communication; Motivation; Time Management and Personal Effectiveness*

John Miller, manager of laundry and linen for City Medical Center, dreaded the one day each month he had to spend doing the statistical report for his department. Miller was responsible for all laundry and linen activities in the 800-bed hospital, two smaller satellite facilities, and several municipal agencies whose linen needs were filled by the hospital. At one time the report had been relatively simple, but as Miller's scope of responsibility grew and administration requested increasingly more detailed information each month, the report had become more complicated. Miller had simply modified his method of preparing the report each time a new requirement was placed upon him, so there was no written procedure for the report's preparation.

Faced once again with the time-consuming report—and confronted, as usual, with several problems demanding his immediate attention—John Miller decided it was time to delegate the preparation of the report to his assistant, Bill Curtis. He called Curtis to his office, gave him a copy of the previous month's report and a set of forms, and said, "I'm sure you've seen this. I want you to take care of it from now on. I've been doing it for a long time, but it's getting to be a real pain and I've got more important things to do than to allow myself to be tied up with routine clerical work."

Curtis spent perhaps a half minute skimming the report before he said, "I'm sure I can do it if I start on the right foot. How about walking me through it—doing just this one with me so I can get the hang of it?"

Miller said, "Look, my objective in giving you this is to save me some time. If I have to hold your hand, I may as well do it myself." He grinned as he added, "Besides, if I can do it, then anyone with half a brain ought to be able to do it."

Without further comment Curtis left the office with the report and the forms. Miller went to work on other matters.

Later that day Curtis stopped Miller in the corridor—they met while going in opposite directions—and said, "John, I'm glad I caught you. I've got three or four questions about the activity report, mostly concerning how you come up with the count and percentages for the satellites." He started to pull a folded sheet of paper from his back pocket.

Miller barely slowed. "Sorry, Bill, but I can't take the time. I'm late for a meeting." As he hurried past Curtis, he called back over his shoulder, "You'll just have to puzzle it out for yourself. After all, I had to do the same thing."

The following day when the report was due, Miller found Curtis's work on his desk when he returned from lunch. He flipped through it to assure himself that all the blanks had been filled in, then scrawled his signature in the usual place. However, something caught his eye—a number that appeared to be far out of line with anything he had encountered in previous reports. He took out two earlier reports and began a line-by-line comparison. He quickly discovered that Curtis had made a crucial error near the beginning and carried it through successive calculations.

Miller was angry with Curtis. The day was more than half gone and he would have to drop everything else and spend the rest of the afternoon reworking the figures so the report could be submitted on time.

Miller was still working at 4:30 PM when Pete Anderson, the engineering manager, appeared in the door way and said, "I thought we were going to rework your preventive schedule this afternoon. What are you up to, anyway?"

Miller threw down his pencil and snapped, "I'm proving an old saying."

"Meaning what?"

"Meaning, if you want something done right, do it yourself."

Instructions:

- Miller committed several significant errors in "delegating" the activity report to Curtis. Identify at least three such errors in the case description.
- Using as many steps as you believe necessary, describe how this instance of delegation might have been properly accomplished.

Case 20

Sixty Minutes or Less

Primary Topic—*Time Management and Personal Effectiveness*
Additional Topics—*Communication; Methods Improvement*

When business office manager Judy Morrison returned from a 2-day seminar, she found her desk half covered with telephone message slips and her in basket overflowing with other work. As she glumly surveyed the pile of work before her, department secretary Ann Rose reminded Judy that she was due at a major meeting in barely an hour and would probably be tied up for the rest of the day.

"Just look at this mess," said Judy. "I knew I shouldn't have gone away. Now I'll take forever getting back to normal."

Ann suggested, "You don't have anything at all on your calendar for tomorrow. And you have almost an hour available right now."

Judy sighed and said, "An hour doesn't seem like much time in the face of this pile of work. I don't know what I could possibly accomplish in only an hour."

Ann indicated the array of telephone messages and said, "Maybe some phone calls. You could probably return most of the important calls within an hour."

"But how do I know that the calls are what I should really be working on? It might make more sense for me to use the time to go through everything and sort it all according to priority and plan how I'm going to attack this backlog."

"Okay, you could do that," Ann said. "You could also check quickly through everything and pick out a couple of important items that you can resolve within the hour. That way you would be trimming the pile down at least a little bit."

"Well, I'd better do something," said Judy. "I've already used up 5 minutes of my hour just wondering where to begin."

Questions:

In the conversation between Judy and Ann, three approaches to the use of the available hour were suggested:

1. Return the telephone calls, concentrating first on the more important calls.
2. Sort everything according to priorities and develop a work plan.
3. Select one or two important items for immediate resolution.

Which of these three approaches would you recommend? Why?

CASE 21

IS IT INSUBORDINATION?

Primary Topic—*Authority*

Additional Topics—*Criticism and Discipline; Decision Making; Leadership; Motivation; Rules and Policies*

Peter Hamilton, the hospital's maintenance department supervisor, was sure that the announcement he had to make would not be well received by many of his employees. He did not like the idea of having to place limits on when his employees could take their vacations, but after several meetings with his boss, the director of environmental services, Pete was convinced that he would need his full staff plus outside help for a particular 6-week period.

At a November staff meeting, Pete Hamilton announced, "Those of you who figure on vacations during the first half of the year, we're going to have to ask you to leave May 15 to June 30 out of your planning. The new admitting offices will open May 15. Demolition of the old west wing will start July 1, timed with some work on the adjoining property. That means we've got just 6 weeks to gut and remodel the old admitting area so we can get accounting out of the west wing by the end of June. We'll need all the hands we can find for those 6 weeks. So, if you have vacation in mind, either schedule it so you're back by May 15, or wait and go some time after July 1."

There was some muttering in the group, but no voices were raised in immediate protest. However, just as Pete thought that perhaps there would be no trouble, a single hand went up. The person was Ed Mason, a long-time employee and one of the hospital's two electricians.

Mason said, "I've always taken the same 2 weeks in June, every year almost as long as I've been here. You trying to tell me I can't go then?"

Hamilton repeated his explanation and added a general appeal covering the need for all of them to pull together to get a difficult job done in a limited amount of time. Ed Mason uttered a one-word obscenity that was clearly audible to all in the room. Mason's expression was one of anger and his manner might have struck some as threatening.

Pete dismissed the group, but ordered Ed Mason to remain. When the others had left, Mason said, "I've been here 17 years, and for the last 12 years I've taken vacation the same 2 weeks in June. There shouldn't be any reason why I can't do the same next June. I always have my request in first. The others in the department know that, and they're all used to doing without me during that period."

Pete responded, "This applies to all of us in maintenance, myself included—I usually go the last part of May, around Memorial Day."

"You can't change that on me," Ed said stubbornly. "That vacation is my right, considering my seniority here."

"Ed, maybe we all need reminding that vacation is scheduled at management's discretion. Sure, we try to give you exactly the time you want if we can, providing—like the policy says—that it's convenient to the functioning of the department and the hospital. This is one time when it isn't convenient. You don't seem to appreciate all the work that needs to be done and how limited we are with present staff."

"Nuts to that," said Mason as he headed for the door. He added, "My seniority ought to be good for something. I'm not changing my plans for you or anybody."

Instruction:

Put yourself in Peter Hamilton's position and decide how you would deal with the problem presented by Ed Mason's reaction to the vacation restriction.

Case 22

Get Back to You in a Minute

Primary Topic—*Communication*

Additional Topics—*Authority; Leadership; Time Management and Personal Effectiveness*

You are the laundry manager at Community Hospital and you report to the director of support services. You have just been through a particularly trying week, and you have concluded that your relationship with the director of support services is not in the best of shape. You review the contacts you had with your boss during the week.

Monday morning a personnel problem arose that you felt could require severe disciplinary action. You thought you had better clear the action with your boss. However, you could not reach him. You called his office three times; each time you spoke with his secretary who said she would have him return your call. Monday ended without a response from the boss.

Tuesday you encountered your boss in a basement corridor when he was going in the opposite direction. As you moved directly toward him so as to nearly block his passage, you told him you needed to see him on a matter of some importance. Without slowing, he detoured around you and called back over his shoulder, "Something's up—can't stop. Get back to you in a minute." You didn't see him again that day. When you called his office you were told he was in a meeting.

Wednesday morning you decided to visit the boss's office. However, you found he had two visitors. He saw you at the door and shrugged, smiled faintly, and waved you away. That afternoon you telephoned the boss's office. His secretary was away from her desk and he answered his own phone and immediately told you he was tied up with someone and added, "Buzz you back as soon as I'm free." You remained nearly an hour after quitting time but he did not "buzz you back." When you left you noticed that his office was dark.

Thursday you made no effort to contact the boss. Rather, because the item you had been holding open since Monday was still plaguing you and someone needed an answer, you went ahead and used your best judgment and took care of it. You felt you were perhaps overstepping your authority a bit, but you knew that further delay would only cause harm.

Friday you encountered the boss twice while you were moving about the lower level of the building. The first time you told him you needed to get a few minutes of his time. He told you he was on his way to the president's office but he would get back to you shortly. Nothing. On the second occasion he saw you before you saw him, and he called out, "Hey, we need to get together. I'm on the way to a meeting, but catch me in my office at about 4 o'clock." The boss was not in his office at 4:00 PM. Neither was he there at 4:30 PM, the normal quitting time, nor was he there at 5:00 PM when you left for the weekend. You learned on the way out of the building that the boss's meeting had ended at 3:30 PM.

Upon review you felt that the week, taken in its entirety, looked pretty grim. Unfortunately, you had experienced too many such weeks.

Instructions:

There are two general approaches you can adopt to handle the problem of working with this particular boss. You can:

- Mount an all-out effort to get his attention, focusing on getting him into situations in which he cannot avoid dealing with you for at least a few minutes.
- Decide to do your own thing, doing your job as you see fit and handling all decisions that arise regardless of where they fall relative to your scope of authority.

Determine how you might develop these approaches, including what specific steps you might consider in either or both cases, and identify all possible pitfalls and hazards present in both.

CASE 23

THE DELEGATED DIGGING

Primary Topic—*Delegation*

Additional Topics—*Leadership; Motivation*

John Kaye, director of biomedical engineering, was discussing an information need with his boss, Peter Gideon. Both agreed that their equipment maintenance and repair records were not providing them with the kind of information they needed—nature of breakdown and failures, maintenance problems, and unique situations encountered—to design an effective preventive maintenance program.

Asked Gideon, "Since we started your department 18 months ago, haven't we kept records of all the work done by you and your technicians?"

"Sure we have," answered Kaye, "but they won't tell us anything useful without lots of digging. We have 18 months worth of completed work orders filed in chronological order."

"Could someone sort through all of the work orders and separate them by kinds of problems? Perhaps see if there are any patterns to the various kinds of work required?" asked Gideon.

"I suppose so," Kaye said, "but I certainly don't have the time to do it myself, and both of my techs are swamped with open work orders. I guess I could always delegate it to my secretary, Sharon—just tell her what I want and let her go about collecting it in her own way."

Gideon asked, "Does Sharon know the language? Know all of the work order codes? Perhaps you might want to provide her with some detailed instructions and maybe even give her a deadline for completion or a schedule for finishing various steps of the project."

"I don't see much point in delegating the job if I'm going to have to do all that work just to get ready," said Kaye. "It ought to be enough for me to give her my objectives, suggest an approach, let her add her own ideas to it, and turn her loose."

Gideon asked, "Could this become a regular part of her job?"

"It should. Hers or somebody's. Then we could monitor the kinds of information we need rather than having to dig for it like we are now," Kaye answered.

"Between us, we seem to have thrown out three ways of using Sharon on this project," said Gideon. He outlined the three possibilities:

1. Tell her what is wanted and let her do it in her own way.
2. Provide her with expected results, a procedure or other instructions, and a schedule or a deadline.
3. Tell her what is wanted, recommend an approach, and turn her loose.

Instructions:

- Assuming Sharon is qualified for the project, what should determine whether John Kaye does indeed assign the task to her (as opposed to doing it himself or looking for another way)?
- Identify the advantages and disadvantages of the three possibilities outlined by Peter Gideon.
- Which of the three approaches would you recommend in this instance? Why?

CASE 24

THE SECOND CHANCE

Primary Topic—*Delegation*

Additional Topics—*Leadership; Motivation; Time Management and Personal Effectiveness*

John Kaye, director of biomedical engineering, felt the pressure of having too much to do. He knew he was not giving a number of matters the attention they deserved, including a special work-order analysis project he had hastily assigned to his secretary, Sharon. Sharon had already interrupted him with questions five times this week—and today was only Tuesday. He fully expected another such interruption at any time, and he had decided that when it occurred he could react in one of three ways. He could:

1. Review what Sharon had accomplished so far, show her where she might be going wrong, and help her plan out the rest of the task.
2. Assume active responsibility for the project and finish it himself.
3. Thoroughly and patiently answer her current question and hope that this would be sufficient to keep her going without having to interrupt him again.

Questions:

1. To which of the three foregoing questions should John Kaye give the most serious consideration?
2. Why?

Case 25

The Bungled Assignment

Primary Topic—*Delegation*

Additional Topics—*Communication; Criticism and Discipline; Leadership; Motivation*

"I'm afraid that this report of yours is practically useless," said John Kaye, director of biomedical engineering, to his secretary, Sharon. "You used some wrong numbers in several critical places, and I've found enough errors in arithmetic to make me doubt the value of any of the percentages you came up with. Frankly, Sharon, I'm surprised. This isn't your kind of output at all."

"I know it isn't," Sharon said. "I didn't feel good about it while I was doing it, but I did the best I could do with what I had. Remember, this isn't my normal kind of work at all."

Kaye said, "You might have asked a few more questions if you had doubts about where you were going. When I didn't hear from you these last several days I felt that everything must have been going okay."

"That wasn't so," said Sharon. "I was snowed, and I knew it. I asked you four or five questions during the first 2 days, remember? But you seemed annoyed with the interruptions. You made me feel like I shouldn't be bothering you. So I decided to tough it out and do the best I could by myself."

"That was the wrong decision," Kaye said. "You may have done no more than remind me that I should never delegate an assignment unless I know for certain that the person is qualified to handle it."

"It seems to me that if you need that kind of certainty you'll never delegate anything. Or at least anything that's new and different."

Kaye shrugged and asked, "What do you think went wrong here? Didn't I communicate my needs clearly when I assigned the job?"

"Yes, you did," Sharon answered. "At least I felt that I knew what you wanted of me. But once I got into the job the questions began to pop up—all sorts of things that I didn't expect and didn't know about—and before I knew it I was really in the woods. And you seemed so busy that I quickly came to feel uneasy about bothering you."

"We seem to be left with two open questions," said Kaye. "First, what do we do to salvage this particular assignment? Second—and probably more important—what can we do to keep this sort of thing from happening again?"

Instructions:

Offer your detailed suggestions for dealing with the two questions posed by John Kaye in the final paragraph of the case.

Case 26

It Isn't in the Job Description

Primary Topic—*Employee Problems and Problem Employees*

Additional Topics—*Authority; Communication; Delegation; Leadership; Motivation*

George Morton, the hospital's maintenance supervisor, felt growing frustration with the behavior of mechanic Jeff Thompson. Morton considered Thompson a good mechanic, and this opinion was regularly reinforced by the consistently high quality of Thompson's preventive maintenance work and by his success at difficult repair jobs. The problem stemmed from Thompson's apparent lack of motivation; he seemed always to need to be told what to do next. If not directly instructed, when he finished a job he would take a prolonged break until Morton sought him out and gave him a specific assignment.

Morton's frustration peaked one day when a small plumbing problem got out of hand and became a large problem. He knew that Thompson must have seen the leaking valve, because it was beside the pump on which Thompson had been working. However, when Morton asked why he had done nothing about the valve, Thompson said, "Plumbing isn't part of my job."

"You could have at least reported the problem," Morton said.

Thompson shrugged. "There's nothing in my job description about reporting anything. I do what I'm paid to do, and I stick to my job description."

"You certainly do," said Morton. "Jeff, you're a good mechanic. But you never extend yourself in anyway, never reach out and take care of something without being told."

"I'm not paid to reach out and extend myself. You're the boss, and I do what I'm told. And I do it right."

"I know you do it right," Morton agreed, "but I also know that you usually take longer than you need to. I know you're capable of giving a lot more to the job, but for some reason or other you're not willing to work up to your capabilities."

Again Thompson shrugged. "I stick to my job description and do what I'm told."

Instructions:

Putting yourself in George Morton's position, consider some possible ways of dealing with employee Thompson. Provide a number of steps or guidelines that you might recommend in an attempt to get Thompson to perform more in line with his capabilities.

Case 27

Delayed Change of Command

Primary Topic—*Change Management*

Additional Topics—*Communication; Decision Making; Delegation; Motivation*

With full notice to administration and with the knowledge of his staff, the manager of information services left the hospital to take a more responsible position elsewhere. Within the department it was assumed that Mr. Smith—"Smitty" to almost everyone—would move up from senior systems analyst and become manager. However, a week passed and no appointment had been made.

The week became several weeks. The finance director, to whom the information services manager normally reported, began to make the administrative decisions for the department. Smitty was left with the growing task of overseeing the functions of the group in addition to performing his regular work.

Department personnel became aware that the hospital was advertising for an information services manager and that the finance director was conducting interviews. However, nobody was hired. Finally, after the group had been without a manager for 6 months, Smitty was elevated to data processing manager and was immediately authorized to hire a replacement systems analyst.

Questions:

1. For the period during which there was no manager, how would you assess Smitty's position from the department's viewpoint? The finance director's viewpoint? Smitty's own viewpoint?
2. How would you assess Smitty's position after he was finally made manager?

CASE 28

THE TIGHT DEADLINE

Primary Topic—*Time Management and Personal Effectiveness*

Additional Topics—*Decision Making; General Management Practice*

"Just one day out with the bug and the work comes pouring in," said nursing office manager Susan Wagner. "You won't believe everything I've got to do. It took half an hour to sort this stuff and decide what my priorities are."

"What's first?" asked secretary Betsy Adams.

"The hottest item of real importance is the monthly overtime report. It's due the day after tomorrow. Trouble is, it takes 3 to 4 hours and right now I've got just"—Susan looked at her watch—"three-quarters of an hour before I jump into a series of interviews that will last the rest of the day."

"I know that report is a bear," Betsy said. "Remember, I'm the one who types it. When are you going to have it ready?"

"I was thinking of getting it started right now and finishing it tomorrow morning, though it's a pain to try to pick up the calculations again once they've been started and dropped."

Betsy said, "Our next 2 days are fairly open." She grinned as she added, "Maybe wait and do it on the day it's due? There's nothing like a little deadline pressure to make us work efficiently."

"More pressure I can do without," Susan responded. "I'm half thinking that I should jump into it tomorrow and save the final day as a buffer in case I get interrupted or something goes wrong."

Betsy shrugged and said, "Well, I'll be ready when you're ready for me. When can I probably expect it?"

Instructions:

In their conversation, Susan and Betsy identified three choices for approaching the overtime report:

1. Start now and finish tomorrow.
2. Do it entirely tomorrow.
3. Do the report on the day it is due.

Put yourself in Susan's position and select the approach you would take. Justify the approach by describing its advantages and by noting the disadvantages of the other alternatives.

CASE 29

TEN MINUTES TO SPARE?

Primary Topic—*Time Management and Personal Effectiveness*
Additional Topics—*Decision Making; General Management Practice*

You are the hospital's manager of supply, processing, and dispatch (SPD), and you report to the director of material management.

This morning you returned to work following a 3-day absence to find your in basket overloaded and your desk littered with telephone message slips. You were greeted by your secretary, Ellen, who informed you that you were expected to substitute for your boss at an outside meeting today. You will have to leave no later than 9:30 AM to get to the meeting on time, and you know you can plan on being gone for the remainder of the day.

You are left with 1 hour during which you can start making order of the chaos on your desk before leaving for the meeting. True to your usual pattern, you set about reviewing the items on your desk, message slips as well as the contents of the in basket, and creating separate stacks according to apparent importance or likely priority. You feel that you can perhaps get sufficiently organized to begin work the following day with emphasis on your most important tasks.

Halfway through your hour of organizing, Ellen enters to say, "The finance director, Mr. Wade, is here. He says he wants 10 minutes of your time to discuss a minor question having to do with last month's operating expense report. Shall I tell him you'll call him? Or that he should give you a memo about it?"

You cannot help feeling that the last thing you need at this moment is an interruption, especially for something that is not urgent. It occurs to you that Ellen has described two possible choices for you, to which you have quickly added another, so that you have the following three options:

1. Say that you cannot get involved at the moment, but that you will call Mr. Wade the following morning.
2. Ask for a memo detailing the problem so that you can take care of it when time is available.
3. Grant the request for a meeting then and there, and try to limit the discussion to 5 to 10 minutes.

Instructions:

- Identify the advantages and disadvantages of each of the three choices.
- Indicate your most likely choice, and give your reasons for making this decision.

Case 30

Assignment and Reassignment

Primary Topic—*Delegation*

Additional Topics—*Communication; Leadership; Motivation*

Carol Ames was director of inservice education at James Memorial Hospital. She reported to Ann Baker, assistant director of nursing, who in turn reported to Helen Carey, director of nursing.

One morning, as Carol sat working in her office, Ms. Carey entered and said, "Come and have a cup of coffee, Carol. There's something I'd like to talk with you about."

When they had gotten their coffee and found seats in a quiet corner of the cafeteria, Ms. Carey said, "How busy are you these days, Carol? There's something I'd like you to do for me."

Carol answered, "I'm almost overloaded right now. I don't have much time to spare."

"I didn't think your teaching schedule was too full just now, at least not since you finished the nursing leadership program," Ms. Carey said. "What's taking up your time?"

"It's true that my class schedule is only moderate right now. That's probably why Ann just gave me a couple of new assignments."

Ms. Carey asked, "What assignments?"

"For one thing, she's given me just 2 weeks to compile an inventory of instructional materials and training aids throughout the hospital. Also, she's having me do a report about the costs of supplying employee education. It's long and complicated, and it has to be submitted to the State Hospital Association by the first of the month."

Ms. Carey said, "Well, it has suddenly become very important that we get moving on the development of our new nursing audit criteria. I think you suspected this was coming. We're under pressure from administration to do something about nursing audits, and we don't have much time to do it."

Carol asked, "Where do I fit in?"

Ms. Carey answered, "You're in the best position to take charge of the nursing audit committee. It will be up to you to convene the committee as necessary and get the criteria developed on time."

"But what do I do about the inventory and the cost report? Surely I'm not going to have time for everything."

"Of course you won't have time for everything," said Ms. Carey. "Ann will have to find some other way to get the cost report done, and the inventory will just have to wait."

"Is Ann aware of this?" Carol asked.

"No," responded Ms. Carey. "I want you to bring her up to date. And please stress the importance of the audit activity."

At this point Ms. Carey excused herself. Carol got a second cup of coffee and sat by herself to ponder the situation. She felt that her immediate supervisor, Ann, had been quite clear about what she expected over the coming weeks. However, Carol now found herself wondering how to tell her boss that her commitments had been changed by higher authority.

Questions:

1. What fundamental management error was committed?
2. What would you recommend that Carol Ames do about the situation in which she finds herself at present?

CASE 31

THE UNREQUESTED INFORMATION

Primary Topic—*Employee Problems and Problem Employees*

Additional Topics—*Authority; Communication; Leadership*

One morning more than a half hour before the start of your department's normal working hours you were enjoying a cup of coffee in a quiet corner of the cafeteria, sorting through some low-priority reading material, when you were approached by one of your employees. The employee, Nellie Morris, one of your most senior staff in years of service, seated herself across from you without invitation and said, "There's something I have to talk to you about—I've simply waited far too long."

Nellie Morris proceeded to tell you—"In strictest confidence, please, I know you'll understand"—that another long-term employee, Marge Greely, has been making a great many derogatory comments throughout the department about you and your management style and generally calling your competence into question.

You heard a considerable number of "she saids" and "she dids" and a smattering of apparently second-hand or twice-told tales, but no specific incidents that you could identify jumped out at you and initially you were too surprised to ask for clarification.

For the greater part of 10 minutes Nellie showered you with criticism of you, your management style, and your approach to individual employees, all attributed to Marge Greely. On exhausting her litany Nellie proclaimed that she did not ordinarily "carry tales," but that she felt you "had a right to know, for the good of the department—but please don't tell her I said anything."

Questions:

Should you:

- Thank Nellie for her concern and ask her to report anything else she might hear?
- Acknowledge her concern for the good of the department, but ask her to bring you no further stories?
- Thank her, ask her to say nothing to anyone else, and decide for yourself to keep an eye on Marge Greely?

What would you do instead of or perhaps in addition to taking one of the preceding three approaches?

CASE 32

DID HE HAVE IT COMING?

Primary Topic—*Criticism and Discipline*

Additional Topics—*General Management Practice; Leadership; Motivation;*

"That was an absolutely idiotic thing to do," said Peter Jackson, the hospital's chief operating officer.

"In what way?" asked recently hired purchasing manager Dan Smither, reddening noticeably at his boss's words.

"You fiddled around with your price break calculations so long that you stalled us right into a significant price increase. Thanks to this one move of yours, we'll go about $10,000 over budget on paper products for the year."

"So I made a mistake," Smither retorted.

"Mistake? More like a major blunder. Ten thousand bucks out the window. I don't know what ever convinced you that you know the paper market. The way prices have been going, you know you've got to get in and cut a contract fast once the suppliers know what you need."

Jackson shook his head and repeated, "Ten thousand!"

Smither glared down at Jackson. "So I slipped—and I know it, although the way we jump around among group contracts and our own deals, I can hardly blame myself. But I do know that in the 2 months I've been here I've saved twice $10,000 in other areas. How come I don't hear about those?"

"Because that's your job," Jackson snapped.

"Well, maybe I need a new one," Smither said, and stormed out of the office.

Instructions:

- Respond to the title question: Did he have it coming?
- Assuming that Jackson was right and that Smither's error did constitute a major blunder, how should Jackson have proceeded with the discussion?

Case 33

It's His Job, Not Mine

Primary Topic—*Delegation*

Additional Topics—*Leadership; Motivation*

As administrative manager of the hospital's diagnostic imaging department, you have found your workload increasing to the extent that you now definitely need assistance, especially with some of your nonmanagerial duties. One of the first tasks that comes to mind as available for delegation is your monthly statistical report. The report itself is fairly easy to create, but gathering the data is a time-consuming activity.

You select an employee to do the report, and you provide the necessary instructions. In doing so, you are certain to choose an employee who you believe is capable of doing a decent job and who has sufficient time available. The individual you select expresses no opinions or feelings for or against taking on the report.

Two days after assigning the task, you find that the report has not yet been started. You remind the employee; the employee tells you that completion of other work has delayed the data gathering. You emphasize the need to get the report done on time, but the assigned person seems in no particular hurry to get into the task.

One day later you accidentally overhear a portion of a conversation in which the employee to whom you have assigned the report says to another employee, ". . . his lousy statistics, and I think he ought to do it himself. It's in his job description, not mine."

Instructions:

- Describe what you might have done incorrectly in delegating the statistical report to this particular employee.
- Decide what, if anything, you can do to try to correct the employee's attitude as revealed by his comments to the other employee.

Case 34

I Used to Run This Unit

Primary Topic—*Change Management*

Additional Topics—*Decision Making; Delegation; Leadership*

For several years Community Hospital, a small, rural institution, had difficulty finding enough registered nurses to fill all of the positions ordinarily held by RNs. As a result of this shortage, for nearly 2 years Unit 2-A had a licensed practical nurse, Ms. Adams, serving as head nurse. She had been appointed as "acting" head nurse, but she was in place for so long that the "acting" designation had fallen out of use.

Recently a registered nurse, Ms. Williams, was hired as head nurse of 2-A. Ms. Adams was left within the unit as one of the staff. Although the change was clearly a demotion for Ms. Adams in terms of leaving supervision, her pay was left unchanged. In fact, she had recently received an increase after a favorable performance evaluation. However, these changes left her "red circled," carrying more than the maximum rate for an LPN with no room left for further financial advancement.

Ms. Adams said little about the change for some weeks, but neither was she particularly friendly or communicative. When finally Ms. Williams was able to get Ms. Adams to speak about the change in her assignment, Ms. Adams said, "I can see why the hospital prefers a registered nurse in charge of the unit. But I ran this unit for 2 years. My evaluations have been good; I've gotten regular raises and there's never been any real criticism of my work. Sure, I was called "acting" head nurse at first; but that got dropped after a while, and since then I've been given no reason to believe that the job was anything but permanent."

Questions:

1. How should Ms. Williams go about managing Ms. Adams so as to minimize hard feelings and gain her cooperation?
2. If Ms. Adams becomes resentful to the point of being uncooperative, what alternatives can Ms. Williams pursue?
3. How could this problem possibly have been avoided in the first place?

CASE 35

YOUR WORD AGAINST THE BOSS'S

Primary Topic—*Communication*

Additional Topics—*Authority; General Management Practice; Leadership*

In many ways it is a typical day. You find yourself at a meeting chaired by your department head. Also present are another department head and four first-line managers other than yourself. The subject of the meeting is the manner in which the organization's supervisors are to conduct themselves during the expected union organizing campaign. Your department head seems not in the best of moods, possibly because this important meeting started late and most parties feel pressured to hurry so as to make subsequent commitments.

Your boss makes a statement about management's behavior during organizing. You are surprised to hear what he said. Earlier that same day you had read a legal opinion that was exactly opposite to the boss's statement and made his intended direction illegal. In other words, were he allowed to proceed along the lines of his statement he would be actively advocating illegal management activity.

You interrupt with, "Excuse me, but I don't believe it can be done quite that way. That might leave us vulnerable to an unfair labor practice charge."

Obviously annoyed with the interruption your department head snaps, "This isn't open to discussion. You're wrong."

You open your mouth to speak again but think better of doing so on seeing the boss's expression.

You are certain the boss had inadvertently reversed a couple of critical words and described a "cannot-do" action as a "can-do" action. Unfortunately, you have been abruptly silenced, and you are in a conference room full of people while the document that could prove your position is in your office.

Question:

1. What do you believe you can do to set the matter straight without incurring further disfavor with your boss?

Case 36

You're the Boss

Primary Topic—*Delegation*

Additional Topics—*Communication; Employee Problems and Problem Employees; Leadership; Motivation*

"I don't think this is the approach to take at all," said accountant Harold Winslow to his manager, finance director James Ross.

This response had not been unanticipated; Ross, in his second month on the job, had already come to expect Winslow to oppose almost every assignment he handed out or every course of action he recommended. Ross was especially frustrated with his less-than-satisfactory relationship with Winslow because he recognized this long-time employee of the hospital as a capable accountant who was highly knowledgeable of healthcare finance and reimbursement.

Ross asked, "And why do you think it isn't right?"

"It just isn't, that's all," said Winslow, who then added, "It's unlike anything we've ever done. If this sort of thing really worked we'd have done it long ago."

"Was this plan ever considered? Or one like it?"

Winslow shrugged. "Don't know."

Ross took a deep breath. "Look Harold," he began, "I've got my orders—and there *are* orders involved—and I believe this is probably the best way of doing what we've got to do. And since you have more knowledge of this area than anyone else in the organization, I'll need you to take the lead on this project."

"Of course I'll do it, if that's what you're telling me to do," said Winslow.

"More than that," said Ross. "I need you to own the project, to innovate, to look at it in ways that never occurred to me. I need you to do the best job you can do on this."

Again Winslow shrugged, his mask of skepticism unchanged, and he said, "You tell me to do it, I do it. You're the boss."

After they parted Ross could not help feel uneasy about the assignment, even though Winslow was technically the best person available.

Questions:

1. What can Ross do to try to get Winslow to willingly apply his full knowledge and experience to the assignment?
2. What might be behind Winslow's apparent lack of motivation, and how should Ross address this problem overall?

Case 37

The New Broom

Primary Topic—*Change Management*

Additional Topics—*Communication; Delegation; Employee Problems and Problem Employees; Leadership; Rules and Policies*

Shari Daniels, the new nurse manager for the emergency department, was not feeling particularly happy with her lot in organizational life. She was just 1 month into her new role and already she felt like walking away from the job.

The problem, she decided, was staff resistance to change. She knew that a certain amount of resistance to a new manager and her ways of doing certain things was inevitable, but it seemed to Shari that everything she said or did was resisted simply because it came from her. There was so much she needed to do—the department had coasted literally for years under an apathetic manager, and the emergency department customarily received little attention from top management—that she had hardly known where to begin. And with so much to be done, she had jumped in and begun fixing everything that needed fixing as rapidly as possible.

As Shari related to her friend Sue Ross, also a nurse manager at the hospital, "I resurrected the dress code and brought it up to date; you have no idea what was being tolerated in the way of appearance. And I put a fast stop to personal telephone calls and the use of food and drink and reading matter within view of the public. In addition, I've started to enforce the hospital's policies on attendance and tardiness; I can't tell you how long those people have been allowed to wander in and out almost whenever they felt like it.

"And what do I get? A nearly complete lack of support except, fortunately, for some 'It's about times' from a couple of the older staff. I've held a staff meeting every week since I started, and I've tried hard to sell them all on the need to improve the general appearance and level of professionalism of the department. But all I get is a lack of support, lots of apparent bitterness, and resistance to everything I say."

Sue asked, "It sounds like you inherited a terrible mess. But are you sure you're not trying to do too much too quickly?"

"But it's such a mess that I've got to move quickly," Shari answered. "Besides, we're less than a year away from our next Joint Commission survey. What am I going to do about that?"

Questions:

1. Based on just the preceding information, what do you believe is probably causing most of the resistance Shari is encountering?
2. How would you recommend that Shari proceed in addressing the situation she faces?

Case 38

No Better Than I Used to Be?

Primary Topic—*Communication*

Additional Topics—*Change Management; Employee Problems and Problem Employees; Leadership; Motivation*

Supervisor Carrie Johnson was not at all comfortable with the way the performance appraisal interview with Helen West was going. Helen seemed uncommunicative; she would speak only when asked something, and then only briefly, and Carrie's two or three attempts to warm the atmosphere with some light remarks had no visible effect.

Except for a brief probationary review of sorts 3 months after Helen's transfer to Carrie's unit, this was the only real opportunity made available for a thorough review of Helen's performance. Helen had initially seemed eager to have this meeting with Carrie, but upon sitting down together and laying out the completed appraisal forms Helen fell largely silent and seemed to withdraw.

Growing increasingly frustrated with Helen's apparent unwillingness to participate, Carrie finally stopped in the middle of trying to make a point and said, "Helen, something about this discussion is bothering you. Out with it."

"Nothing's bothering me," answered Helen.

"I know you well enough to know that you're upset about something. Out with it, so we don't simply wind up wasting our time here."

For a moment Helen said nothing. Then she rapped a fingertip against the appraisal form and said, "It's this—my rating."

"There's nothing wrong with it," Carrie said. "It's comfortably above standard performance and very close to the average of a very good group of people on this unit."

"It's lower than any score I ever got from Sue Collins," Helen said, mentioning her previous supervisor. "I know I've done at least as well here as I ever did there, but you've given me my lowest score in nearly 5 years."

"Helen, this is a good evaluation score," Carrie insisted.

"I can't agree," Helen said. "All of you who do these use the same forms and the same job descriptions, and the evaluations ought to be consistent. Compared with Sue, are you telling me that after all my hard work I'm still no better than I used to be? Or even that my performance is slipping because I had a higher score last year?"

Questions:

1. If you found yourself in Carrie's position, how would you try to explain the differences in evaluation scores to this employee?
2. What, if anything, do you believe the organization should be doing about its performance appraisal system?

CASE 39

THE INCOMPATIBLE EMPLOYEES

Primary Topic—*Employee Problems and Problem Employees*

Additional Topics—*Authority; Communication; Criticism and Discipline; Leadership*

"I'm so frustrated by the situation in my department that I'm ready to get rid of two fairly good employees just for the sake of tranquillity," said supervisor Annette Johnson.

"I don't see why you'd want to get rid of good employees at all," commented fellow supervisor Barbara Wilson. "Sometimes the good ones are pretty hard to come by."

Annette said, "I said *fairly* good; the two of them would be practically ideal if I could keep them out of each other's way. But they work in the same office—like we all do, 12 or 13 people in one large area—and they just don't get along."

Barbara asked, "Personality conflict?"

"Don't know, but it's a possibility. If one of them says something's black the other says it's white, seemingly just for spite. If anything's at all wrong with one's work input or anything's out of place at one station, the other is always blamed. They seem always to be competing, and if one sees the other as gaining favor in any way the jealous behavior becomes intolerable."

"Maybe they deserve each other," Barbara said. "Why not just stick the two of them in the farthest corner of the department and leave them be?"

"I can't," Annette said. "They both have to relate to about half of the rest of the staff on any given day, and when they're not getting along the tension affects others in the work environment. It gets so bad that sometimes these two people—who are supposed to be communicating regularly during the day—will speak to each other only through a third party."

"Childish," said Barbara.

"Childish, yes," said Annette, "but the effects of their behavior are serious. And they've been talked to about it, a couple of times in fact, but even though things simmer down a little when they're spoken to they're back at each other's throats in a week."

Instruction:

Putting yourself in the position of supervisor Annette Johnson, describe how you would go about addressing the problem presented by the incompatible employees.

Case 40

Where Does the Time Go?

Primary Topic—*Time Management and Personal Effectiveness*

Additional Topics—*Communication; General Management Practice*

Kay Thatcher, director of staff education, decided she had to get organized once and for all. Recently her work days had been running well beyond quitting time, cutting noticeably into the time required by her family responsibilities, but instead of going down, her backlog of work was growing.

Inspired by an article she read about planning and setting priorities, Kay decided to try planning each day's activities at the end of the preceding day. This past Monday Kay came to the office with her day planned out to the last minute. During the morning she had to complete a report on a recent learning needs analysis, write the performance appraisals of two part-time instructors, and assemble the balance of the materials for a 2-hour class she was scheduled to conduct that afternoon. After lunch she had to conduct the class, complete a schedule of the next 3 months' training activities (now 10 days overdue), and prepare notices—which should have been posted this very day—for two upcoming classes.

Kay got off to a good start; she finished the report before 10:00 AM and turned her attention to the performance evaluations. However, at that time the interruptions began. In the next 2 hours she was interrupted six times—there were three telephone calls and three visitors. The calls were all business calls. Two of the visitors had legitimate problems, one of them taking perhaps 30 minutes to resolve. The other visitor was a fellow manager simply passing the time of day. Neither performance appraisal was completed, and the training materials were assembled in time for the class only because Kay threw them together during lunch while juggling a sandwich at her desk.

Kay's afternoon class ran 20 minutes overtime because of legitimate discussion and questions. When she returned to her office she discovered she had a visitor, a good-humored, talkative sales representative from whom Kay sometimes bought materials, who "happened to be in the area and just dropped in." The sales representative stayed for more than an hour and a half.

Once again alone, Kay spent several minutes simply wondering what to do next. The performance appraisals, the 3-month schedule, the class notices—all were overdue. Deciding on the class notices because they were the briefest task facing her, she dashed off both notices in longhand and asked the nursing department secretary to type them, run them off, and post them immediately. Then she set about to tackle the training schedule.

When Kay next looked up from her work it was nearly an hour past quitting time. She still had a long way to go on the schedule and had not yet started the two performance appraisals. As she swept her work aside for the day she sadly reflected that she had not accomplished two thirds of what she intended to accomplish that day in spite of all her planning. She decided, however, to try again; when she could get a few minutes of quiet time late in the evening, she would plan out her next day's activities.

On her way out of the hospital she paused at the main bulletin board to assure herself that the class notices had been posted. The small satisfaction she felt when she saw the notices vanished instantly when she discovered that both were incorrect—the dates and time of the two classes had been interchanged.

Questions:

1. What errors did Kay commit in her approach to planning and the establishment of priorities?
2. In what respects could Kay have improved her use of time on the Monday described in the case?

Case 41

Sylvia's Choice

Primary Topic—*Employee Problems and Problem Employees*

Additional Topics—*Communication; Hiring and Placement; Motivation*

When head nurse Sylvia Miller was faced with the opportunity to promote one of her staff members to a charge nurse capacity, she found that she was not lacking apparently qualified employees. In fact, after sorting through several possibilities Sylvia was left with two equally appealing candidates. Jane Wilson and Hilda Ross, in Sylvia's opinion the two best nurses on the floor, appeared equal in qualifications and experience in just about every respect.

It was evident to Sylvia that Jane and Hilda both wanted the position; each had made her desires known to Sylvia upon first learning that the position would be available. Jane and Hilda were energetic, willing, and apparently career oriented.

Sylvia eventually made her choice and promoted Jane Wilson to charge nurse. Although she did not discuss the ultimate basis of her decision with anyone, Sylvia admitted to herself that her decision was based largely on personality—Jane seemed friendlier than Hilda and more able to relate to other people on a one-to-one basis.

Jane Wilson eagerly accepted the promotion and plunged into her new role with enthusiasm. Hilda Ross expressed some initial disappointment, which seemed, at least to Sylvia, to dissipate rapidly.

However, 6 weeks after Jane's promotion it was plain to Sylvia that Hilda Ross had changed both her outlook and her behavior. Where previously Hilda had always seemed willing to do more than her share of work, she now seemed content doing just enough to get by. Although never overly talkative or socially outgoing, Hilda now seemed all the more silent and withdrawn. Worst of all, at least to Sylvia, was Hilda's apparent practice of resisting instructions from the new head nurse and creating obstacles for Jane.

Sylvia realized that she had a problem requiring her active involvement when she overheard Hilda Ross grumbling about how "a person has to be the head nurse's buddy to get anywhere around here."

Questions:

1. How might unintended personal bias here have intruded in Sylvia's selection of Jane over Hilda?
2. What do events subsequent to Jane's promotion have to say about Sylvia's choice of a charge nurse?
3. How should Sylvia go about dealing with Hilda Ross?

Case 42

Ultimatum

Primary Topic—*Employee Problems and Problem Employees*
Additional Topics—*Communication; Leadership*

You are the administrative director of the hospital's department of radiology. One of your more troublesome areas of late has been special procedures; you have chronically had difficulty recruiting and retaining special procedures technologists. You presently have your allotted full staff of three special procedures technologists, but these people are fully utilized and at least two of them have recently made comments about the staffing level being inadequate for the workload.

Your senior technologist, Arthur Morris, has been especially vocal in his comments claiming understaffing in the department. Several times, and as recently as Monday of this week, Morris spoke with you concerning his perception of the need for another special procedures technologist. Today, Wednesday, September 9, you received the following note from Morris:

"As I suggested I would do in our conversation of Monday this week, I am going on record notifying you that additional technologist help for special procedures must be available by Monday, September 21. If you are unable or unwilling to provide another special procedures technologist, I will be unable to continue in my present position beyond Friday, September 18."

Questions:

1. What should you do about the ultimatum delivered by Arthur Morris? Why?
2. Identify the key issue in the case and describe why it presents a significant problem.

Case 43

To Motivate the Unmovable

Primary Topic—*Motivation*

Additional Topics—*Communication; Delegation; Leadership; Rules and Policies*

"My hands are tied," said laboratory supervisor Melissa Wilson. "Because of the way this place is organized there's absolutely nothing I can do to motivate the employees in the laboratory. I should have listened when I was told 2 years ago that I wouldn't be free to supervise normally in this environment."

"What's wrong with this environment?" asked Melissa's manager, assistant administrator June Allen.

Melissa spread her hands and lifted her shoulders. "You know as well as I do, June. Goodness knows you've worked under it long enough—government. We're a municipal hospital, an arm of local government."

"But we're still a not-for-profit general hospital," said June. "What makes motivating employees any different here than it would be almost anywhere else?"

"Almost everything," said Melissa. "Look what our governmental status and the civil service system does to us."

Melissa bent down the little finger of her left hand and said, "First, I can't give an employee a pay raise or a bonus for good performance because that's not allowed." She gathered the next finger with the small one and continued, "Second, I can't promote a good performer because there's no career ladder structure and I can't advance anyone unless something opens up; and third," she said as she drew the middle finger into a bundle with the other two, "creating a new position falls somewhere between impossible and taking forever; and finally if an opening occurs or I manage to get another position approved I'm usually required to go by the results of some examination in filling the job."

June Allen shrugged and said, "Civil service has its drawbacks, that's true, but I think maybe you're looking in the wrong places for most of the motivators."

"I don't know, June," Melissa responded. "Oh, I've heard all this stuff about how money supposedly doesn't really motivate. If that's so, why do our employees talk about money so much? As far as I'm concerned, I've about decided that 'thank you' goes only so far and that's not far enough."

Instructions:

Putting yourself in the position of assistant administrator June Allen, prepare a response for your subordinate supervisor Melissa Wilson. Be sure to include some clear direction for Melissa to follow in seeking more effective ways of motivating her staff.

CASE 44

WHO'S THE BOSS?

Primary Topic—*Employee Problems and Problem Employees*

Additional Topics—*Authority; General Management Practice; Leadership*

"Since we began our total quality program I've gotten genuinely confused about who's really running the department," said supervisor Carrie Block. "I certainly don't feel like it's me these days."

"Why is that?" asked her friend, Janet Mason.

"We've got all these employee project groups working on a lot of things that used to tie me up so much, and maybe that's good. But it seems like I'm just not doing some of the things I've always been paid to do."

Janet asked, "Like what?"

"Like making some of the really hard decisions, like scheduling—who's going to work when has always been touchy—and like deciding on capital equipment purchases. These have always been tough, but I accept that. After all, it's what they pay me for. But I seem to have lost control."

Carrie continued, "It isn't bad enough that I've got a dozen people going off in their own directions talking about this 'empowerment' stuff. There's also the problem of Freddie the Expert."

"Who's that? I haven't heard you mention a Freddie before."

"Just hired him a couple of months ago," Carrie explained. "He seemed bright and willing to work, maybe too much so. Willing—to take over, apparently. He's never managed anything in his young life, but he's taken a couple of management courses and he has all the answers."

"Thus the 'expert?'"

Carrie nodded. "All the answers," she repeated, adding, "and always absolutely right—just ask him."

Carrie sighed wearily and said, "Between Freddie always challenging what I say and telling everyone how to do their jobs, and these quality project groups who seem bound and determined to make all the decisions, I'm left feeling like I've been deposed. Who's the boss, anyway? And if it isn't me, what am I here for?"

Questions:

1. What would appear to be the major problems Carrie is experiencing with her organization's total quality process, and what should be her true role in the organization?
2. What should Carrie be doing about "Freddie the Expert?"

Case 45

But I'm Really Sick!

Primary Topic—*Employee Problems and Problem Employees*
Additional Topics—*Criticism and Discipline; Rules and Policies*

"I'm really up a tree as to what to do with Kelly," said nurse manager Jane Babson. "I know she's genuinely ill quite often, or at least I know she's asthmatic and some of her absences seem to relate to that. She's out often enough that her sick time is always used as fast as it's earned, and she's chipped away a lot of her vacation bank to cover illness. Yet she's never out long enough to go on disability so I could get some reliable temporary coverage for a while."

Personnel representative Diane Jones asked, "What happened with the other absence problem you mentioned some time ago? Wilson? Or was it Williams?"

"Wilson," Jane said. "That one's pretty clear cut. Sick time taken as fast as accrued, patterned absences—always before or after scheduled days off. Good health, at least by all appearances. She's even been seen at the mall a couple of times when she was supposedly sick."

"No problem dealing with Wilson," she added. "A file full of warnings—next time she's out."

"What about Kelly?" Diane asked.

"I've tried to work with Kelly about the time she's missing. After all, I've got a unit to staff and whether somebody is truly ill or just faking it, the work still isn't getting done. And Kelly's pretty quick to claim that she's really sick—not like those others and their so-called mental health days, as she puts it—and she's come pretty close to threatening me with some kind of legal action if she gets disciplined for absenteeism."

Jane sighed heavily and asked, "Diane, what can I do about Kelly? And can I do something different about Wilson?"

Diane leaned forward in her chair and began, "Let's consider what we've got here, and then we'll look at options. First, ..."

Instructions:

Put yourself in the position of personnel representative Diane Jones and summarize the advice you would present to Jane Babson.

CASE 46

ALL THAT EMPOWERMENT JAZZ

Primary Topic—*Delegation*

Additional Topics—*Authority; Communication; Leadership; Motivation*

"As a middle manager, I've got five supervisors to deal with on a daily basis," said business office manager Susan Benton to Craig Williams, the hospital's training manager. "Over the past several years, I've tried as hard as I could to use true participative management techniques in dealing with them, but this effort seems to be backfiring on me."

"How so?" asked Craig.

"Well, I've tried to delegate to them faithfully and completely—or I guess I should say I've tried to empower them, using today's more acceptable terminology—and I've encouraged them to do the same with the people who report directly to them."

Craig asked, "What's wrong with that? As long as you're clear and up-front in dealing with the supervisors, they should be able to do the same with their employees."

"The problem is that most of the five supervisors act like all I'm doing is trying to shift my duties and responsibilities to them. The one who's been toughest to deal with, Ellie Patrick in the billing section, told me she wouldn't dream of backing away from her responsibilities by sticking someone else with them."

Craig nodded. "Kind of a 'the buck stops here' reaction?"

"Exactly," said Susan. "Ellie used that precise phrase in describing her attitude toward her responsibilities. And her attitude toward my responsibilities as well, I guess, when she told me directly, 'Don't try to hand me all that empowerment jazz, either.'"

Questions:

1. What is the difference between true delegation or empowerment and simply shifting duties and responsibilities?
2. How should Craig Williams advise Susan Benton to proceed in dealing with her five supervisors?

CASE 47

WHY DOESN'T ANYONE TELL ME?

Primary Topic—*Communication*

Additional Topic—*General Management Practice*

On Monday of this week, business office manager Carrie Owens learned that one of her key staff members had decided not to return to work after her maternity leave. Carrie learned this first from one of her employees, but it was confirmed later that day by the hospital's employee health service.

That same day, she was asked by two employees whether the hospital's new policy on vacation accruals would affect their vacation banks. Since she had heard nothing on this subject, she asked them where their concern had come from. One employee said she saw it in writing in the accounting office; the other said, "Barry told me." (Barry was the director of patient services and, not incidentally, Carrie's immediate superior.) It was Wednesday before Carrie received a copy of the policy change.

The two foregoing occurrences left Carrie feeling that she was a step behind most of her employees in receiving information of importance to her department. This feeling was intensified on Thursday. That day she received a call from a fellow manager asking why she was not at an important meeting that was already starting. Hastily saying that she knew nothing about the meeting, Carrie dropped everything to attend. When she returned to her department after the meeting, she found an announcement for the meeting in her mail tray. It had not been there that morning when she emptied the tray as she did each day, but it was dated 5 days earlier.

By the end of the week, Carrie was feeling considerable frustration with communication practices within the hospital organization. As she said to a good friend over breakfast on Saturday, "I feel totally out of the mainstream of information, especially when my employees hear about things before I do. Why doesn't anyone tell me what's going on?"

Instructions:

Unlike previous cases, this is not asking the reader to describe what is wrong in the situation. We can safely conclude that, for whatever reasons, communication within

Carrie's hospital organization leaves much to be desired. Rather, you are asked to suggest what Carrie can do—what actions she can take and how—to improve her overall communication posture in the organization and generally increase her chances of receiving the information she needs to do her job. In other words, what can she do to improve organizational communication for herself?

CASE 48

THE DEDICATED HIP-SHOOTER

Primary Topic—*Employee Problems and Problem Employees*
Additional Topics—*Communication; Delegation; Motivation*

"We're not a really large organization as maintenance departments go," said plant engineering manager Dan Stevens, "and because of our size I don't have real full-time supervisors in the different sections. Rather, we use working leaders, people who do lots of the work themselves and supervise maybe two to five others. My problem is Bob Wade, the lead electrician, who has to manage two other electricians and a helper in addition to looking after his own workload."

Assistant administrator Elias Woods asked, "What makes Wade a problem? The guy has spent most of this life here and he lives and breathes for this place. He treats every last circuit and device around here like it was his child."

Woods shrugged and added, "If a person with Wade's dedication is a problem, I can say only that we need a few more problems around here."

"I'm not questioning Bob's intentions at all," said Stevens. "I know he's incredibly dedicated to this place."

"So?"

"So he's still a problem, even though he's an outstanding electrician," Stevens answered. "He's a working boss—emphasis on working. He pays most attention to what he—personally—is doing at the moment, and there's no apparent rhyme or reason to how his task of the moment is chosen. There's no visible organization in the group. Anything that comes up—well, Wade just shoots from the hip. Jobs get done well, but all the group's efforts seem haphazardly applied, there are always problems and complaints—especially complaints about things that need attention—and except for Bob himself, nobody seems to know what to work on at any given time.

"I'd truly like to know," Stevens added, "how to get this guy and his group focused on the job they're supposed to be doing."

Instructions:

Put yourself in the position of the assistant administrator and suggest how Dan Stevens might begin to turn around Bob Wade and the electrical group and make them more efficient and productive.

CASE 49

THE PAPERWORK SIMPLY ISN'T IMPORTANT

Primary Topic—*Employee Problems and Problem Employees*
Additional Topics—*Authority; Criticism and Discipline; Motivation*

"I've got this absolutely brilliant employee—probably the best patient-contact person out of the two dozen in the department, and clearly the most successful in terms of results—who drives me nuts by not keeping up with her documentation." Manager Sharon Ward slapped the file folder on the desk in front of her and added, "Truly, Julia gets more positive results than anyone else, yet she consumes more of my time than any other two put together, even the ones who bend the attendance rules."

Employee relations manager Jean Howell asked, "How can this person be so good—so 'absolutely brilliant,' as you put it—if she doesn't document what she's doing?"

"Because everything else is great," said Sharon. "Her productivity is high, maybe the highest in the group, so that means she's a revenue producer. Quite simply, she sees more patients on a consistent basis than just about anybody else, and her results are generally better, at least based on the number of personal referrals she's received and the minimum number of complaints I've ever had about her work."

"Isn't documentation part of the job description?" Jean asked. "We generally require that anything done with, for, or on behalf of a patient be documented, and usually there are payment implications as well. That is, if certain documentation isn't provided, we don't get paid."

Sharon said, "Hmmpf! Minimum documentation for billing purposes is just about all we get, and we have to drag that out of her. Our therapists are all on a productivity arrangement, so they know—even Julia knows—that their own income as well as the division's depends on timely and accurate billing."

"Then what's the real problem?"

"A chronic lack of complete visit reports. Almost never any real progress notes." Sharon spread her palms in a gesture of helplessness and continued, "Julia's charts are a time bomb waiting for a state inspection or external audit, not to mention a professional standards review. Yet every time I try to address the issue she brushes me off. I even caught her at a quiet time the other day and tried to bring up the problem, but she just gave me one of her standard little flip responses, something like, 'You worry too much, Sharon. The paperwork just isn't that important!'"

Instructions:

Put yourself in the position of employee relations manager Jean Howell and recommend a course of action for supervisor Sharon Ward to pursue in dealing with the professional with the delinquent documentation problem.

Case 50

Why Should I Always Go the Extra Mile?

Primary Topic—*Communication*

Additional Topics—*Authority: Leadership; Motivation*

"I practically have to set a trap for my boss to get him to stand still and listen to me for 2 minutes," complained maintenance supervisor Harry Jones.

"I could almost say that you're lucky," said Millie Phillips. "I wish I could get my boss off my back. All she's ever doing is communicating." Millie spoke the word "communicating" with considerable scorn.

Harry shrugged. "I wouldn't have thought there was such a thing as too much communication. Half the time I'm in the dark as to what's expected of me and my crew. Outside of scheduled preventive maintenance, that is."

"There is such a thing as too much communication. I know my job, but I'm always being reminded how to do it. And if I'm being given a simple assignment I don't have to have it explained three times and then asked five times along the way if I've got any questions. It's a big, big pain."

"I think I could use a little of that pain," said Harry. "To get a few words in sideways with that guy I've got to follow him down the hall at top speed, trying to talk while I'm nearly running."

"How about department staff meetings?" asked Millie. "Or your regular meeting? You do have a regularly scheduled meeting with your manager? Every supervisor I know has one."

"If so it's everybody but me. And staff meetings are as rare as major natural disasters. Lots of staff meetings regularly scheduled, but always canceled for one reason or another."

Millie inquired, "Have you ever asked about a staff meeting? Or requested a regular time for you to meet with him?"

"No."

"Or put any of your concerns in writing to him? Tried to nail him down to answering on paper?"

"I don't think that's my place," said Harry. "He's responsible for the operation of the whole department, not me. He ought to have a real interest in communicating, and communicating well. I don't see why I should have to reach out because he's not doing what he should. Why should I always go the extra mile?"

Instructions:

Develop some individualized advice for both Harry and Millie to apply in dealing with their separate communication problems with higher management.

CASE 51

DON'T TELL THEM I SAID SO

Primary Topic—*Employee Problems and Problem Employees*
Additional Topics—*Authority; Communication; Leadership*

Admitting supervisor Rita Malloy occasionally stayed an hour or so after normal business hours in search of some quiet time to catch up on mail and project work. The majority of the department's staff went home at 4:30 PM, leaving two admitting representatives to cover later hours. However, one admitting representative had been making it almost a habit to seek out Rita on her late days and talk about other members of the department. This tale-carrying employee, Molly Nelson, worked a different shift from all others, starting at noon and ending at 8:30 PM, straddling two regular shifts to provide needed additional help during the afternoon and early evening.

Last Thursday, Rita had barely gotten organized and into her planned after-hours activity when Molly showed up at her door. Molly began as she usually did, with a pained expression and urgency in her voice, "Rita, there's something I have to talk with you about for the good of the department."

Molly proceeded to relate what went on when Rita was away at an all-day conference 2 days earlier, how three specific people—Molly named them without hesitation—had overstayed their lunch break by fully a half hour and how they could be counted on to do this every time Rita was absent.

Rita noted that Molly made regular reference to "the group," an apparent clique of employees that centered about the three alleged lunchtime abusers. Rita had to agree that her staff seemed divided between the "ins" and the "outs," with Molly, perhaps at least partly because of her unique schedule, definitely one of the "outs" as far as "the group" was concerned.

Although the lunchtime-abuse story was quite specific, complete with names, Molly's comments became more general as she continued, "And I swear I don't know how some of them have time for any real work, what with coupon clipping and all those personal telephone calls!"

Close to 10 minutes of reporting included, in addition to the foregoing, a strong suggestion that someone in the department was an active substance abuser while at work and a direct accusation that members of "the group" had been actively and openly criticizing Rita's management of the department. When she had apparently exhausted her supply of information for this particular visit, Molly concluded with, "Really, Rita, some of these people have really got it in for you. They're hurting this department, and something ought to be done about them. But don't tell them I said so!"

Instructions:

How should Rita deal with Molly Nelson and the information she furnishes? Specifically, should Rita:

- Take any action concerning the abuse of scheduled lunch breaks?
- Do anything—if indeed there is anything she can do—about the effects of "the group?"
- Encourage Molly's reports, but ask her to be more specific?
- Discourage Molly's reports altogether?
- Initiate any follow-up concerning the alleged substance abuser?

CASE 52

THE OIL-AND-WATER EMPLOYEES

Primary Topic—*Employee Problems and Problem Employees*

Additional Topics—*Authority; Communication; Criticism and Discipline; Leadership*

Feeling nearly at the end of her rope in dealing with two constantly bickering employees, supervisor Carrie Wilson sought counsel with personnel specialist Janet Baker.

"Janet," Carrie began, "I truly don't know what to do about Ellie and Nellie."

Janet responded, "Ellie and Nellie? Sounds like twins."

"Hah! More like bitter enemies. But maybe you're onto something," said Carrie. "They're about as much alike as some twins I've known—they're both stubborn, uncompromising, and short-tempered."

Carrie continued, "You know I've got a fairly small group. We're stuck in an extra-small office where we're always bumping into each other, and anyway we're really required to work together closely most of the time."

"So what's the problem?" asked Janet.

"Ellie and Nellie are the problem. Almost totally incompatible. Almost any conversation between them quickly degenerates into arguments and name-calling. They essentially do the same job and are forced by circumstances to work side by side most of the day."

"How good are they at what they do? Any performance problems, either of them?"

Carrie answered, "Both are fairly highly productive, in fact the two best in the group as far as output is concerned. If I had to choose, though, I'd say Nellie is just a bit better. Nearly perfect work records, both of them, at least until I had to start talking to them about their disruptive feuding."

Janet asked, "How disruptive?"

"The tension in the group is becoming unbearable. And although Ellie and Nellie appear to be keeping up with the work very well, other staff's productivity is beginning to suffer."

"Where do things stand right now? Today?"

Carrie said, "Big blowup this morning." She released a long sigh and continued, "I thought someone was going to get her eyes scratched out. Worst of it, though, was the effect on others. One of them, young Lorraine, finally screamed at both of them to shut up and ran bawling from the office. It's really a mess, Janet, and unless you've got a better suggestion I'm going back to the department and give them both a strong written warning for misconduct, for actions disruptive to the department's functioning."

Instructions:

Putting yourself in the position of personnel specialist Janet Baker and develop an approach for Carrie to follow in dealing with the apparently incompatible employees.

CASE 53

GETTING OFF THE FENCE: JUMP, FALL, OR PUSHED?

Primary Topic—*General Management Practice*

Additional Topics—*Decision Making; Leadership; Motivation*

Without being aware she was doing so, Myrna Wallace was actually summing up the concerns of a number of her fellow supervisors in the Supervisor Skills Development Program when she said, "As a first-line manager I always find myself 'straddling the fence.' I came up out of this same group that I'm supervising. Because I have to work so closely with all these hourly employees—most of whom were my peers for a long time, not to mention my friends as well—I'm considered by many to be one of them, to be treated as they're treated."

Encouraged by several nods of assent within the group of 15 mostly new supervisors, Myrna continued, "On the other hand, my boss expects me to act like a member of management and certainly to perform as a manager."

"On the fence is a lonely and thankless place to be," came a mutter from the rear of the room.

Myrna smiled and added, "I wouldn't put it quite that dramatically, but it can be an uncomfortable position. I really don't like this on-the-fence feeling. I want to know how to handle my situation, given that I'd like to continue getting along with these people I've known for so long, but I'd also like to do what my boss expects me to do."

The voice from the rear of the room said, "First thing, you're going to have to get off the fence."

Myrna turned and asked, "How?"

Myrna turned again as the group's instructor said, "You can jump off the fence as you choose, fall off if you're not careful, or get pushed off from one side or the other. Only partly your choice, but if you don't jump down on your own you'll eventually fall or be pushed. How do you want to do it?"

Instructions:

Advise Myrna how she could best approach getting "off the fence," balancing her concerns for relations with the work group with the needs of her manager.

Case 54

The Vocally Unhappy Camper

Primary Topic—*Employee Problems and Problem Employees*

Additional Topics—*Communication; Criticism and Discipline; Motivation*

"I have a problem with one employee that's affecting the whole department's performance," said business office manager Carol Jamison, "and I'm wondering if I can refer that person to you to help find out what's going on."

"What does seem to be going on?" asked employee health nurse Agnes Wilson. "Who's the employee?"

"It's Jean Todd," Carol answered. "A really longtime employee, one of the most senior in the group."

Agnes nodded and said, "I've known her for years. What seems to be the problem?"

"I don't know. As long as I've been there—you're aware that I came in as manager from the outside, just 4 years ago—Jean's projected an extremely negative attitude. She's been here lots longer than I have, but I don't know if she's always been like that."

"She's been here over 20 years, and no, she hasn't always been that way."

Carol said, "Jean turns out good work. In fact, it seems that a tall pile of work or a minor workload disaster is made to order for her capability. She's really very productive most of the time, but to listen to her constant griping you'd think she was the most unhappy person you ever met."

Agnes asked, "What does she usually complain about?"

"Just about everything. Me and my style. The hospital's policies. Her coworkers. Her pay and benefits. The work itself."

"What about her life outside of work?"

"I think something's going on but I don't know what. She complains about life in general just about as much as she gripes about work. And don't ever get her on the subject of her oldest child!"

"If her work is so good, what's the real problem? Outside of having her attitude in the middle of the department?"

Carol said, "I'm worried mostly about the other employees. Jean has alienated almost everyone. About once a week she has one of the others in tears, and two people have asked me to move their work stations farther from hers. One of my best billers has threatened to quit if I don't do something about Jean."

"That bad?"

"Truly that bad. How can I turn her around before the other employees start leaving?"

Instructions:

Respond to Carol's question. How would you advise her to proceed in dealing with this employee whose attitude seems so disruptive?

Case 55

To Manage the Manager

Primary Topic—*Employee Problems and Problem Employees*

Additional Topics—*Authority; Communication; Leadership; Motivation*

From the look on the face across the desk from her, human resources representative Margie Olson thought she had better pay special attention to what supervisor Nancy Wright was saying. Not ordinarily given to emotional displays, Nancy was clearly on the verge of tears as she spoke of increasing frustration and pressure that she apparently felt was to the result of the behavior of another supervisor.

"Please understand," Nancy was saying, "that my job and the jobs of Linda Williams and Mark Allen are extremely interrelated. The three of us work at the same level and report to the same boss. Mark does just fine, and I don't have any problems because of him. But Linda is making my life miserable and I don't know how to change things."

Margie asked, "Miserable how?"

"Linda simply will not address any real problems that arise and she continually puts off any decisions that have to be made."

"How does that affect you?"

"It means I do her work, and so does Mark. At least the more difficult stuff. She schedules disciplinary conferences to happen when she's conveniently not going to be here. In the same way she procrastinates on decisions until someone else—usually Mark or myself—is forced to make them."

Margie asked, "Why are you and Mark always so conveniently available to bail her out?"

"The way we're organized, the three of us are set up to cross-cover each other's areas on virtually a minute's notice. Jane Worth set it up that way."

At the mention of the three supervisors' mutual boss, Margie asked, "What about Jane? Isn't she aware of what's going on with Linda?"

"I don't know how aware she really is. Anyway, it seems like any time Jane calls Linda on the carpet for anything, Linda manages to shift the blame to someone else. Usually Mark or me. Remember, Linda was on the scene before I came here and before Mark was promoted. Linda and Jane go a long way back, and anyway I've never felt I could go to my boss with a complaint about a peer supervisor."

Nancy was silent a moment, strain evident in her expression. At last she said, "I don't know how to fix this. I only know I can't remain on this job forever picking up the slack for a supervisor who refuses to be accountable."

Instructions:

Put yourself in Margie's position and advise Nancy how to proceed in the matter of the apparent responsibility dodging by a fellow supervisor.

CASE 56

THE WEEKLY STAFF MEETING

Primary Topic—*Meeting Leadership*

Additional Topics—*Communication; Leadership; Time Management and Personal Effectiveness*

There are 15 people in your department. It has been your longstanding practice to hold a weekly staff meeting at 3:00 each Wednesday afternoon. Rather, we should say you attempt to hold it at 3:00 PM because about half of your employees are more than 5 minutes late, and two or three of them are usually late by 15 minutes or more.

You have made repeated announcements about being there on time, but to no avail. Come Wednesday at 3:00 PM, you usually find yourself and the same six or seven punctual attendees present and waiting for the latecomers.

Question:

Without immediately turning to disciplinary action (which you should always regard as the last resort), what can you do to encourage punctuality in attending your staff meetings?

CASE 57

WHERE ARE THEY WHEN I NEED THEM?

Primary Topic—*Employee Problems and Problem Employees*
Additional Topics—*Delegation; General Management Practice*

Jenny Lee is nurse manager of 3-West, a 40-bed geriatric unit that is nearly always fully occupied. Many of the patients spend several hours each day in wheelchairs, but most return to their beds for 2 or 3 hours in the afternoon.

Jenny has been concerned that her limited staff is only marginally able to fulfill all the needs of the elderly patients. She has spoken with many patients concerning needs that volunteers could possibly fill for them, and she has developed a list of volunteers who indicated they could make themselves available to help. Jenny developed a 30-day schedule for volunteer support.

On the first day of the schedule three of the five volunteers did not show up. On the second day, two did not appear. Only one showed up on each of the third and fourth days, and on the fifth day there were no volunteers present in the unit. Jenny abandoned her schedule.

Jenny was thoroughly discouraged by what she perceived as the volunteers' lack of dependability. Further, since Jenny had made no secret of her volunteer program, a number of patients were similarly discouraged and several complained.

Questions:

1. What has Jenny been doing wrong?
2. What might she consider doing to correct the situation that she has gotten herself into?

Case 58

The Unnecessary Task

Primary Topic—*Delegation*

Additional Topics—*Authority; Communication; Criticism and Discipline; Motivation*

The health information management (HIM) department of Memorial Hospital was considered able to function for a day or two at a time without a manager when necessary. However, when Mrs. James, the director of HIM, was hospitalized for several weeks, administration asked Guy Smith, the director of admissions, to look in on HIM on a regular basis. In his previous position with another, smaller hospital, Smith had supervised both HIM and admitting.

About noon one day Smith noticed a completed form entitled "Daily Census Report" on the corner of a clerk's desk in the medical records department. It caught his eye because in his months at the hospital the only census report he had seen was the computer-generated report he received each morning. He became even more curious when he noticed that the hand-generated report was dated for that day. He asked the clerk who created the report and why.

"I do it," she said, "but I don't really know why." She proceeded to describe the process: Each morning she took the previous day's record department count of admissions and discharges and merged it with the information obtained from copies of the midnight census report generated by the head nurse in each nursing unit. This took her about an hour and a half each day.

Smith asked, "Who uses this report?"

"I don't think anybody uses it."

"Then let me put it this way," said Smith, his frustration beginning to show, "Who receives the report?"

"Nobody," the clerk answered. She went on to explain that some time earlier the hospital experienced problems with its computer system and certain census information was being lost. Mrs. Victor, who was her supervisor then, showed her how to do the report and told her where to leave it. For about 4 weeks the report was picked up faithfully at noon every day.

"Why hasn't it been discontinued?" asked Smith.

"It was discontinued, once," the clerk answered. "By me. And I got into plenty of trouble over it. It got picked up regularly only for about 4 weeks. After that, before I knew it I had eight or nine on my desk. I tried to ask Mrs. Victor about it but I still couldn't get an answer—you couldn't get her to stand still for 10 seconds—so I just stopped doing it on my own because I couldn't see any sense in it. When Mrs. Victor found out I dropped it, she gave me the chewing out of my life and said that I'd better never do anything like that again without a direct order."

Smith said, "But Mrs. Victor has been gone more than a year. Did you mention this to Mrs. James?"

"Yes, but I'm not sure it ever sank in. She's just as busy as Mrs. Victor ever was, and the only people who seem able to get her attention for more than a minute at a time are administration and the physicians. She said she'd look into it, but I haven't heard anything. And I'm not sticking my neck out again."

Guy Smith spent a few more minutes with the clerk looking over some of the reports. In that time he discovered that the clerk had done neat, accurate work, taking as long as 90 minutes a day, for nearly 25 months. And 23 months' worth of this work was never seen by anyone other than the clerk herself.

Questions:

1. Who do you see as responsible for the duration of this task? Why?
2. What fundamental errors do you believe caused this to happen?
3. What should Smith do with his newly acquired information?

CASE 59

YOUR WASTEFUL FRIEND

Primary Topic—*Employee Problems and Problem Employees*
Additional Topics—*Communication; General Management Practice*

You are one of two supervisors in the central supply department. You take your job seriously, and in light of a current economic pinch, you are keenly aware of the necessity to economize wherever possible.

You are also aware that your fellow supervisor does not share your attitude and outlook and is costing the institution unnecessary expense through failure to exercise what you consider to be common sense cost control. You have attempted to control costs closely because you see this as part of your job and because you believe cost control to be necessary. However, the other supervisor makes no effort to control costs and openly resists any economy-oriented changes you attempt to make.

Higher management, from the central supply manager on up, seems to be paying no attention to what is going on in the department. The other supervisor whose attitudes and actions seem constantly to frustrate your own is supposedly a close friend of yours, so you are reluctant to "blow the whistle."

Question:

1. What approaches could you take, considering that you are in a bind between the dictates of your conscience and a personal relationship?

CASE 60

ONE BOSS TOO MANY

Primary Topic—*Leadership*

Additional Topics—*Authority; Communication; Decision Making; General Management Practice; Motivation*

The engineering and maintenance groups of Memorial Hospital are headed by three first-line supervisors. These supervisors and a department secretary report directly to a manager of engineering and maintenance, who in turn reports to the director of environmental services.

The institution is in the midst of a prolonged period of growth and expansion owing mostly to merger and acquisition. Almost weekly some organizational unit or other is being located to new quarters or drastically rearranged within its original area. The institution promises to be in a chronic state of change for some time to come, with much extra effort required by engineering and maintenance as numerous areas are opened, renovated, or rearranged.

The position of director of environmental services was created at the start of this period of major change. The incumbent was hired specifically for his apparent ability to get a new operation up and running through active involvement of personnel at all levels.

The director was quick to discover that his immediate subordinate, the manager of engineering and maintenance, came across as a man of considerable inertia who moved slowly, was reluctant to change, and usually defended "the way we've always done things."

Although the manager had longstanding relationships with the three supervisors, the director began avoiding the manager and dealing directly with the first-line supervisors. Most matters, however, found their way back to the manager, who would then take action or give instructions contrary to what the director had done.

After several weeks in this mode of operation, one of the first-line supervisors summed up the circumstances as follows: "We now have two bosses, and they're opposed to each other on everything. What one decides, the other reverses; what one puts together, the other tears apart. They can't even agree on anything as basic as an obvious need for disciplinary action. How do we go about maintaining effectiveness in dealing with our employees, and how do we prevent morale and inefficiency from going straight down the drain?"

Instructions:

Deal with the question posed by the supervisors in the final paragraph of the case. Based on what you believe to be sound management practice, develop an approach the three supervisors might take. State any assumptions you may have to make, and fully explain the reasons for your recommended approach.

Case 61

How Time Flies

Primary Topic—*Time Management and Personal Effectiveness*
Additional Topics—*Authority; General Management Practice; Leadership*

You are the business office manager at Community Hospital. At 9:00 AM your boss, the controller, called you into his office for, as he put it—"a little chit-chat, 10 minutes or so, on where we stand on getting the new procedure manuals done." You scooped up the proper papers and went into his office, bracing yourself because you knew how frustrating these sessions could be.

After you entered and sat down, the controller shuffled through the clutter on his desk looking for a particular document. At the same time he found the document he also found a pink telephone message slip apparently left over from the previous day. He said, "Oh-oh, should have done this yesterday. Excuse me just a minute. Sit tight."

The "minute" turned out to be a quarter of an hour as he transacted a bit of business and engaged in some social conversation. You fidgeted, wondering as you did at such times whether you should get up and leave and return when he was free.

You were perhaps 5 minutes underway with the true subject of your meeting when the telephone rang. Your boss answered it himself, although his secretary was in her usual place. This time it was fully 10 minutes before you could return to the subject of the meeting. Before you concluded your business, your boss had taken two more calls and made a brief additional call for something that he had "just remembered."

When at last you were finished to the boss's satisfaction, you rose to leave. He rose also, reaching for his empty coffee mug. On the way out of his office he glanced at his watch and said, "Wow, 10:00 already. Time sure flies."

You made no comment. You were well aware that the pile of work on your desk had gotten no smaller while you were tied up for a full hour trying to accomplish about 10 minutes' worth of true work.

Questions:

1. What assumptions about the value of your time and his time are implicit in the boss's behavior?
2. What can you possibly do or attempt to do to encourage your boss to show more respect for your working time?

Case 62

Your Unhappy Duty

Primary Topic—*Authority*

Additional Topics—*Communication; Criticism and Discipline; Leadership; Motivation; Rules and Policies*

You are the manager of purchasing and general stores for Ajax Memorial Hospital. In the 1 year you have been there you have come to know your four employees quite well. They are generally a happy, cohesive, and cooperative group, usually joking among themselves, but getting the work done more than satisfactorily. All of them seem to give a great deal to the hospital, and it is obvious to you that they care about what they are doing. A couple of them usually come in a bit early, going over their plans for the day's work over coffee before starting time, and although quitting time is 4:30 PM, all of them generally stay a few minutes later to finish what they happen to be working on at quitting time. You have felt all along that you could not ask for a better group of employees.

This afternoon, however, things changed. You returned at about 3:00 PM from an outside meeting to be met by four grim faces reflecting varying degrees of gloom and anger. The department secretary, Carol, said, "The CEO is looking for you. In fact, three calls in the last hour—although I said you weren't due back until 3:00."

The telephone rang. Carol answered it and after a few seconds said, "Yes, he just walked in. He'll be right there."

Without an inkling of the problem you hurried to the CEO's office, where you were greeted with a stern look and a firm instruction to close the door before seating yourself.

"I want to know whether you think you're running a hospital department or a social club," the CEO snapped.

"What do you mean?"

"I was walking along the corridor near your office when I heard an awful racket coming from the stockroom. Laughing, practically shrieking, so loud I could hear it two hundred feet up the hall. I went in and found all four of your staff eating lunch in the stockroom. Actually eating lunch in the department. Were you aware that they did so?"

"Certainly. They've always done that. I wondered about it when I was new here, but I did enough digging to convince myself there was no rule against it."

"There are common sense rules of behavior I insist on. These should be sufficiently plain that they need not be written. And eating in the department is an obvious case. Why do you suppose we provide a cafeteria?"

You said that you agreed as far as certain areas were concerned. For instance, you said that it would not look good for someone to be eating lunch at the admissions desk. You believe it does not really matter in the case of the stockroom because this is a closed area never entered by patients or visitors.

"What's good for one department is good for all departments," the CEO responded. "And that goes for the coffee pot. I don't permit coffee pots in the departments. Your people can get their coffee in the cafeteria at specified break times just like everyone else."

Not quite biting your tongue you said, "There's a coffee pot in the dictating room health information management. Of course that's used by doctors as well."

Your remark triggered a few choice comments about your attitude, and you found yourself on the receiving end of a spontaneous and rather critical "performance evaluation" until a few minutes before quitting time. Although you tried your best to defend your employees, citing their good-humored cooperation and flexibility, you nevertheless departed with a clear message to take back to your employees: We are running a healthcare organization in businesslike fashion, and that means no boisterous laughter, no eating in the department, and no coffee pot.

You arrived back in your department at exactly 4:30. Your four employees, grim faces and all, were the first persons in line at the time clock in the corridor. It was the first time you ever knew any of them to leave at 4:30 on the dot.

Questions:

1. Assuming you disagree with the CEO's directive, but recognizing that you are under orders to see that it is followed, how are you going to get the word across to your staff?
2. Because staff morale has already been adversely affected and you have yet to reaffirm the order they received during the CEO's surprise visit, what can you do to blunt the demotivating effects of this turn of events?

Case 63

The Independent Employee

Primary Topic—*Delegation*

Additional Topics—*Authority; Leadership, Motivation*

Maintenance supervisor Jim Wood often felt that he has his hands full getting electrical repairman Bob Trent to follow his instructions. A case in point: On Monday of this week Wood realized that the laboratory air conditioning unit was due for its semiannual servicing and inspection, a task that either Bob Trent or the one other mechanic usually accomplished. He further realized that if this job was not done by the end of Wednesday it was not likely to get done for some time; some new equipment was scheduled to arrive on Thursday, and Trent's fellow mechanic would be gone on vacation the following week.

Wood customarily tried to assign Trent 2 or 3 days' work at a time, because once he was underway Trent could usually be found (or not found, as often was the case) just about any place in the building tackling his assigned tasks—and often a number of unassigned tasks—in seemingly random order.

Wood gave Trent the file on the laboratory air conditioner and said, "You don't necessarily have to do this first, but I'd like you to take care of it today or tomorrow. In any case, it has to be finished by noon Wednesday."

Trent simply shrugged and took the file. Wood did not see Bob Trent again until Thursday morning coffee break. The laboratory air conditioner had not crossed Wood's mind until the sight of Trent reminded him of it. He approached Trent and asked, "Any trouble with the lab air conditioner?"

"Haven't done it yet," said Trent.

"Why not? I specifically told you it had to be finished by noon Wednesday."

"I almost got started on it," said Trent, "but the assistant administrator collared me and told me he wanted the fan coil unit in his office fixed right away. I had to tear the whole thing down to do it, but I figured that was more important than the air conditioner in the lab."

Wood felt a sense of frustration. he said, "Bob, this is the fourth time at least that I can think of when I told you specifically to do something and you went and decided something else was more important. Just what do you think I mean when I delegate something to you, anyway?"

Trent shrugged and said, somewhat defensively, "I don't know, Mr. Wood, but I figure when I see something that's more important than what I'm doing at the moment I better take care of it. Anyway, if the lab air conditioner was so all-fired important, how come you didn't say anything about it until now?"

Instructions:

Analyze the foregoing occurrence of incomplete delegation, criticizing the conduct of both employee and supervisor as necessary. Spell out those steps you believe Jim Wood should take in the future to assure that Bob Trent does not decide that other tasks are "more important" than duties specifically assigned by Wood.

Case 64

Here We Go Again

Primary Topic—*Change Management*

Additional Topics—*Communication; Leadership; Motivation*

The position of business office manager at Memorial Hospital has been a "hot seat," changing incumbents frequently. When the position was vacated last May the four senior employees in the department were interviewed. All were told that because they were at the top of grade and the compensation structure for new supervisors had "not yet caught up with that of other jobs," the position would not involve an increase in pay. All four declined to pursue the position, and all were given the impression that they were not considered fully qualified anyway, but that they might be considered for supervision again at a later date.

That same month a new business office manager was hired from the outside, and the four senior employees were instructed to "show the new boss all you know." Over the following several months the finance director told all four employees that they had "come along very well" and would be considered for the manager's position should it come open again.

In October of that same year the manager resigned. However, none of the four senior employees got the job; the process described in the preceding was repeated, and again a new manager was hired from the outside.

Questions:

1. How do you believe the four senior employees would feel, having gone through the foregoing process twice?
2. What do you believe would be the attitude of the business office staff toward the organization?
3. What do you believe would be the attitudes of the four senior employees toward the finance director?
4. Is the apparent inequity in the organization's wage and salary structure at all justifiable? Why, or why not?

CASE 65

THE FORCEFUL ORGANIZER

Primary Topic—*Labor Relations*

Additional Topics—*Communication; Decision Making; Leadership*

Your are the hospital's admitting manager. This morning you were called to attend a meeting concerned with possible union organizing activity.

On your way to the meeting you observe a man backing one of the housekeepers into a corner. The man's back is turned to you, and you do not recognize him. The man appears to be trying to get the housekeeper to take a card and a pen he is holding.

You cannot hear what is being said, but the housekeeper appears to be close to tears, and she is effectively trapped in a corner. Your first thought is of active solicitation of interest in a union election.

You move closer in an attempt to see the man's face.

Questions:

1. What will you do if you recognize the man as an employee?
2. What will you do if you are certain the man is not a hospital employee?
3. Whether or not you recognize the man as an employee, what should be your first action?

Case 66

The Requested Favor

Primary Topic—*Employee Problems and Problem Employees*
Additional Topics—*Authority; Communication; Rules and Policies*

You are head nurse of a 40-bed medical/surgical unit. This morning one of your nurses, Mrs. Allen, came to you with a request for a "small change" in her hours of work. She asked to be permitted to start and end her shift 30 minutes earlier than scheduled. She explained that this was necessary because her husband's hours had changed (he works evenings), and she has to be home before he leaves so the children will not be unattended.

You told her that you would have to think about the request and get back to her. Your thoughts seemed to resolve into three alternatives:

1. Deny the request.
2. Grant the request.
3. Grant the request on a temporary basis, giving her some time to work out a permanent arrangement.

Questions:

1. What are the advantages and disadvantages of all three options?
2. Which option do you believe you should choose? Why?

Case 67

Boss? Who Needs One?

Primary Topic—*Change Management*

Additional Topics—*Authority; Communication; Leadership*

Kay Morgan is assigned to the reception desk at Community Hospital. Her job also includes sorting mail for distribution, and metering and bundling all outgoing mail. She has been doing this same job since the hospital opened nearly 15 years ago. She has always worked independently and has never been assigned to any particular supervisor. She never appears on an organization chart, and she considers the administrator, whom she rarely saw, to be her only "boss."

During a period of internal growth it was considered necessary to establish the position of business manager. You are hired from the outside to fill this new position. One of the activities placed under your direct supervision is Morgan's mail and reception area.

You cannot tell from your initial visit with Morgan if her seemingly quiet and stern manner is natural to her or perhaps indicates resentment. Your visit was not preceded by any announcement concerning your arrival as her supervisor.

Instructions:

Develop an approach that will help you "start out on the right foot" with Kay Morgan. Do not assume at the outset that she will resist your authority. You actually have no idea how she will react, although showing up without notice does create some basis for concern on her part.

CASE 68

CHOICES

Primary Topic—*Hiring and Placement*

Additional Topics—*Communication; Employee Problems and Problem Employees; Rules and Policies*

You have a position open in your department, and you have been presented with three candidates for consideration. All are equally qualified. They are:

1. A young woman, 19 years old, who has one child and is separated from her husband.
2. A woman, 31 years old, who had been unsuccessfully seeking work for several months and whose husband is disabled.
3. The daughter of a fellow employee. This young lady actually desires to get into a different department, but would like to have this job until there is an opening in the department of her choice.

Much of the little you know about the first two candidates (as noted) is "forbidden information" in that you are not allowed to ask for it on an application or an interview. However, the candidates themselves volunteered this information. What you know about the third person came to you from the fellow employee who wants you to hire her daughter.

Questions:

1. What are the points of "forbidden information?" Why are you not allowed to solicit this information?
2. What are some of the potential problems coming with the hiring of any of the three?
3. Under what circumstances would you be likely to rule out all three candidates?

Case 69

Shortage of Help

Primary Topic—*Hiring and Placement*

Additional Topics—*Authority; Communication; Rules and Policies*

You are director of nursing in a hospital that recently completed an expansion program and opened a new 36-bed medical/surgical unit. Recently you have not done too badly in keeping your nursing staff up to required levels in spite of a general shortage of nurses in your geographic region, but the opening of the new unit has strained your resources to the extent where you are short several registered nurses. This shortage is particularly evident on the evening shift (3:00 PM to 11:00 PM). You have more than enough people willing to work days, and you have long had a thoroughly stable crew who prefer to work nights.

In response to your long-running recruiting efforts, a well-qualified registered nurse has applied for employment. You are impressed with her; she seems energetic and personable, and she is immediately available. Also, she is quite willing to take a position on the evening shift.

Unfortunately, although she is willing to work 3:00 PM to 11:00 PM, she has also stated during her initial interview that she cannot work any weekends. She will say only that weekend work causes severe inconvenience in her family life, and she repeats her willingness to work evenings, but only Monday through Friday.

You have not yet explained to her that scheduling practices in your hospital require everyone below the level of day, evening, or night supervisor to work every other weekend.

Questions:

1. Conscious of your critical need for nursing help on weekends, what are you going to tell this applicant?
2. If you adhere to your scheduling policy and the nurse refuses the job, what problems will you be facing?
3. If you alter your scheduling policy and offer the applicant a Monday-through-Friday position that she accepts, what problems are you likely to face?

CASE 70

WHO ANSWERS TO WHOM?

Primary Topic—*Employee Problems and Problem Employees*

Additional Topics—*Authority; Communication; Criticism and Discipline*

As a recently hired housekeeping supervisor at County General Hospital, Will Ross has put a great deal of effort into trying to tighten up housekeeping operations and improve staff productivity. Every day he provides each member of his crew of housekeeping aides with a work plan to follow, and he stresses that his employees are not to deviate from this plan. He has arranged his employees' work so that the workload is not unreasonable or overly demanding, but the employees have to work steadily to stay on schedule.

One afternoon housekeeping aide Tom Mooney was buffing a corridor in a medical/surgical unit when the unit's head nurse hurried up to him and said, "Shut that thing off and come with me. We need to clean up a mess in room 211." Without shutting off the buffer Mooney responded, "Sorry, but I've got a schedule of things to do and only so much time to do them. Mr. Ross says I'm not to take on any extra jobs unless he tells me to."

The nurse replied, "I don't care what Mr. Ross says. Right now you're in my nursing unit, and when you're in my unit you'll do what I tell you to do. Now come with me."

Mooney shut off the buffer but did not move. Rather, he said, "I think we need to call Mr. Ross."

The nurse snapped, "We don't need to call anyone. Now, if you're interested in keeping your job you'd better do as I say."

Instructions:

Decide how this incident should be handled and by whom it should be handled. In developing your tentative solution, consider the question of authority: To whose authority must Mooney ultimately respond? Why?

CASE 71

WHEN DO YOU STOP BEING GENERAL?

Primary Topic—*Criticism and Discipline*

Additional Topics—*Communication; Employee Problems and Problem Employees; Meeting Leadership*

You are supervisor of transcription at City General Hospital. Your group includes several transcriptionists who handle all the dictation from the laboratory and x-ray, and the typing for several department managers, as well as all transcription of physicians' dictation.

You are in the habit of holding a brief informational meeting with your staff early each month. At your June meeting you felt obligated to point out that quality was slipping and word processing errors were on the increase, and that more care had to be taken with keyboarding. At your July meeting you made the following statement: "The overall quality of transcription has not improved at all in the last month; in fact, it has gotten worse. I expect all of you to begin improving your typing quality immediately."

It is now almost time for your August meeting. In your estimation, and backed up with error-rate statistics and complaints, quality has not improved in the least.

Questions:

1. Do you continue to deal with the group at large? Why, or why not?
2. How do you believe you might approach the problem of making your criticism increasingly more specific?

CASE 72

AN ACT OF NEGLIGENCE

Primary Topic—*Criticism and Discipline*

Additional Topics—*Communication; Employee Problems and Problem Employees; Leadership*

This morning you entered the work room of your nursing unit just in time to see Jenny Walters, an aide whom you considered a usually careful worker, commit an act of negligence. There was little room for doubt, and Jenny's behavior resulted in several pieces of costly glassware being broken before your eyes. In addition to Jenny, three more of your employees were present when you entered and witnessed the incident.

Questions:

1. Should you reprimand Jenny on the spot, while the incident is fresh and the other employees can take your criticism as a warning; or, should you separate Jenny from the group and deliver the reprimand in private?
2. Which of the foregoing options did you choose? Why?
3. How can you improve upon your chosen option?

Case 73

It Wasn't My Decision

Primary Topic—*Change Management*

Additional Topics—*Authority; Communication; Meeting Leadership*

Within the finance division of City Hospital, a problem developed in the processing of receiving reports from the receipt of incoming material to the completion of payment. The purchasing manager, Mr. Sampson, first recognized the problem and pointed it out to the assistant administrator. Sampson said he believed he understood the situation and knew how it should be corrected. However, five different departments were involved.

Sampson was directed to "get together with the other four supervisors and work out a solution."

On extremely short notice Sampson called a meeting of the affected supervisors. Only two of the four were able to attend; the others were out of the building when Sampson decided to get together. Nevertheless the three persons who were present went to work on the problem.

The three supervisors developed a solution that required no implementation on their part but called upon the other two supervisors to take all of the required action. Sampson put the results of their decision in a memo to the two supervisors who were expected to translate the decision into action.

Questions:

1. Assuming the solution Sampson and his companions arrived at was the most reasonable answer available, could there be any legitimate reasons for resistance from the two supervisors who were expected to carry it out.
2. If you were one of the two supervisors left out of the decision process, how would you react to the "directive" from Sampson? What would you do about it?

Case 74

The Dodger

Primary Topic—*Criticism and Discipline*

Additional Topics—*Communication; Employee Problems and Problem Employees; Motivation*

Jane Wilson had considerable difficulty developing the schedule for her nursing unit for the coming 2 weeks. The nursing department was in marginal position overall as far as available nurses were concerned, so her flexibility was limited. To make matters worse, within hours after Jane developed the new schedule, Alice Johnson, a part-time licensed practical nurse, submitted a request for a personal day on one of the days she was scheduled to work.

The request caused Jane to realize she had been seeing Alice's name in connection with scheduling difficulties often in recent months. Looking back over the preceding 6 months' schedules she discovered that the current request was the fifth time in 6 months that Alice had requested time off on a scheduled weekend day. Even more significant was the pattern of Alice's use of sick time. She had called in sick four times, all of these on Saturdays or Sundays. All in all Alice had worked only about half of the weekend days she was scheduled to work over a period of 6 months.

Jane was displeased with Alice's attendance and unhappy with herself for not discovering the problem sooner. She felt she had to talk with Alice about it, but she also felt that her unit could ill afford to lose a nurse. Nevertheless she believed that she could not allow Alice's attendance pattern to continue uncorrected.

Questions:

1. What are the hazards Jane faces in (a) dealing firmly with Alice's behavior? or (b) ignoring Alice's absences and saying nothing?
2. Assuming Jane is seriously considering talking with Alice, how might she approach the subject of the attendance problem?

Case 75

Yours, Mine, and Hours

Primary Topic—*Rules and Policies*

Additional Topics—*Communication; Employee Problems and Problem Employees*

You were recently hired as director of health information management (HIM). Among your first official acts was the hiring of an assistant director and an additional medical transcriptionist.

On the first morning of your fourth week on the job, and the second week for your two new employees, your new employees came to you with a complaint. They said they just discovered they were working 40 hours per week, but the other employees in the department—five in all—were working only 37.5 hours. This was the first you had heard of anything less than a 40-hour week.

You questioned the other employees one by one. You learned that the former director of HIM, who had been there many years, hired all of these people, one by one, with promises of a 37.5 hour week. You told each employee, as you felt you must, that the basic work week throughout the hospital is 40 hours, and there is no policy that states this department is entitled to operate on the basis of a shorter work week.

Your employees agree that nothing was ever written down about a 37.5 hour week, but each claimed that this was promised orally as a condition of employment. All of them insisted that the hospital is honor-bound to observe what is apparently an unwritten policy established by the former director of medical records. As one employee put it, "This place has always had a pretty good reputation as an employer; I didn't think we had to have everything in writing."

Questions:

1. What are you going to do about the predicament in which you find yourself?
2. Who else may you have to involve in the solution to your problem? Why?

CASE 76

AN EXPENSIVE GAME

Primary Topic—*Hiring and Placement*

Additional Topics—*Authority; Decision Making; Motivation*

Dr. Gable, chief of anesthesiology, said to vice president Arthur Phillips and human resource director Charlie Miller, "There are no two ways about it—we're going to have to raise the pay of our nurse anesthetists by at least 10 percent. With Don Williams leaving—he's going to Midstate University Hospital for a lot more money—we're going to have to pay more than we're now paying to fill that spot. Of the ten hospitals in this city, our nurse anesthetists are by far the lowest paid."

Charlie Miller said, "Since we talked about this same matter a week ago, I've obtained an up-to-date survey of the community. We're not the lowest paying of the ten. In fact, we're the third highest paying."

Dr. Gable shook his head. "That doesn't wash," he said. "Some of our people moonlight at the other hospitals and they've told me the hourly rates they're getting for part-time work. They said they can bring in pay stubs to prove it."

Arthur said, "A week ago you said they were going to bring you pay stubs from other places. You didn't get them yet?"

"No, they forgot."

Miller said, "Moonlighting rates aren't relevant. Most of these places pay their per diem nurse anesthetists a rate that amounts to more per hour than their full-time employees get. That's because the per diems work only when called and they don't receive vacation, sick time, or other benefits, and they don't get retirement credit."

Arthur asked, "How about Midstate University Hospital? I understand that it has more than one pay scale for nurse anesthetists, with a second scale that might not be readily shared with the agencies who do our salary surveys."

Miller nodded and said, "That's right. Midstate is the highest paying hospital in the area, based on this sort of hidden scale that they apply to some of their people. They pay up to 15 percent more to this one small group, all of whom have agreed to an extra-long work week and a certain amount of weekend call. But it's not really comparable to our situation."

Arthur said, "In all the years I've been here, it seems I can depend on this same exercise coming up every time one of our nurse anesthetists leaves. I've also come to count on it happening with radiologists and pathologists every few years—they go to work on one hospital to get their compensation increased, then they use this new pay leader as a wedge to get the other hospitals to pay more."

Charlie Miller said, "I'm sure that all of the nurse anesthetists in town know what the others earn. All it takes is a few people in one hospital to get a strong advocate to go to bat for them, and the pressure to bump pay rates is felt throughout the region."

Dr. Gable said, "I take it that you're seeing me in that strong advocate role." Miller did not respond.

Arthur said, "Anyway, Dr. Gable, you obviously see the nurse anesthetist pay rates as a problem and we're willing to listen to any potential solutions you may have to offer. However, the budget year is barely one-third over and there is no more money to play with until the first of next year. As a first pass at the problem, we'll be happy to take a close look at any creative solutions you can come up with that lie within the limits of this year's budget."

Questions:

1. What does this case suggest about the supply of nurse anesthetists in the area? And what might come of Dr. Gable's arguments if the realities of supply were different?
2. Do you believe that the interorganizational "bumping" of pay rates, if indeed a fact, is appropriate professional behavior? Why, or why not?
3. Because it might be reasonably suggested that the nurse anesthetists in the area are acting together, at least in a loosely organized way, one might be tempted to suggest that the area's ten hospitals get together and establish fair and consistent pay rates for nurse anesthetists. Comment on this as a potential approach.
4. How do you suggest Phillips and Miller proceed in their consideration of Dr. Gable's request?

Case 77

The Reclassification Request

Primary Topic—*Communication*

Additional Topics—*Authority; Decision Making; Hiring and Placement; Motivation*

"All of the justification for upgrading the position of hematology supervisor is right here," said Dr. Smithers, indicating the two-page memorandum that lay in front of human resource director Carl Miller. Laboratory administrator Lori Brandon, seated alongside Dr. Smithers, added, "I know that you folks need to do your magic by cranking it through some kind of job evaluation process, and for that you need a new job description. Just tell me what I need to write to get this job moved from Grade 6 to Grade 7 and I'll take care of it."

Carl said, "The hematology supervisor—Pat Forrest, I believe you said—where does he stand in Grade 6 in terms of pay?"

Apparently ignoring the question, Dr. Smithers said, "I don't see where a job evaluation system has anything to do with it. I'm director of laboratories, and I want the position of hematology supervisor upgraded."

Lori responded to Carl's question with, "He's at the top of the grade. We won't be able to give him an increase the next time around, and the only chance he'll have to get more money is when the range for Grade 6 moves with the whole structure."

"I must insist on the continued ability to reward people financially for work well done," said Dr. Smithers. "I don't want to lose Pat the way we've lost so many other good people, taken away by local industry for more money."

Lori Brandon said, "As I understand it, job evaluations are comparative in nature. How can we really evaluate a job like hematology supervisor when there's only one in the house?"

Carl said, "We can come pretty close by assessing the various elements of the position such as educational requirements, level of decision-making authority, number of employees supervised, and the like. We also can and frequently do make comparisons using surveys of the other hospitals in our region."

Lori asked, "Can you do that for hematology supervisor? Survey the other hospitals?"

"It's already been done, through the Regional Hospital Association," Carl answered. "By a narrow margin, Pat Forrest appears to be the highest paid hematology supervisor in the region. But in terms of job responsibility he commands only the third largest of seven hematology sections in the region."

With a flip of his hand Dr. Smithers said, "Comparisons with other laboratories are simply not valid. This hospital is different, this laboratory is different, and our hematology supervisor position is different from all the others. Frankly, I'm tired of a personnel department that uses a so-called system simply to prevent deserving people from getting more money."

Carl said, "The system calls for re-analysis of a job at the request of the department manager. If Ms. Brandon will provide an updated job description, I'll see that it's analyzed thoroughly in every respect. Believe me, I'll give it a fair shake. I can't tell you that the possibility of an upgrade is strong because it isn't. But I'll look into it and make a recommendation for the chief operating officer to consider—because he must approve all individual upgrades."

As Carl's visitors rose to leave, Dr. Smithers grumbled, "Bah! And I'll be going directly to the chief executive officer if necessary."

Questions:

1. What is the major problem in the request to upgrade the position of hematology supervisor?
2. Is an upgrade a valid reaction to the threat of the loss of a valued employee to local industry? Why or why not?
3. If Carl's analysis simply reaffirms that the position should not be upgraded, how far may he realistically be able to go in enforcing his recommendation?

CASE 78

SEEKING THE LIMITS

Primary Topic—*Authority*

Additional Topics—*Criticism and Discipline; Decision Making; Leadership*

When you accepted the position of manager of engineering and maintenance, your boss, assistant administrator Peter Jackson, told you that you would not find a great deal of decision-making guidance written out in policy and procedure form. As Jackson put it, "Common sense is the overriding policy." However, Jackson cautioned you about the necessity to see him about matters involving employee discipline because the hospital was especially sensitive to union overtures in the service and maintenance areas.

Early during your third week on the job, a matter arose that seemed to you to call for disciplinary action of a routine nature. Remembering Jackson's precaution, you tried to see the assistant administrator several times over a period of 3 days. Being unable to get Jackson and receiving no response to your messages specifically describing the situation, you went ahead and took action rather than risk losing credibility through procrastination. When you were finally able to obtain a meeting with Jackson some several days later you described both the situation and the action you had taken. Jackson agreed with you, and of your apparent concern for getting to him quickly he said, "What's the big deal? As I said, common sense is the best policy and yours was a sound, common-sense decision."

When a similar situation arose some weeks later and you could not get to Jackson although you tried to reach him several times, once again you took action. However, this time the disciplinary action involved an employee whom you later learned was a vocal informal leader of a sizeable group of discontented employees. Your disciplinary action blew up in your face and provided the active union organizers with an issue that they instantly took up as a rallying point.

Jackson was furious with you, accusing you of deliberately overstepping your authority by refusing to bring such problems to his attention as he had directed.

Instructions:

1. Develop a tentative approach to the determination of the limits of your decision-making authority.
2. Since the limits of your authority are ultimately those limits set by your boss—and your boss here is the aforementioned Peter Jackson—develop a possible approach for getting Jackson to help you define the limits of your authority.

Case 79

A Peer Problem

Primary Topic—*Employee Problems and Problem Employees*
Additional Topics—*Authority; Communication; Leadership; Motivation*

Sally Lowe and Carl Stratton were two of the seven physicians' assistants (PAs) assigned to the emergency department of City Hospital. Scheduling was such that there was at least one PA on duty at all times and two PAs on duty during the busiest periods.

Sally was experiencing some difficulty in her working relationship with Stratton. She felt that her work was being made more difficult and more demanding by Carl's conduct, specifically by his lackadaisical attitude and apparent unwillingness to do more than absolutely necessary to get by. As Sally confided to her friend Jane, also a PA, but assigned to the department of medicine, "I really don't know what to do about working with Carl Stratton. He's never been a real ball of fire, but he was better when he first started here a year ago. Now it seems as though he's either lazy or simply doesn't care."

Jane asked, "Doesn't care in what way?"

"About much of anything," Sally answered. "As you know, sometimes there are two PAs on together in the emergency department. Lots of times there's just one, but often there's about an hour's worth of overlap because of our staggered shifts.

"About the only time I can count on Carl to even come close to what he's supposed to do is when our boss, Dr. Markis, is around. He's at his best—if I can call it that—when there's a chance Dr. Markis might see him in action. Most of the time, though, he's late getting started, takes more coffee breaks than any other two people together, and seems to take forever at lunch. I know he's making life more difficult for the other PAs and for others on the staff, although the only one I've heard say anything about it is Helen Jones, one of the nurses."

Jane asked, "Do you suppose that any of the other PAs feel the way you do?"

"I don't know. I know that I'm the one who has most of the working contact with Carl, and I know—and I'm not being paranoid—that I'm doing a lot of the work he should be doing. And it isn't just amount of work; it's quality as well. I can think of a dozen times when I've taken over his cases at shift change and had to redo half or more of what he did."

Jane said, "It sounds like you have a real problem, but I can't see how you can do much about it."

Sally sighed wearily and said, "The trouble is that it's two problems. One problem is wondering how to address the real problem. Carl Stratton and I are peers, supposedly equals. We're both supposedly professionals in the same field. Even though he and his performance are affecting me and my performance, I don't know how to go about getting anything changed."

Instructions:

List and briefly explain at least three alternative approaches that Sally might consider in addressing the problem with her peer. Fully identify all apparent advantages and disadvantages of each alternative, and on the basis of these advantages and disadvantages recommend which approach Sally should try first, which she should hold for second as necessary, and which to apply as a last resort.

CASE 80

THE ORPHAN SUPPLIES

Primary Topic—*General Management Practice*
Additional Topics—*Communication; Decision Making*

When Jerry Bennett joined the John James Memorial Hospital staff as an administrative intern, he was assigned to study the organization's structure and the apportionment of departmental responsibilities.

Early in his travels about the hospital to visit the supervisors of various departments, Jerry encountered a condition that disturbed him. In the basement of the main building, just outside of central supply, several dozen large cartons of paper products were stored in the corridor. The large cartons were stacked three deep against the wall along nearly 200 feet of the corridor. Although the corridor was wider than most and the cartons did not impede normal traffic, materials stored there placed the hospital in violation of local fire codes.

Because examining departmental responsibilities was part of his basic charge, Jerry decided to see if he could determine who was responsible for this material and find out why it could not be stored elsewhere. Because the supplies were stored outside of central supply, he made that department his first stop.

The manager of central supply explained, rather indignantly, that the boxes belonged to purchasing and stores; they had put them there because there was no room in their own storeroom. Because the boxes had been undisturbed for some months, it was probably a case of "purchasing fouling up and overordering again."

Jerry next visited purchasing, where he asked the manager about the supplies. The answer was, "Those belong to central supply. They didn't know what to do with them, so they just stuck them in the hall as usual."

Jerry Bennett's investigation hit a dead end when he could find no paperwork that could tell him to which department the supplies belonged. The purchase orders and accounting's records of payment were all on file. However, the purchase requisitions had been only partially completed; there were no signatures, and the receiving copies of the purchase orders were nowhere to be found.

What Jerry found most disturbing was that of the four products that made up this cache of material, one of them represented a 10-year supply of the item.

Questions:

1. What are the systems problems Jerry has begun to uncover?
2. What can be said about the state of departmental authority versus responsibility in the case of the supplies?
3. What do you recommend doing with the orphan supplies?

CASE 81

THE EMPLOYEE WHO IS ALWAYS RIGHT

Primary Topic—*Communication*

Additional Topics—*Criticism and Discipline; Employee Problems and Problem Employees*

"I know what I heard, and that's all there is to it," staff nurse Janice Wayne said curtly. The muscles of her face were tensed, and she spoke in the righteous tone that head nurse Wilma Paul had heard so many times.

"Dr. Gordon says otherwise, Janice," said Wilma. "He told me in no uncertain terms that the instructions he gave you were just the opposite of what you actually did. And he really came on strong."

"He's wrong, period," snapped Janice.

"He says that you were wrong, and he seemed quite sure about his position." Wilma paused thoughtfully before adding, "He went to the trouble of explaining the whole situation to me, and I have to admit that I understood his instructions. At least I was able to repeat his directions in my own words so he was satisfied that I understood what he said."

Janice scowled, then shrugged and said, "Then Dr. Gordon changed his story between the time we talked and the time he spoke with you."

"Are you suggesting that he lied to me?"

"I didn't say that. I'm only saying that he told me one thing and then apparently told you something different. Maybe he didn't realize what he was saying to me. You know how he just kind of rattles off something quickly and runs away."

Wilma sighed and said, "Janice, did you consider the possibility that you didn't understand? It isn't hard to misinterpret a message when things happen so fast and—"

"I know what I heard," interrupted Janice. "When I know I'm wrong, I'll say so. If I even think that I may be wrong, I'll say so. But in this case I know I'm right. It's not even remotely possible that I could have misinterpreted Dr. Gordon."

Feeling that Janice had given her cause to speak up about something that had been nagging her for quite some time, Wilma said, "It seems to me that you're never wrong, Janice."

Janice Wayne glared at her supervisor. "What do you mean by that?"

Wilma took a deep breath and offered her explanation. "I've been head nurse of this unit for 3 years, and in all that time I've never known you to admit being wrong about anything. This problem with Dr. Gordon is just one more example of how you always turn things around so that you look innocent or correct. Is it so necessary that you be right about everything?"

Janice's tone, already cool, became colder. "As I said, I'll admit that I'm wrong—but only when I am wrong. And I want to know the other times you're talking about, the times when I supposedly 'turned things around.'"

Wilma began, "Well, there was—" She stopped, shook her head, and said, "No, I was thinking about something else. In any case, you ought to know what I'm talking about. Think about it and you'll know what I'm saying. You seem to have an answer for everything, and it's always an answer that places you in the right."

"You can't think of any specific incidents because there haven't been any," said Janice. She rose from her chair and continued, "You may be my supervisor, but I don't have to listen to this. Is there anything else you wanted to say about *Dr. Gordon's problem*?" She glared down at Wilma.

Wilma rose to her feet. "Just that the incident is not to be considered closed. Dr. Gordon insists that it be written up for disciplinary dialogue—a verbal warning."

"I'll protest, of course," said Janice. "I won't accept a warning that I don't deserve, and I won't say that I'm wrong when I know I'm right."

When Janice left the office, Wilma began to regret having spoken to Janice as she did. She was convinced, however, that she had to try to get through to Janice about her apparent need to be right whenever a disagreement or misunderstanding arose.

Questions:

1. When Wilma left the specific incident to talk about Janice's overall conduct, she made a mistake that is embodied in the words "You always turn things around so that you look innocent or correct." What was Wilma's mistake, and why was it a mistake?
2. How would you recommend attempting to determine the cause of the misunderstanding involving Janice and Dr. Gordon?
3. Taking Janice's departure from Wilma's office at the end of the case as your starting point, how would you propose to deal with the employee who is always right?

CASE 82

THE DRILL SERGEANT

Primary Topic—*Authority*

Additional Topics—*Communication; Criticism and Discipline; Employee Problems and Problem Employees; General Management Practice; Leadership*

One day when nurse manager Diane Cowan was in the supermarket, she encountered Ruth Miller, a neighbor and acquaintance and also one of the nurses in Diane's unit. After a bit of social conversation, Diane asked Ruth, "I know that since you went part-time you've been working every other weekend. Eve Bonner, our new weekend charge nurse, came in about the same time you changed. How do you like working with her?"

Ruth hesitated a moment, then said, "Quite honestly, Diane—and just between the two of us, outside the hospital—I don't like working for her at all."

"May I ask why?"

"It's her whole manner and approach," said Ruth. "She's curt and snappish, and she doesn't ask people to do things or even give instructions—she just barks orders. Most of the time she sounds more like an army sergeant than a charge nurse."

Although she realized that it was only a single person's view, Diane was nevertheless disturbed by this informal report on a weekend charge nurse whom she had appointed. It was true that Eve Bonner appeared no more or less qualified than a number of other nurses on the unit, but Eve had no objections to working weekends and seemed to Diane even to welcome the opportunity. For 3 days each week Eve was simply one of the capable nurses on Diane's unit. However, Diane had to admit that she knew nothing about how Eve was functioning as weekend charge nurse because she had never seen Eve in action in that capacity. Until her conversation with Ruth, Diane had received no reports about Eve's performance.

Diane decided that although the need to evaluate Eve Bonner as a weekend charge nurse was months away, she had nevertheless better look into the matter of Eve's performance. Over the course of 2 weeks Diane sought out most of her unit's weekend workers for individual discussions. In each discussion she was no more pointed in her initial questioning than, "How are you getting along with our new weekend charge?" However, this approach was sufficient. Diane had known most of these people for several years, and, given that opening, the majority of them spoke freely.

In the process of her one-on-one meetings Diane learned that several weekend employees were convinced that Eve's conduct was directly responsible for the resignation of one nurse who cited "personal reasons" for her departure. From her discussions Diane was also able to glean the following comments:

- "During the week when she's not in charge she's fine to work with, but on the weekends she's a terror."
- "She dictates like a drill sergeant."
- "She doesn't do much herself—just tells everybody else what to do."
- "I think being in charge has gone to her head. She really likes to lord it over everyone."

All in all, Diane was quite disheartened by all the secondhand information she had acquired about the style of her weekend charge nurse, Eve Bonner.

Question:

How should Diane proceed in addressing the problems of the weekend charge nurse? Outline your steps or options, and supply a complete rationale or justification for each.

Case 83

The Tyrant

Primary Topic—*Employee Problems and Problem Employees*

Additional Topics—*Authority; Communication; Criticism and Discipline; Leadership*

Wende Carlson, office manager for the hospital's ambulatory services division, was secretly happy that her half-day conference had been in the morning and not the afternoon. Mornings in the office were so hectic that it was a relief to get away once in a while. The afternoons were relatively quiet, and Wende had hopes of getting caught up on some delinquent paperwork. However, when Wende arrived at her office after lunch, she was greeted by four angry expressions and one empty desk.

Indicating the empty desk, Wende asked the others, "Where is Sue? And what's going on around here?"

"Sue went home," Eleanor said.

"She had to go home after Dr. Greer got through with her," said Kay. "I think I would've spit in his eye and walked out for good."

Wende asked, "What in the world happened?"

Eleanor explained, "Sue had the misfortune to make a simple booking mistake when Dr. Greer was at his busiest. He's a bear most of the time anyway, and we all know how he's been lately with the group running one physician short."

Wende said, "We obviously shouldn't make booking errors, but as hectic as it gets around here, they're bound to happen once in a while, and there's usually nothing serious about them."

Kay said, "You'd think they were life threatening the way he took off on her. He called her about ten different kinds of an idiot and said he was going to have her fired for incompetence. He literally screamed at her, in front of the four of us and Dr. Wilson and at least three or four patients in the waiting area."

"No class, rotten style," Eleanor muttered. The others nodded in agreement.

"Why did Sue go home?" Wende asked.

Eleanor answered, "Greer really leveled her and ordered her out of the office. She cried in the ladies room for nearly half an hour, but even after she calmed down a bit she was afraid to come back in. She just signed out and went home."

In further discussion with her four staff members, Wende learned that Sue had stated there was no way she could continue working where she was treated in that fashion and that Dr. Greer had announced for all to hear that she was forbidden ever to touch his schedules again.

Questions:

1. How should Wende Carlson approach the discussion of the incident with Sue?
2. Recognizing that Dr. Greer is neither her employer nor her organizational superior, how should Wende approach the discussion of the incident with Dr. Greer?
3. How should Wende proceed in general to deal with the situation outlined in the case? List a number of possible steps or actions and provide reasons for each.

Case 84

The Busy Boss Delegates

Primary Topic—*Delegation*

Additional Topics—*Authority; Communication; Leadership*

Director of materials management Tom Netter was responsible for activities divided among five managers, some with subordinate supervisors. As someone responsible for a wide range of activities and many tasks, Tom had always espoused a belief in active delegation of authority and active participative management as far as his five direct-reporting managers were concerned.

It seemed to Tom as though a common response throughout the hospital to many problems and questions that arose was, "That's Netter's responsibility." In a way it made him feel good to be identified so strongly with many important activities.

Among Tom's many responsibilities was membership, on behalf of the hospital, on several product committees of the region's group purchasing program. He also served on at least four hospital committees, including the product evaluation committee and the safety committee.

As is often the case with a growing healthcare institution and with the expanding field of health care, Tom Netter's job continued to grow until it reached a point at which he became painfully aware that he could no longer cover all of the bases as he had been doing for so long. He was missing committee meetings and failing to completely fulfill a number of his other responsibilities.

In an attempt to gain some relief, Tom delegated representation on several committees to some of his subordinate managers and likewise delegated some other tasks that he had become too busy to handle. He thought that doing so would be wise for both him and his subordinate managers, so he was surprised to discover that his five managers were quite resentful of their newly delegated assignments. He inadvertently heard one manager say to another something about "Netter dumping off his responsibilities on us." Another, purchasing manager Bill Marlowe, said to Tom directly, "Of all things, why did you have to stick me with the safety committee? Couldn't you take it any more?"

Questions:

1. What in the brief description of Tom Netter's role in the hospital suggests that the seeds for resistance to his delegation may have been long present?
2. What was Tom Netter's primary failing in his working relationship with his subordinate managers?
3. Having met with resistance from his subordinate managers, how might Tom readdress the matter of proper delegation so they might better appreciate the value of the tasks being delegated?

CASE 85

THE MANAGEMENT EXPERT

Primary Topic—*General Management Practice*

Additional Topics—*Authority; Communication; Criticism and Discipline; Delegation; Employee Problems and Employee Problems*

Several weeks ago physical therapist Walt Palmer said to his boss, director of physical therapy George Jackson, "You know, George, the way that we develop the budget in this department doesn't make much sense. All we do is take last year's actual expenses and add on an inflation factor and make some other guesses. What we really ought to be doing is budgeting from a zero base, making every line item completely justify itself every year."

George said something about simply following the budgeting instructions issued by the finance department and doing it the way he was told. He pursued the matter no further.

Within a few days of the budget question, Walt approached George with, "Don't you think the way this place does performance evaluations ought to change? Certainly most smart managers know it's better to evaluate employees on their anniversary dates than the way we do it."

George again answered to the effect that as a manager he was simply doing what he had to do to comply with the policies and practices of the organization. They discussed the matter for perhaps 5 minutes, and although George was not about to start working to stimulate change in the performance appraisal system, he nevertheless felt led to concede that Walt had brought up a number of good points. It struck George that his employee was idealizing an evaluation system in almost textbook terms; it seemed flawless in theory, but George had been through enough actual systems to be able to recognize a number of potential barriers to thorough practical application.

In the ensuing 2 to 3 weeks Walt had more and more to say to George about how the organization should be managed. And it took Walt only a matter of days to get beyond generalized management techniques—such as budgeting and appraisal—and begin to offer specific advice on the management of the physical therapy department.

Quickly George Jackson came to realize that he could virtually count on Walt to offer some criticism of most of his actions in running the department and most of administration's actions in running the hospital. George did not appreciate this turn in his relationship with an otherwise good employee. George had always seen Walt as an excellent performer as a physical therapist, perhaps somewhat opinionated but not to any harmful extent. Recently, however, he had come to regard Walt as a sort of conscience, a critical presence who was monitoring his every move as a manager.

The worsening situation came to a head one day when Walt attempted to intercede in a squabble between two other physical therapy employees and, when George entered the situation, proceeded to criticize George's handling of the matter in front of the other employees.

George immediately took Walt into his office for a private one-to-one discussion. He first told Walt that although he was free to offer his suggestions, opinions, and criticisms regarding management, he—Walt—was never again to do so in the presence of others in the department. George then asked Walt, "It seems that lately you have a great deal to say about management and specifically about how I manage this department. Why this sudden active interest in management?"

Walt answered, "Last month I finished the first course in the management program at the community college, a course called Introduction to Management Theory. Now I'm in the second course, one called Supervisory Practice. I know what I'm hearing—and quite honestly, it's pretty simple stuff—and when I see things that I know aren't being handled right, I feel that I have an obligation to this hospital to speak up."

George ended the discussion by again telling Walt that he expected all such criticism and advice to be offered in private and never again in front of other employees. Overall, the conversation did not go well; more than once George felt that Walt's remarks were edging toward insubordination. Because of the uneasy feeling the discussion left with him, George requested a meeting with Carl Miller, the hospital's vice president for human resources.

After describing the state of the relationship between him and Walt in some detail, George spread his hands in a gesture of helplessness and said to Carl, "I'm looking for your advice. Apparently on the strength of a course or two of textbook management, this guy suddenly has all the answers. What can I do with him?"

Questions:

1. If Walt does indeed act as though he has all the answers, what can George do to encourage modification of this attitude?
2. If you were Walt, how should you best proceed in applying your newly acquired knowledge of management? Explain and provide an example.
3. What are the possible reasons behind George Jackson's growing aggravation with Walt Palmer? List a few possible reasons and comment on the validity of each.

Case 86

No Longer Pulling Her Weight

Primary Topic—*Employee Problems and Problem Employees*

Additional Topics—*Criticism and Discipline; Decision Making; Leadership*

Head nurse Mary Bennett felt that she had a problem of considerable dimensions involving staff nurse Eleanor Collins. As Mary explained to her manager, associate nursing director and day supervisor Ruth Wells, "I just don't know what to do about Eleanor any more. She's simply not pulling her weight, and I have to recognize that."

Ruth asked, "Has she been having health problems? Or do you think she's another burnout case?"

Mary responded, "She's definitely not a burnout case. She still seems to care about nursing, and she's a pretty cool head most of the time. She just seems completely unable to keep up the pace on the job. Let me take a few minutes to fill you in on where she's at and the things I've been thinking about."

Mary talked to Ruth for 15 minutes or longer. The following list summarizes the major points of her presentation.

- Eleanor had experienced some apparently minor health problems within the recent 2 years, but she did not seem to be troubled by anything chronic and her recent attendance record was better than average.
- Eleanor was older than the hospital's minimum retirement age as stated in the pension plan. However, she was still short of becoming completely vested in the plan and short of the minimum eligibility age for social security.
- Eleanor was always pleasant and always cooperative, but it invariably took her 8 hours to accomplish the same amount of work that others were doing in 5 or 6 hours. Her slowdown had been sufficiently gradual that Mary could not truthfully indicate a point in time at which her productivity began to drop.

Because staffing was marginally tight, a condition prevailing in all units, everyone in the unit had to put forth maximum effort at all times. Mary was getting complaints from other staff members about Eleanor's inability to keep up with the pace. Most of these complaints were offered kindly and with some reluctance; however, Mary had received information—admittedly secondhand and unverified—that she,

Mary, was being accused of "covering up for the dead wood" because she had done nothing about Eleanor's obviously diminished productivity. Mary felt that most of the other staff members liked Eleanor and felt sympathy for her, but that these kindly feelings were in danger of being crowded out by growing resentment for having to work harder because of Eleanor.

Mary had considered urging Eleanor to seek transfer opportunity, but Mary did not know if Eleanor would be amenable to a transfer or even if there were any other positions in the department where Eleanor would not likely experience the same problems.

"In short," said Mary, "Eleanor is a nice person but her inability to keep up is causing harm within the unit, and I have to do something about it."

Question:

If you were in the position of day supervisor Ruth Wells, how would you advise Mary to proceed in the matter of staff nurse Eleanor Collins?

Case 87

She's Having a Rough Time

Primary Topic—*Employee Problems and Problem Employees*

Additional Topics—*Authority; Criticism and Discipline; General Management Practice; Leadership*

Janet Carling, manager of the business office for Wilson County Hospital, a small rural facility serving a geographically large but sparsely populated area, was having difficulty covering her office's essential functions for five 8-hour days each week because of one particular staff member. In addition to Janet, the business office consisted of just two full-time and two part-time employees. Janet felt she could not count on Dale Hamlin, one of the full-time employees and second only to Janet herself in hospital longevity, to be regularly available when needed.

"Most of the time it doesn't seem to be Dale's fault," Janet said to her friend and fellow supervisor, Harriet Redding, over coffee one morning before work. "I know she has a chronic health problem that keeps her out on short, unpredictable absences and sends her off to medical appointments on short notice. It's a day here, a half day there, once in a while 2 days, and never more than 3 days—I think it was 3 days just once—all without any real notice."

Harriet asked, "How does Dale cover her time off? If she's as bad as she sounds I can't imagine she has any sick-time bank at all."

"None. She has no bank, and she long ago passed the point where she was using up sick time as fast as she earned it. In fact she uses all of her vacation time to cover these bits and pieces of time off."

"As I understand the policy, her supervisor—that's you kiddo—is supposed to approve vacation requests in advance," said Harriet. "You're not obligated to approve all these little 'vacations' of hers, especially if you haven't been given notice."

Janet spread her hands in a gesture of helplessness. "What am I supposed to do? One way or another she's going to be off, and if I don't approve vacation she'll have to take the time without pay. As it is it looks like she'll go through all of her vacation well before year's end and will get stuck with unpaid time anyway."

Janet went on, "I feel sorry for her, I really do, but I can't even plan 1 week's worth of coverage of all activities given her unpredictability. And I have three other employees who are getting just as tired as I am of having the whole group's schedule subject to her comings and goings."

"Have you spoken with Miller?" Harriet's reference was to Scott Miller, the hospital's chief financial officer and their mutual boss.

"Yes, for all the good it's done."

Harriet smiled knowingly. "Nothing from *Mister Indecision*? My, my, imagine that."

"Less than nothing," Janet said. "I told him I wanted to do something with Dale's status. You know, make her part-time, change her hours, something that will give me more flexibility. You know, I'm even way past the point where I should be taking action based on chronic absenteeism, so now I'm backed into a place where I'll probably have to cut the others some extra slack so I'm not accused of differential treatment of employees. But all I get from Miller when I try to talk about Dale is, '*She's having a rough time, so don't pressure her.*'"

Harriet glanced furtively to her right and left and lowered her voice. "You *do* know—or maybe you don't know—that Dale is related to Miller's wife? Cousin, I think."

Janet rolled her eyes toward the ceiling. "Great. I've got a sweet lady for an employee but she's turning into a liability, and I can't deal with the situation because I get no backing from my boss. What am I supposed to do?"

Instructions:

Suggest one or two possible courses of action Janet Carling might consider in addressing the problem presented by Dale Hamlin's circumstances and the absence of higher management support or assistance.

CASE 88

DISCHARGE FOR CAUSE

Primary Topic—*Criticism and Discipline*

Additional Topics—*Authority; Employee Problems and Problem Employees; General Management Practice; Leadership; Rules and Policies*

William Short is chief executive officer of Benton Memorial Hospital, a 120-bed institution serving a fairly widespread semirural area. He has been in his position for 8 months. Before his arrival the hospital operated for 4 months without a CEO after the abrupt and unexplained departure of the former CEO.

The previous CEO appeared to have been extremely well liked by his management group but at the same time was at constant odds with the hospital's board of trustees. This former CEO had been considered easygoing, low-key in style, and relatively slow to act in many matters. William Short stands in stark contrast to his predecessor; his pace is rapid, his manner is brusque and forceful, and many find his size and demeanor to be intimidating. It is generally believed he was brought into the organization to apply pressure to the management team and perhaps to weed out certain individuals. It is, then, no surprise that his arrival was greeted with some apprehension and resentment, and his personal style has only supported those initial impressions.

Among several members of management remaining cool toward Short was Clara Jackson, RN, an employee of some 9 years who for the most recent 5 years has been emergency department supervisor.

It took Short the better part of his initial 8 months to work his lengthy priority list down to one particular problem: overtime authorization and approval. One of the departments with consistent overtime use out of proportion to the rest of the hospital was the emergency department.

Short asked Clara Jackson to turn over her overtime logs. These included the names of persons authorized to work overtime, dates, hours, and authorizing initial of either the director or assistant director of nursing service. Clara's cool response was that she had misplaced the logs, and anyway she "saw no good reason why he should need them." All he had to do, she claimed, was check the time cards retained by the payroll department. Nevertheless, Short repeated his request several times and finally directed Clara to stop stalling and locate the logs.

When Short received the overtime logs he was initially struck by the fact that all of the entries were in the same color ink and the same style of writing. He took this as an indication that all of the entries may have been made by the same person at the same time. This indication became a certainty when he noticed that the date on which the most recent log pages had been started was some 3 weeks before the date appearing in the lower left-hand corner as the reprinting date of the form. Further investigation revealed that the initials of the director and assistant director of nursing were not authentic.

When Clara was confronted, she first denied creating the logs and then reversed her story and admitted doing so. She claimed she did so because Short was applying pressure and she was afraid to admit she had lost the originals. She resisted Short's allegation that she had never maintained the logs in the first place but had simply authorized overtime herself, entered it on the time cards, and put it through without following policy, a practice already proved to have occurred in two other departments.

Short's allegations were largely supported by the director and assistant director of nursing who claimed it had been a year or more since they were last asked to authorize overtime for the emergency department. When asked why this did not seem to concern them, their answers suggested that under the former management policies such as the one for overtime authorization were neither observed nor enforced.

One the basis of violation of policy and falsification of records, William Short discharged Clara Jackson. Clara strongly objected to the firing and appealed directly to several trustees. Her personal appeals were unsuccessful, so she filed a complaint with the State Employment Commission charging that her discharge was arbitrary and unjust.

William Short was called to a Commission hearing to show cause why Clara Jackson should not be reinstated.

Instructions:

Consider the information provided in the case description and prepare to offer a decision that either supports the firing of Clara Jackson, or orders Clara Jackson to be reinstated in her position. Explain why you decided as you did, enumerating the factors that prompted your decision, and describe what you believe to be the management errors that permitted the situation to occur.

Case 89

The "Demanding" Manager

Primary Topic—*Change Management*

Additional Topics—*Authority; Communication; General Management Practice; Leadership*

Alan Mack was recruited from out-of-state and brought into County Memorial Hospital as director of biomedical engineering. In addition to Alan, the department's staff consisted of one senior biomedical engineer, two junior biomedical engineers, and three biomedical engineering technicians. The job of the department was to maintain, calibrate, and repair as necessary all of the hospital's electrical and electronic medical equipment except for those pieces in sizeable fixed installations, such as analyzers in the clinical laboratories that were under maintenance contracts with manufacturers.

Alan was introduced to his new group by his predecessor, the retiring Fred Richards, during Fred's final few days on the job. Fred emphasized the difficult nature of much of the work, noting that in his opinion much of the equipment they had to maintain had outlived its true useful life; for financial reasons, the hospital had been stalling certain replacement purchases. Old equipment notwithstanding, Fred also noted that he felt the employee relations aspects were the most important dimensions of the job. He believed, said Fred, that what worked best with this group was letting them work independently at their own pace and learn from their own mistakes. This was, Fred boasted, a cohesive group of people with high morale and upbeat attitudes.

During his first few weeks Alan made no changes to existing departmental procedures. Instead, he concentrated on getting to know the staff and sometimes actually working with an engineer or technician to get the feel of some of the more difficult tasks they faced. Alan soon concluded, however, that total amount of work turned out was quite low considering the size of the staff. It seemed there was always a considerable backlog of repairs and calibration work, yet relations with the line departments they served were generally good.

Alan discovered that by personally working together with someone in the group on the more challenging repair jobs, the more quickly certain problems were isolated and the faster the equipment went back into service. He concluded that his employees were not working efficiently, nor were they putting forth their best efforts.

Rather than expressing his observations to the staff, Alan decided to require individual productivity reports from each person on a weekly basis and use these to track individual productivity. Each report was to enumerate: the number of PMs (preventive maintenance jobs) performed; number of repairs, including time spent on each job and the problems encountered; and the amount of calibration activity.

With the introduction of the reports, Alan was pleased to see an immediate increase in the total amount of work accomplished and a corresponding reduction in the department's backlog. However, it seemed there was now a more strained relationship existing between Alan and the group.

About 6 weeks after the weekly reporting was started, one junior biomedical engineer and one technician, employees of 4 and 2 years, respectively, gave notice of their resignation. They both cited as their reason for resigning the pressure of work, specifically, as one expressed it, "the unrealistic demands of the department director." This came as a complete surprise to Alan, who felt, compared with industry standards and other organizations with which he was familiar, that his staff, following recent improvement, was barely operating at average efficiency for a department its size.

Questions:

1. What do you believe to be the character of the problem that Alan has encountered, and how did it likely become a problem?
2. Because Alan cannot back up and start over with this group, what do you believe he will have to do to stand a chance of restoring good working relationships with the employees?

Case 90

The Uncooperative Colleague

Primary Topic—*Communication*

Additional Topics—*Authority; General Management Practice*

Irene West, day shift supervisor in Central Processing at County General Hospital, usually did not take her problems outside of the department. She rarely complained to anyone about the frustrations she experienced from time to time. However, what was heavy on her mind must have shown on her face when she joined her friend from Human Resources, Melinda Walters, for coffee in the employee cafeteria shortly before the start of the Tuesday's work day. Melinda took one look at Irene and said, "Wow, why the storm clouds? What's bugging you?"

Irene hesitated, waging a brief internal struggle over whether she should speak up to her friend. Frustration and anger won out, and Irene said, with considerable vehemence, "Tami Dean's what's bugging me. If I can't do something about her, I'm going to walk off the job one of these days and put this place behind me forever."

"Tami? The one who's got your job on second shift?"

"The very same," Irene muttered sarcastically, "Tami the let's-leave-most-of-messes-for-the-day-shift, my evening counterpart who's divided her work into two categories: the stuff she ignores, and the stuff she does wrong."

"Like what?"

"Like almost everything. Packs assembled incorrectly by her people, work left half done or undone, inventories and stock reports done wrong or ignored, even normal housekeeping ignored—I can always tell what she had for lunch by looking at the top of our shared desk."

Melinda asked, "What have you tried to do about it?"

"I've talked to Tami until I'm sick of talking. She either brushes aside my remarks as unfounded or she becomes so defensive that there's no talking with her. Whenever I try talking with her about problems we're having on days because of something the evening shift has done—or hasn't done, as the case may be—she shuts down on me immediately."

"What about her employees? Does she seem to get along with them?"

"Oh, they all get along for the most part. It's a small staff on evenings, no heavy demands. And the staff all love Tami, not surprisingly; she practically lets them come and go as they please and work at their own pace—whatever that pace may be.

"But much of what Tami does is affecting me and my shift," Irene continued, "and I seem totally unable to get through to her. I'm getting really tired of trying hard to do my best while this person just coasts along while she makes more work for me and my people."

Instructions:

Put yourself in the position of Melinda Walters—and remember, Melinda works in human resources—and outline some possible actions for Irene to consider in her ongoing conflict with the evening shift supervisor.

CASE 91

THE INFORMANT

Primary Topic—*Communication*

Additional Topics—*Criticism and Discipline; Employee Problems and Problem Employees*

Admitting manager Estelle Porter felt she was in a quandary concerning a faithful volunteer who spent a great deal of time in the department. As Estelle described to her friend, Kathy Wilson, a manager in another department that frequently used volunteers, "You know that I rely fairly heavily on volunteers, especially when it comes to running the desk in the front lobby and the information center near the cashier's office."

"Sure do," said Kathy, "even more than I do. And if your volunteers are anything like mine, you're overjoyed to find an occasional one who can actually be depended upon to show up when needed."

"That's not a problem with the situation that's bugging me. I've got this one particular volunteer, Edwina Marsh. I think you know her, or at least know who she is. She puts in lots of hours and I can always depend on her to show up. She's small and soft-spoken, the kind of person who does her work and bothers no one. She's so inconspicuous that it's easy to forget she's even there much of the time. And I think that's a lot of the problem."

Kathy asked, "How so?"

"I have a few staff members who sometimes act out when I'm not around. And—"

"Join the club," said Kathy.

"—and since they don't pay much attention to Edwina they're not bashful about goofing off when I'm not there."

"And the problem?"

"Although Edwina does wonderful work, she seems to feel like she's got to keep me clued in on all of the errors and shortcomings and behavior problems of the regular staff. She usually comes to me with a standard opening like, 'There's something I think you ought to know.' But of course a lot of what I get from her I can't realistically use without getting Edwina into trouble with the others."

"Why not just tell her to keep her observations and comments to herself?" asked Kathy.

"Because—and this is the scary part—*every time I've been able to check out something she's told me, it turns out that she's absolutely correct.* How should I deal with her, and how can I constructively use what she's bringing me?"

Instructions:

Put yourself in Kathy's position and suggest how Estelle should deal with Edwina and how, if at all, she can constructively use the information Edwina brings.

Case 92

Managing the Drama Queen

Primary Topic—*Employee Problems and Problem Employees*
Additional Topics—*Communication; Criticism and Discipline*

Janice Jenkins, one of several supervisors within the business office structure at Mammoth Medical Center, had an ongoing problem with one particular employee, a biller named Helen Benjamin. As Janice attempted to explain to her immediate manager, Casey Sutton, "I'm at a loss as to how to deal with Helen Benjamin. She's not the poorest performer in the group, but she's far from the best and she makes her share of mistakes. But every time I criticize her or try to get her to change the way she's doing something, I get a pretty wild reaction. It's not always the same reaction from one time to the next, and we seem never to get anything accomplished."

Casey asked, "Wild in what ways? What's she doing?"

Janice thought a moment before saying, "The mode I see her in most often is defensiveness. I'll try to correct something she's been doing wrong. First, she'll deny wrongdoing, sometimes quite vehemently. Almost always her first reaction to criticism of any kind is that she just doesn't make mistakes. Then when we've reached a point where she really can't successfully deny the mistake, she'll demand to know whether this incident is going to appear on her next evaluation. And she lets me know that if it does appear as part of her evaluation, she'll file a grievance."

"What else?"

"Her other significant approach is even tougher for me to deal with. I'll take her aside concerning something that's been done improperly—and it's always aside, always in private, and when it's Helen I always try to approach the situation as gently as possible—and she'll burst into tears and carry on about how unfair everything is, how she does her honest best all the time, and how the stress of the job and the way she's treated are driving her crazy. Whether she's in her defensive mode or her weeping mode, she carries on as though she's trying to impress an audience."

Casey asked, "Is she treated differently from the others at all?"

"Only to the extent that she takes up more of my time than any other employee. Believe me, I do my best to play no favorites. But I have 14 employees overall and I treat them all the same, and Helen is the only one who consistently gives me trouble. Seems to me she has no clue as to how to take criticism like an adult."

"How does she relate to the rest of the group?"

"She seems to get along with coworkers just fine. In fact, I don't think the others know what I go through with Helen. Whether it's been one of her defensive tirades or a weeping-and-whining session, she seems to be back to normal 30 seconds after leaving my office."

Instructions:

1. Offer two or three possible reasons that might at least partially explain the behavior of "the Drama Queen."
2. Recommend a course of action for Janice to consider in dealing with Helen. Be sure to provide justification for your recommendations.

CASE 93

THE HOLIDAY SWITCH

Primary Topic—*Rules and Policies*

Additional Topics—*Communication; Employee Problems and Problem Employees*

Nurse manager Carrie Williams had a complaint about licensed practical nurse Sue Marvin. According to Carrie, Sue was unfairly working the hospital's scheduling practices to her own advantage. As Carrie explained to assistant director of nursing Dana Daniels, "I think I've gotten stung at least twice by Sue Marvin's schedule switching. She came to me a couple of weeks ago and volunteered to work the upcoming holiday, for which she wasn't scheduled. And you know how tough holiday scheduling is, so we're usually overjoyed when someone offers to work the holiday."

"For time and a half, of course," offered Dana. "I think I know where this is going."

"And I think you're probably right. Sue then had the option to choose another day as her 'holiday.' Which she took several days before the actual holiday she was now scheduled to work."

"Which our policy allows her to do. She can pick any replacement day before or after the holiday as long as it falls within the same 2-week pay period."

"Correct," said Carrie.

"The problem? I bet I can guess."

"No bet. I'm sure you've seen this more than once. She took her replacement day off for something that was apparently important to her. Then she reported to work on the actual holiday but worked barely half of the shift before pleading illness and leaving. Making us one person short for 4 critical hours."

Dana asked, "She's done this before?"

Carrie nodded. "At least once that I can remember. That time she claimed an urgent family situation as her reason for leaving early. It seems that Sue has been able to get certain days off that she specifically wants without honoring her end of the agreement."

Instructions:

Imagining yourself in the position of nursing assistant director Dana Daniels:

1. How would you advise Carrie in dealing with Sue Marvin?, and
2. What might you consider doing in an effort to curtail such occurrences in the future?

Case 94

The Elusive Employee

Primary Topic—*Employee Problems and Problem Employees*
Additional Topics—*Communication; General Management Practice; Leadership*

Laboratory supervisor Vera Simpson was expressing her frustrations with employee Daniel Brandon to her friend, human resources representative Ginny Flavin. Said Vera, "Most of the time I really have no idea what Dan's doing, since I hardly ever see him. He works what I refer to as our crazy shift, and most of the time his hours overlap the other shifts. And he's alone much of the time, completely on his own."

Ginny asked, "Is he getting the work done?"

"He seems to be, but at any given time it's awfully hard for me to tell because I just don't see him. And a couple of times when I tried to call him from home—times he was covering nights in clinical chemistry—I couldn't reach him. He claimed he was responding to a stat call, but I couldn't verify that. And at least twice the night nursing supervisor said it took 10 or 15 minutes to track him down when she needed something."

"So you're concerned about whether he's really working all the time? Or that his work is up to standard?"

"I've never found his work to be anything but acceptable. That is, at least when I'm aware of what he's doing. My concerns are really twofold: How can I adequately supervise an individual who I'm able to see for only about 10 percent of an average shift, if that? And, how can I do an honest performance evaluation of someone working in his circumstances?"

Question:

As noted in the preceding paragraph, how can Vera adequately supervise this employee given the small percentage of time he's actually in her presence?

CASE 95

THIS PLACE OWES ME

Primary Topic—*Employee Problem and Problem Employees*

Additional Topics—*Communication; Criticism and Discipline; Leadership; Motivation*

"I have a particular part-time employee who is giving me a great deal of grief," said business office manager Darlene Swift, "and I'm looking for advice on how to deal with her."

"What's she doing?" asked human resources representative Ellen Francis who then added, "Are you going to tell me it's Jennifer Wilson again? The one we spoke about maybe 6 months ago?"

"Yes, the same. I'd forgotten we talked about her briefly. I tried counseling like you suggested, but nothing changed. If anything, things have gotten worse."

"How so? Fill me in; I don't recall the particulars of our earlier discussion."

Darlene offered, "Jennie's still part-time, 20 hours a week. But she takes more sick time than any full-time employee. She's out frequently, and whenever she returns she automatically expects that someone will have completed anything she left unfinished. She expects someone else to clear up her backlog any time she's out, and unfortunately that's what's been happening."

Darlene continued, "And whenever she's asked to work extra time help cover for vacations or others' illnesses, she always refuses. With what usually sound like good reasons."

Ellen asked, "How long has she been employed here?"

Darlene sighed. "Maybe that's part of the problem. She's been here forever—close to 25 years. In fact, she told me recently that she'd given her share of extra effort to the hospital over the years and that it was about time the hospital gave back to her. As she puts it, 'This place owes me.'"

"Have you talked about her behavior recently? Specifically, the absences?"

A shrug. "I tried counseling. About absences. That's when I got the speech about expecting the hospital to give back to her."

"Still concerning the absences, any disciplinary actions?"

"No," Darlene answered. "I don't believe she's ever been disciplined for anything."

"Okay," said Ellen. "Let's take a look at her file, access her attendance records, and see what we might be able to do about Jennifer."

Questions:

1. Imagining yourself in the position of human resources representative Ellen Francis, what advice would you offer Darlene for dealing with her troublesome employee, Jennifer?
2. How could Darlene have avoided—or at least minimized—the present problem?
3. What personnel policies are likely to be in place to assist Darlene in addressing difficulties such as those presented by Jennifer?

Case 96

He Didn't Work Out

Primary Topic—*Hiring and Placement*

Additional Topics—*Authority; Decision Making; General Management Practice; Leadership*

Bill Young, an all-around mechanic and electrician, was hired by James Memorial Hospital as supervisor of engineering and maintenance. Although he had 15 years experience in the field, this was Young's first supervisory position.

Shortly after Young's arrival a maintenance helper job became available. This was an important job because of the numerous preventive maintenance tasks involved, and Bill Young recognized the need to fill this position as soon as possible. Immediately after receiving the departing helper's resignation, Young asked the human resource department to locate several candidates for him to interview.

Young's immediate supervisor, chief operating officer Peter Jackson, chose to sit in on the interviews, giving as his reason Young's newness to management. Jackson indicated that since Young had never interviewed or hired before he should be assisted in the process.

Young and Jackson jointly interviewed five candidates. Of the five, two appeared to be reasonably qualified for the job. One of these was a young man named Simmons who was employed in the hospital's food service department. The other was a young man named Kelly who had not worked recently but had had several months of building-and-grounds experience at a school.

After the interviews Young expressed his desire to hire Simmons from food service because he appeared to have the aptitude and ability and exhibited a strong desire to better himself. Young also reasoned that selecting Simmons would show that the hospital was genuinely interested in developing employees within the organization. However, Jackson disagreed with Young, told Young he could do the hiring "the next time a job opened." Jackson himself made the decision to hire Kelly and personally communicated the offer to Kelly.

As the 30-day probationary period progressed, it became increasingly evident to Bill Young that Kelly was not shaping up as a satisfactory employee. Even with being sure to give Kelly all reasonable orientation and guidance, and extending every benefit of the doubt because he had been "the boss's choice," Young could conclude only that they would be making a mistake keeping Kelly on past the introductory period.

On the 28th day of Kelly's employment Bill Young went to see Jackson. He had kept Jackson advised of Kelly's poor progress and lack of response to guidance, so it was no surprise to Jackson when Young said they should let Kelly go and start all over again.

"Okay," was Jackson's reply, "let Kelly go."

Young hesitated, wondering a moment if he should say anything, and finally said to Jackson, "I don't believe I should be the one to let him go. I'm not the one who hired him."

"He's your employee," Jackson responded. "You get rid of him."

Questions:

1. Do you believe Jackson dodged responsibility by ordering Young to get rid of Kelly? Why, or why not?
2. In what other way could this situation have been more equitably handled?
3. What effect is the Kelly incident likely to have on the future relationship between Young and Jackson?

CASE 97

TAKE YOUR CHOICE

Primary Topic—*General Management Practice*

Additional Topics—*Authority; Change Management; Time Management and Personal Effectiveness*

You are a registered nurse with 20 years of hospital experience, and you have spent 10 years as nursing director in a 60-bed rural hospital. You recently applied for the position of assistant director of nursing at a 375-bed city hospital. During your initial interview the nursing director posed four sets of "conditions" and asked you to state which of these best described the circumstances under which you believed such a position should be taken. The "conditions" are:

1. You step into the job with the full authority and responsibility of the position as experienced by your predecessor.
2. You assume the full authority of the position but have somewhat reduced responsibility because of your newness to the job.
3. You have equal responsibility and authority but at a lesser level than your predecessor, leaving you room to "grow" in the position.
4. You assume the full responsibility of the position but can exercise less authority than your predecessor (again, temporarily, because you are "new").

Instructions:

Designate the set of "conditions" under which you would consider taking the job, and explain why. In doing so, consider the advantages and disadvantages of each set of "conditions."

CASE 98

WHY SHOULD I?

Primary Topic—*Employee Problems and Problem Employees*

Additional Topics—*Communication; Criticism and Discipline; Delegation*

You are a unit manager in a hospital's clinical laboratory, and you have 22 direct-reporting employees.

You believe that you have comfortable working relationships with all of your employees except one. The single employee in question, a laboratory technologist, continually gives you a hard time regarding assignments. Whenever you give this person a task that she considers not part of her daily routine and is not specifically designated in her job description, her response is, "Why should I? That's not part of my job."

In once recent, frustrating exchange you found yourself responding angrily, "Because I said so, that's why!" This response not only failed to get results, it also generated increased hostility.

Question:

How are you going to deal with this employee?

Case 99

The Drop-in Visitor

Primary Topic—*Time Management and Personal Effectiveness*
Additional Topics—*Communication*

As the door closed behind her departing visitor, central supply supervisor Janet Mills glumly reflected that she had just lost an hour that she could ill afford to lose. She would either have to forgo the schedule she was working on or be later for an upcoming meeting.

The hour had been lost because of a visit from a pleasant but marginally aggressive sales representative trying to acquaint her with "the greatest little thing ever to come along." As was her practice, Janet consented to see the visitor, although she resented the intrusion.

This incident, occurring on a Friday, made Janet realize that she had lost time to four such drop-in visits this week alone. She did not like the idea of simply saying no or otherwise trying to avoid people who wanted to see her, but she was becoming more aware that her work was beginning to suffer because of such demands on her time.

Instruction:

Develop some guidelines that might help Janet and other supervisors deal with the problem of drop-in visitors.

Case 100

Promotion

Primary Topic—*Leadership*

Additional Topics—*Change Management; Communication; Motivation*

You have been employed in the hospital's business office for 12 years. Starting in a clerical capacity, you have worked your way up through several jobs in the department. You consider yourself friends with all 14 other business office employees, and at least two of them you number among your closest friends.

Recently you were appointed business office manager. You willingly accepted the position. You believe that although one or two persons in the department may feel some slight resentment over your appointment, they are, for the most part, supportive. However, you realize that as a supervisor it may sometimes be necessary for you to do things that are inconsistent with your feelings for this group of people, these people with whom you have worked for so long.

Questions:

1. Should you find it necessary to "pull away" to any extent from those people with whom you have worked for so long?
2. How do believe you should go about reestablishing a long-term relationship with your former coworkers?

PART III

RESPONSES

RESPONSE 1

MORE HELP NEEDED—NOW!

One possible solution is for the department manager to simply concede to the request and immediately authorize an additional transcriptionist. On the plus side, a greater amount of work could then be accomplished. However, it is equally possible that the manager, in conceding, would be demonstrating to all employees that he or she is likely to give in to threats.

Another solution would be to ignore the transaction supervisor's threats and allow her to step down from supervision or resign if she should so choose. However, it is possible that by calling her bluff the manager could cause the loss of an otherwise good employee.

A third possible solution would be to require that only documented requests for increases in personnel, complete with justification, can be considered. The supervisor should thus be encouraged to fully document her request. This routine might encourage the supervisor to consider all ramifications of her request. However, it could also possibly discourage a busy employee who may not have time for supervisory duties from generating a proper request.

The department manager appears to be in a twofold trap: The department apparently has employees operating with inappropriate job descriptions and titles; and persons with the title of supervisor have apparently not been given appropriate training in supervision. It is this lack of supervisory training that could well be the main genesis of the existing problem.

Also, there appear to be communication problems; the department manager has ignored the warning signs of frustration up to the point at which the supervisor is desperate for action and will risk her job to get help.

The most serious trap is presented by a threat, seemingly an ultimatum, from an employee. The employee is saying to the manager, "Do it my way or I quit." The employee's drastic step has made the manager fully aware of a problem that needs to be acted upon, but has also put the manager in a position in which immediate action, no matter how well intended, can be interpreted as capitulation to employee pressure.

The list of possible approaches could be much longer. However, any solution attempted should recognize and attempt to correct the communications problems, emphasize the correct way to go about requesting relief, and ensure that investigation and analysis come before action.

Response 2

Up from the Ranks

As the manager of a group of former peers, Julie will have the advantage of already knowing many of the strengths and weaknesses of the people reporting to her. She should also know, based on past behavior, which employees are likely to have attendance or disciplinary problems. As an 8-year member of the unit, she may be privy to personal information or have knowledge of idiosyncrasies that could enable her to select and apply effective motivational techniques. In short, she knows the people.

The disadvantages may be troublesome for Julie. The new supervisor may have difficulty being taken seriously by her former peer group; these people have responded to Julie in a particular way for 8 years, and it may be difficult to change their response patterns. There could also be resentment from others in the group who thought they were more qualified, or that perhaps another specific person should have been promoted instead of Julie. There may even be some who simply resent another's good fortune. Julie may also be uncomfortable giving orders to her friends or pointing out errors to them. Disciplinary matters may also present problems for Julie.

Julie must be prepared to deal with the likelihood that she will no longer be thought of as one of the gang. It is a rare instance in which one who has been promoted can remain a member of group in the same good standing as previously enjoyed. The immediate effects may be mostly negative, and unless Julie's direct superior prepares her for them, she may be in for some difficult times. Her membership in the carpool and the "lunch bunch" may be among the first things to change.

There is often an "us-and-them" mind-set in the working world, suggesting that if you are one of "them," you cannot be one of "us." If Julie realizes this and accepts the fact that she cannot be all things to all people, she should have every chance for success.

RESPONSE 3

THE SILENT GROUP

One way to approach the problem presented by the quiet group begins with trying again at the next regularly scheduled staff meeting. This time, however, do not leave it entirely up to your employees to speak up and volunteer their complaints. Rather, be prepared to prime them with some information that might encourage them to open up about whatever is bothering them.

To encourage your employees to speak up, you be the first to speak. Because you have met with them individually and heard their complaints to the extent of identifying common themes, you have the ideal basis on which to begin. Share with the group these common themes, being careful, of course, to avoid saying anything that is sufficiently specific to be attributed to a single individual. The key is common; tell your group that this information you are sharing came to you in various forms from several of them so there is every reason to address these issues as a group.

At all times, tread lightly and proceed carefully. You are new to the organization, so chances are, you know very little of the history of the organization, and you have not had sufficient time to become acclimated to the environment and corporate culture. It is conceivable that the employees are silent in the group setting because they have been criticized or penalized or have otherwise experienced negative consequences for speaking up in the past. The task you face in earning their trust will be considerable even if the problem lay only with your predecessor; it will be all the more difficult if the problem resided in higher management because chances are, the perceived reasons for distrust of the hierarchy are still in place.

The possibility of one or more employees "carrying tales to administration" presents some interesting concerns. Having been there longer than you, some of these employees may have relationships with higher management that you do not yet enjoy, so you should proceed cautiously. Higher management should of course avoid subverting the chain of command by acting upon any information that comes to them from your subordinates. The very least you can do under the circumstances is to, first, make your group aware that there are concerns about some of them possibly carrying their gripes direct to higher management, and second, for you to do your job as you should, you need to hear their concerns—individually and confidentially, if necessary—directly and not secondhand or through your manager.

Response 4

The Repeat Offender

"You can't make mistakes like this one" could very well be a valid statement, depending, of course, on the nature of the mistake. An error that can result in direct patient harm, or, in the case of the overlooked stat order, can increase the patient's risk of a serious occurrence of some kind, can be considered a potentially serious error. Depending on the requirements of any particular state government, an error like the one Arnold admits to could conceivably cause a state-reportable incident to which the organization will have to respond.

What is wrong with Arnold's description of a warning as a form of punishment is that a warning, properly administered, is an attempt at correction, not a form of punishment. Arnold, however, appears to regard a warning as only another "gotcha!" one more strike that ensures your position "on the list" and one step closer to the door. He has apparently never learned, or perhaps has chosen to ignore, the true purpose of disciplinary action. In all but extreme circumstances that call for immediate termination with no second chances, the essential purpose of disciplinary action is correction of behavior. That is precisely why there is a hierarchy of actions that are progressive in severity—for instance, counseling, oral warning, written warning, suspension without pay, and ultimately termination—to provide plenty of opportunity for correction.

There could be a valid point in what Arnold says about the age of a warning. We do not know how long Arnold has gone between occurrences; however, you will often find in place a personnel policy that declares a warning invalid providing there has been no recurrence of the same kind of behavior for a specified length of time.

The way to deal with Arnold is to be quite specific about the nature of the problem and write the warning to include the potential consequences of recurrence within a particular period of time. And the potential consequences need to be more specific than "you may find that more than a written warning is involved." In Arnold's case, it may be wise to indicate that another such error "may involve disciplinary action up to and including termination." Then if Arnold repeats a serious error within, say, a year, it might mean termination, but if he stays "clean" for longer than a year it may suffice to repeat the last step before termination. In any case, however, laboratory manager Elsie Clark needs to be working with Arnold concerning his attitude toward errors and his apparent lack of concern for quality.

Response 5

A Good Employee?

Housekeeping supervisor Ellie Richards should arrange a counseling interview with the employee. Ellie needs to try to learn firsthand Judy's reasons for her excessive absenteeism and for being absent for several days without calling in.

Ellie can break the ice by stating that she recognizes Judy has problems, but out of fairness to Judy's coworkers, they must attempt to correct the situation. Furthermore, Ellie can indicate that she was hesitant to address the attendance issue because of Judy's otherwise-positive work record.

If Judy is willing to explain her behavior, Ellie will have the opportunity to indicate her understanding and offer support and guidance.

The key questions are: Does Judy have her situation resolved? Or is further absenteeism anticipated? Either way, a timetable for review should be established, perhaps 15 to 30 days or so in the future, depending on Ellie's judgment.

Ellie should make it clear that this counseling session must be recorded, but that it is hoped that Judy will be able to return to her former good behavior. If Judy remains in her job, most likely she will eventually appreciate the action taken. If Judy is unable to get back on track, then further disciplinary action can proceed. The morale of other staff could be at stake if one employee is allowed to get away with behavior that others feel would be grounds for action against them.

Ellie's failure to take action thus far does not affect her ability to take action now. What is done is done, and continued lack of action will not correct the situation. Appropriate action is both explainable and defensible, and if no action is taken, the opportunity to salvage this worthwhile employee may be lost.

RESPONSE 6

THE CLINGING VINE

One of the first responsibilities of a new supervisor is to become fully acquainted with all employees, discuss their jobs with them and determine how they perceive their responsibilities, and communicate to them your expectations as their new supervisor. The discussion should be informal and nonthreatening but, nevertheless, quite specific so that future misunderstandings can be avoided.

As a result of such discussions, a new supervisor following an apparently authoritarian supervisor might anticipate some of the problems that May faces with Brenda. Some employees will welcome a more democratic working environment and will readily accept increased responsibility and freedom in decision making. However, others may lack the desired initiative because of insecurity that is either innate or was instilled by the previous supervisor.

How does one train to think and act independently an employee who has been accustomed to authoritarian supervision? Having clarified new expectations, the new supervisor should concede that complete change cannot be realized immediately. The employee must be allowed to gain confidence as increased responsibility is given and accepted. The supervisor should appreciate that, concerning most tasks, the employee already knows what to do and needs only confirmation and reassurance. Applying this belief, May can ask Brenda to provide her own answers to the questions she brings. As confirmation is provided for Brenda's responses, she should gradually learn that she is capable of handling some situations herself. As Brenda's self-confidence increases, independent action is encouraged, acknowledged, and rewarded until a level of satisfactory performance is achieved.

May will never have enough time to deal with her department's major problems until she can delegate with confidence. Elimination of Brenda's time-consuming dependency must be one of May's priorities if she is to succeed in her supervisory position.

Response 7

The Inherited Problem

Donna, the kitchen supervisor, has every chance of salvaging her problem employee, Sandra. Sandra is possibly a problem only because of improper orientation and training. It is unreasonable to expect an employee to perform at a particular level unless that level of performance is clearly defined in the minds of both the employee and the supervisor.

Correcting the problem must begin with thorough orientation to the department. Sandra should be fully advised of the chain of command, the various functions of the department, and the specific requirements of her particular job. It may also be helpful to include a listing of possible tasks to be done should Sandra have unexpected time available when her regular work is caught up.

Donna has an obligation to tell Sandra, as well as other employees, that practices are necessarily changing, that performance must be monitored, and below-standard performance will be pointed out so that it can be corrected. Donna must also make it a point to commend above standard performance whenever she observes it.

If properly handled, this situation may be a blessing in disguise for Donna. The results of her efforts may serve to firmly establish her in her new position as supervisor. The other employees may judge Donna's ability by her success or failure with Sandra. If Sandra indeed becomes a productive employee, other employees will be favorably impressed. Another result for all employees could be a lessening of the tension inevitably accompanying a change of boss, because the new boss has clarified her expectations and the consequences of nonperformance. The employees will know where they stand. Consistent application of her requirements and expectations will help to ensure Donna's success as a supervisor.

The solution includes the need to formally extend the employee's probationary period. The employee is to be essentially held harmless for her recent unsatisfactory performance because of a supervisor's omissions. A fresh start, with all ground rules out in the open at last, is in order.

RESPONSE 8

THE WELL-ENTRENCHED EMPLOYEE

Although Dave Farren may indeed have felt that "the biggest problem was Mary West's complete lack of an efficient approach to the job," he nevertheless owes it to his employee and to himself to recognize some other long-standing difficulties. If he is to stand a chance of "selling" Mary on the need for change, he should consider the following:

- Carefully studying all of the complaints about mail service, looking for correctable procedural problems
- Doing whatever he can to relieve the physical problems of the "cramped, out-of-the-way mail room," if not through securing a new area, then at least by updating the equipment and the sorting and storage facilities
- Taking steps to determine, through engineering studies or other means, the actual amount of time required for daily sorting and mailing and for daily rounds requiring Mary's involvement in documenting the workload of the mail room so that presently unsubstantiated claims of "too much work" can either be verified or refuted.

Dave will be most likely to win the employee's cooperation if he demonstrates that he cares about the functioning of the mail room, that he cares about Mary's work surroundings and is genuinely interested in getting the work accomplished efficiently with minimum strain on her. He needs to be patient and extend her the benefit of the doubt. Although it may appear that she has been allowed to work independently over the years, it is even more likely that she has simply been ignored.

After 20-plus years of making her own way and following her own apparently meandering path, Mary may not respond to even the best that Dave can offer. However, as the responsible manager, he nevertheless needs to try. If she is not responsive, that is, if she cannot be "sold," then he should implement whatever improvements he can develop without her help, provide her with specific job procedures, spell out his expectations of her, and hope for the best. He should not, however, resort to any disciplinary action until he has clearly given her every reasonable opportunity to improve.

Response 9

The Sensitive Employee

Theresa began this employee counseling session with a negative attitude because of her previous experiences with Barbara. Her approach immediately put Barbara on the defensive. Theresa could have opened the conversation with facts simply stated: "Barbara, on June 30, 2009 (using the date applicable) you received a warning about your absenteeism. Since that date you have taken 10 sick days. This is an excessive number of sick days. Do you have any explanation?"

Emotions cannot always be ignored; they must be dealt with often. However, at the same time, a manager must remain objective in dealing with the resentful and emotional employee. Barbara's outburst of tears might indicate an underlying problem at home that causes her absenteeism. Theresa might want to suggest that Barbara work part-time until she resolves her problems, or that perhaps she change shifts.

If Barbara offers no real reasons for her absenteeism, and it is evident that she is an unreliable employee, then further disciplinary steps can be taken. When a second warning regarding absenteeism is issued, specific corrective guidelines should be set in writing for the employee. At this time, Theresa should define what the organization considers "excessive absenteeism" in terms of number of days allowed in a specified period of time; this is ordinarily specified in personnel policy. The second warning should explicitly state that if improvement is not seen and probation limits are violated, disciplinary action will be taken. Depending on business office policies and the state labor laws, "disciplinary action" can mean suspension without pay, and after a third warning, termination. Barbara then should be placed on probation for at least 3 months with the assurance that her attendance will be closely monitored. At the end of the probationary period, another counseling session should take place with proper documentation of Barbara's adherence to or violation of the probation.

Response 10

The Enemy Camps

Helen should not discipline Sandy on the secondhand evidence provided by a member of the opposite "camp." There is really no clear way of carrying out such disciplinary action without compromising Jeanette. Disciplinary action undertaken on such a basis would destroy the confidence Helen may have established in the last 7 months and would probably solidify the counterproductive positions of the "camps."

An initial action suggested for Helen would be to change the locks in her office. She should make no accusations. Helen should hold a meeting with Sandy and others to seek help in designing and implementing a goal-setting system with the participation of all employees, perhaps in brainstorming sessions to set and prioritize goals and objectives. Sandy, being an informal leader, would be an excellent source of assistance to Helen in furthering her efforts. Helen might also consider having Sandy and an informal leader of "Camp A" cross-train to further integrate the department. Helen needs to outline the general goals, seek input on objectives from employees, and have Sandy and the "Camp A" informal leader put the plan into action, reporting to her often to ensure control. Helen should continue her regular meetings, including time during each to discuss progress toward the departmental objectives.

RESPONSE 11

THE TURNAROUND CHALLENGE

One should first recognize that there are two significant dimensions to this problem and that the overall difficulty may be described as two separate but related problems. The first of these problems is the one described in some detail in the case: the lax department. The second problem to emerge, but the one that may have to be solved first or at least put into a "hold" status, is that of the boss's expectations. By simply demanding to know how soon a problem that took years to evolve can be corrected, the boss is adding an element of pressure that may cause Fred to take shortcuts to find an answer, thereby ignoring some of the people problems that should be dealt with along the way.

Fred should attempt to obtain some clear, detailed expectations from his superior. If those expectations appear unrealistic—for example, the boss expects it to be fixed in 3 months, tops—then Fred is going to have to try to negotiate with his boss. In his negotiations, Fred should suggest objectives aimed at incremental progress and try to sell a long-range program of steady improvement that is far more realistic than an attempt to forcibly alter a situation that took years to develop. Fred and his boss both need to recognize that many of the department's employees came to regard their slow pace and lax environment as normal and that management is now trying to force them to do more than normal.

As part of his overall approach, Fred must make full use of the knowledge and capabilities of his assistant manager, treating this person as a true member of management and delegating responsibility to him accordingly.

The case suggests that Fred is at least partly on the right track. Some improvements have been made, and even though there were some setbacks, if he keeps trying, the net result may be long-term improvement. Neither he nor his boss can necessarily expect every month or every reporting period to show constant improvement.

Much of the challenge referred to in the title lies in the work Fred has to do with the department's employees and their attitudes. He has before him the significant task of building on the improvements made so far by attempting to motivate his workers through pride in their contributions.

Because the department in question is a laundry, there is one seemingly drastic option available that has been used to solve numerous laundries' problems: The hospital could consider going outside to a commercial laundry or to membership in a shared laundry. Productivity problems of the human kind sometimes have an impact in such a decision, but often, the decision to get the hospital out of the laundry business is based on economics. In an increasing number of cases, hospitals are finding it more economical to go outside for this service than to upgrade and modernize their laundries. Thus an analysis of the economic feasibility of retaining the laundry might well be part of the hospital's approach to the laundry problem.

RESPONSE 12

ONE PERSON'S WORD AGAINST ANOTHER'S

The second-shift supervisor should decline Mrs. Carter's request to cosign a written warning for Janet Mills. Further, Mrs. Carter should be advised against generating such a warning. Because there was room for confusion and misunderstanding, on this occasion the employee should be given the benefit of the doubt. Ms. Mills bears some responsibility for asking Mrs. Carter for permission to leave rather than asking the second shift supervisor, however, and it is reasonable to assume that Ms. Mills asked Mrs. Carter only because she was afraid of receiving a negative response from the other supervisor. A cynical view might suggest that this behavior is akin to that of a manipulative child playing one parent off against the other.

The two supervisors should consider meeting with Janet Mills so that both sides of the story can be aired for all concerned parties at the same time. It should then be made plain to Ms. Mills—and reinforced with all employees as a department policy—that permission to leave early (or otherwise alter scheduled work time) must be obtained from the supervisor who will be on duty at the time of the early departure. Furthermore Ms. Mills must be advised that the two supervisors necessarily work closely because of their common responsibilities and that any attempt to play one of them against the other will not succeed. It could in fact affect future performance evaluations and perhaps result in disciplinary action. Both supervisors should become well aware of the hazards existing when an employee reports to two different supervisors in the course of a single shift.

Any employee attempting to play one supervisor against another should be confronted by the involved supervisors and warned of the unacceptability of this practice. Communication between supervisors can be facilitated by brief shift report meetings each day. Also, a daily supervisors' log could be maintained to exchange information. Regular departmental meetings should be held, and at these meetings the work force should see a unified management team.

Response 13

The Grouchy Receptionist

Morris Craig is challenged to determine the cause of Jennifer's poor job performance. Trying to meet individual and departmental needs, having no rationale for the change in Jennifer's behavior, and trying to avoid a confrontation, he is relying on Jennifer to solve her own problems—or rather *hoping* that she will solve them. Unfortunately, she seems unable to solve them and unwilling to discuss them, and Morris's delaying tactics are only compounding the problem.

If the cause is determined, Morris can ascertain what he and the department can do to achieve a solution benefiting everyone. If the trouble is work related (for example, "burnout"), job satisfaction might be improved through promotion, new responsibilities, different hours, additional help, or unit transfer. If the cause is personal (for example, marital problems), a leave of absence or counseling might be appropriate.

Marie Stark's recommendation is an excellent first step, especially with an employee whose past behavior has been acceptable. Jennifer may avoid discussing specific concerns with her male boss but she might talk with a female colleague. This approach emphasizes commitment of the work group to its members and departmental goals, something that the department seems to lack at present.

Morris Craig could complete a performance appraisal for Jennifer. Open, honest dialogue is required. Jennifer knows her responsibilities and is probably aware of her behavior, her perceptions of the job, her role within the department, and adverse influences on her work, so her recommendations are critical in a mutually satisfactory resolution.

As a last resort, disciplinary action may be considered to prevent further disruption. Morris must clearly indicate to Jennifer why such action is required and must describe organizational policy, identify expected behaviors, delineate progressive steps of the action, structure evaluation mechanisms, and provide close supervision. The onus lies with Jennifer: regardless of the cause, she either changes her behavior and improves performance or ultimately is terminated.

RESPONSE 14

WHAT'S THE TRUTH?

This is an extremely difficult case to deal with in any consistent fashion because it does not provide a point of view from which to address the problem presented. One is asked to assess what happened from the perspectives of two participants, but without being firmly positioned in some relationship to the characters, it is possible to be led in any of several directions. One could automatically adopt the viewpoint of any of the three characters, or one could assume an omniscient viewpoint. Thus, four completely different viewpoints—and a number of potential paths toward resolution within each viewpoint—are possible. To further complicate matters, it is also relatively easy to unintentionally change points of view while thinking through the case.

The overall problem is twofold: some clear indications of weakness on the part of the immediate supervisor, Tom Davis; and what would seem to be continuing difficulties with employee Stan Thomas, who apparently "plays the gray areas" and comes across as troublesome while staying out of big trouble with his boss. Thomas seems to have a sense of the extent of Davis's weakness; with many other supervisors, his insubordinate behavior would have already gotten him into big trouble.

Considering where the situation has gone, one is left with little reasonable action that can be taken over the specific incident but much that can and should be done about future communication among the parties. Also, Harry Willis, Tom Davis's immediate superior, needs to make Davis appreciate some of supervision's basic responsibilities. Tom Davis seems to have made his problem Harry Willis's problem, as he was unable to resolve it himself. Also, Davis exhibited weakness in attempting to deal with this apparently troublesome employee; perhaps Davis has little control over his subordinates and feels intimidated by them.

Tom Davis fails to see the need to help Stan Thomas set priorities; it does not appear that the supervisor has done a great deal to ensure the employee's understanding of what must be done and when it must be done. The supervisor's position is further weakened by director of building services Harry Willis, who steps out of his role and into Tom's when he addresses Stan for insubordination.

All reasonable approaches to this case should ideally mention the need to work on communication, and should also suggest the supervisory education and higher-management guidance necessary to help Tom Davis better fulfill his responsibilities.

RESPONSE 15

IN A RUT

There are two basic problems underlying the situation described in the case. First and foremost, Sue has taken it upon herself to come up with all the ideas for the group; she has not involved any of her staff in planning. Second, she has been fairly quick to develop a negative attitude toward her staff and blame them for a lack of progress.

Director Andy Miller has his work cut out for him. He must counsel Sue concerning proper techniques of management, suggesting that she first invite her staff to participate in planning. She must be helped to realize that the employees are her most valuable asset, and that more than likely, those people can offer many good ideas based on their experience if only they are given the chance to be heard. It is of utmost importance to involve the affected people in the setting of both short- and long-range goals.

Sue must also be reminded that no manager is an island; no manager is always expected to come up with all the exciting new ideas. The manager has the job of coordinating, prioritizing, and developing others' ideas. Having access to the bigger picture, the manager can be the judge of where and how a given idea can fit into the overall scheme of things. One of the most pleasing experiences a manager can have is to witness the success—and thus the professional growth and development—of an employee for whom the manager has paved the way.

Also, Sue needs to do some work on her apparent negative attitude. She may need to be actively encouraged to look for the positive a bit more readily.

Response 16

The Up-and-Down Performer

There are some significant issues to consider before dealing with the questions posed in the case:

1. The employee's actions and the possible reasons for them. It is necessary to ask whether she has been thoroughly trained, understands the manager's expectations, and has sufficient time to do all that is assigned to her.
2. The lack of documentation. The manager failed to record all efforts at correction.
3. Failure to follow up. Since the manager did not discuss the employee's marginal performance at the end of the 30-day period, the employee had reason to assume that her performance was acceptable.

With the foregoing in mind, the questions may be addressed:

1. The employee could cause trouble because of the lack of documentation. Termination at the point described in the case could readily be construed as occurring without cause and could lead to a lawsuit or other legal action.
2. At this point the manager needs to go back and reassess the employee's training, capabilities, and assigned workload. Eventually satisfied that the problem is indeed employee performance, the supervisor may then begin the process over again with an oral warning or other appropriate reprimand, making sure to document all efforts and follow up regularly even if behavior seems to be improving over the short run.

Documentation is the key in this case. Whenever such an employee problem lands in court or the hands of an advocacy agency, the employer is required to demonstrate that the employee was given a reasonable opportunity to improve the substandard performance. It does not matter if you have talked repeatedly with a problem employee; as far as employment law is concerned, in most cases if it is not documented, it never happened.

RESPONSE 17

I'LL GET AROUND TO IT

The problem appears to involve poor supervisor–employee communication. Supervisor Mabel may feel that she has little control over housekeeper Ellie because she leaves Ellie alone to do her assigned work and intrudes into Ellie's world only when she has additional work for her. Ellie may well be resistant if she has come to associate communication from her supervisor with more work. Mabel should make a point to find time to communicate with Ellie in a positive way and not always about work. She needs to break Ellie's habit of associating the supervisor with additional work.

Instead of telling Ellie to do something based on information from a third party, Mabel could have said something like, "I hear that the ER entrance is muddy again. Would you please check it out and get back to me?" This type of communication invites dialogue between supervisor and employee. It also implies trust. Mabel should not have to tell Ellie to "take care of it." She need only direct Ellie to the problem area and trust that once Ellie sees that the floor is muddy again, she will clean it up and report back about what she has done. If this approach fails to work the first time, Mabel needs to work at it until she gains Ellie's cooperation.

Mabel might also consider looking into the state of Ellie's job description. If the job description states or can be modified to state that the incumbent is to periodically check certain specific areas (such as the ER entrance) and clean as necessary, this can be used to encourage Ellie to possibly become self-managed in maintaining the area.

Working with employees is a two-way street. Mabel must show an interest in Ellie and her concerns before she can expect Ellie to reciprocate. So long as Mabel simply issues directives, Ellie may continue to respond in borderline insubordinate fashion.

Response 18

The Alternate Day Off

There appears to be no policy violation in this situation. The issue revolves around Susan's action. Was she ill? Or did Susan use the policy to manipulate the nurse manager? If so, this is an ethical issue dealing with Susan's sense of responsibility, her respect for her coworkers, and her duty to the patients. However, claiming illness when one wants time off for other purposes is such a common occurrence that it is understandable that the manager might suspect manipulation.

As Susan's immediate superior, Mabel should review Susan's performance record to identify whether or not Susan has established a pattern of illness or absence. If so, she should then determine whether the pattern is related to holidays and alternate days off. In many organizations' policies, such patterned absenteeism can trigger the start of a progressive disciplinary process. Second, Mabel should schedule a conference with Susan to discuss Susan's behavior, offer Susan the opportunity to express her point of view, and for Mabel, as head nurse, reiterate the responsibilities of an employee. Third, Mabel should document this incident and the subsequent conference.

Regarding the "alternate-day-off policy," Mabel can do little or nothing. The policy is not the issue; it is a broadly stated general policy that serves its purpose. However, there may be no procedure to follow when an employee becomes ill on the job. Perhaps Mabel could suggest to the administration that such a procedure be considered.

About all Mabel could do regarding the policy itself is to suggest that it be clarified to specify the alternate day off as coming only after the holiday. Again, if Susan was not truly ill, the real issue would seem to be her sense of duty to the institution, her coworkers, and the patients. Appropriate change in Susan's attitude and in her sense of commitment to her responsibilities is the real challenge for Mabel.

Response 19

If You Want Things Done Well . . .

Having never put in writing his procedure for preparing his monthly report, laundry manager Miller was not in a good position to suddenly decide to delegate the task. His decision to have Curtis do the report should have been accompanied by a simple note to himself to orient Curtis to the procedure, followed by completion of that month's report himself. Then, unhurried, he should have committed the procedure to writing.

Miller presented the assignment to Curtis as though he was dumping an unpleasant chore that required little skill. Actually, his presentation of the task should have been positive, a recognition of Curtis's abilities and an expansion of his responsibilities. Based on his knowledge of Curtis's learning capability and work style, Miller should have presented the written procedure and copies of past reports and then should have either gone through the procedure with him or allowed him to go over it himself and later ask questions.

Given a previous month's raw data, Curtis should have been asked to do the report and then compare his results with the actual report. Curtis's critical error would have been either avoided because of the written procedure or corrected in a far more positive manner. A regular submission deadline should have been negotiated, allowing for necessary corrections to be made by Curtis after discussion.

Finally, and perhaps most importantly, the report form should have been amended to allow Curtis to sign his own work, with Miller's signature of approval if required. Task ownership and recognition are crucial in effective delegation.

RESPONSE 20

SIXTY MINUTES OR LESS

If forced to select one and only one of the three suggested uses for Judy's available hour, the expected textbook answer would be the second choice, sort everything according to priority and develop a work plan. This is the only certain way of bringing to the surface any true high-priority items that might be buried in the stack. If Judy already knows the relative importance of everything awaiting her attention, she can select one or two important items for immediate resolution as suggested in the third choice.

However, if Judy has no idea of what is there she needs to invest the hour in sorting her work and determining priorities so she can then be assured that she will begin working on the most important items first.

Some people who have discussed this case in time management workshops have suggested that the department secretary could be involved to a greater extent than implied by the short case description. A knowledgeable secretary can at least separate the items that might be of immediate importance from those that clearly can wait. It appears that Judy and Ann, manager and secretary, already enjoy open communication as evidenced by their exchange of feelings and opinions. As long as it was Ann who originally took the numerous phone messages, and as long as Ann is reasonably familiar with Judy's job duties, one approach to making the most of the available hour would be for Judy to ask Ann to brief her on each item or call and thus help arrange the work in priority order.

Since Judy has nothing on her calendar for the following day, that would be the best time to start actually working on the listed items. Also, if Ann considered any of the telephone calls to be urgent, perhaps Judy could have Ann relay brief messages to those particular callers or at least let them know that Judy would get back to them early the following day.

RESPONSE 21

IS IT INSUBORDINATION?

It is a manager's responsibility to balance organizational needs with employees' rights. Personnel policies exist to provide equity between the employee and the organization. In the instance described in the case, Mason does indeed exhibit insubordination to Hamilton during and after the staff meeting.

Hamilton restricted vacation time as a management strategy to ensure adequate worker availability. Recognizing the potential hardship the time restriction may have on his employees, Hamilton shows sensitivity by announcing his intentions a full 6 months before the actual restriction. Even though Hamilton has the right to schedule according to the organization's needs, he provides employees with rationale and time that helped foster their acceptance of the change.

If Mason had not used a group forum for his outburst, Hamilton would have had more room to negotiate a settlement. Now if Hamilton decides to allow an exception to his policy and gives Mason time off, he must address two issues: the responsibility for rewarding negative behavior, and the impact of his decision on the morale of the work group.

Supervisor Hamilton needs to assess whether Mason's belligerence was blatant insubordination or a subconscious strategy by Mason to garner peer support for time off; that is, "With his attitude, let him take off." Regardless of Mason's motivation, Hamilton needs to initiate dialogue and take appropriate corrective action to prevent future outbursts.

In joining an organization an individual in effect agrees to follow its rules. It is the manager's position to uphold the work of the organization; that is, the creation of a secure and successful work climate for the employees. Hamilton may have to exercise his management right to restrict Mason's vacation, a right based on work demand.

As long as Hamilton applies his ruling on vacations consistently throughout his staff, he has every right to insist that everyone—Mason included—schedule vacation as directed.

Pete Hamilton should also advise his manager and human resources of the necessity for the vacation restriction and the situation with Mason, because it is possible that Mason may take his complaint up the chain of command. We do not know to what extent Hamilton may have planned the vacation restriction, but if he has approached it responsibly, both his manager and human resources will have been consulted and agreed to the change.

RESPONSE 22

GET BACK TO YOU IN A MINUTE

This is a truly frustrating situation for a manager. The description of this one particular week illustrates a king-size problem by highlighting the frustrations involved in reporting to a manager who seems never to have time for subordinate supervisors.

Neither mounting an all-out campaign to get the boss in situations in which he has to talk to you, nor doing your own thing may be appropriate answers. You might best proceed by:

- Examining your relationship with the boss before this terrible week. Ask yourself to recall a time when the boss listened to you or paid attention to the needs of your department.
- Considering how you can replicate that situation to get his attention now.
- Trying to identify the boss's priorities.

All of the contacts made with the boss were either by catching him on the run or telephoning. He does not appear to respond well to either of these methods. Perhaps he places greatest importance on scheduled or emergency meetings, so making an appointment with his secretary to discuss concerns on a regular basis might be helpful. Right now, he seems to perceive your attempts to talk with him as interruptions or distractions.

We are given no indication that he pays attention to written communication, but in case he does, it could be helpful to try writing your concerns and asking for a reply. You may be surprised at the speed with which you get an answer; then again you get no response at all. This may cause you to be more flexible in your style.

You may be comfortable doing business as you run into people, but your boss's style is different. Being aware of that and making adjustments will improve your relationship with your boss.

There is one technique you might consider when something of importance is pending and you cannot get at the boss directly: Briefly write out the problem, clearly state what you believe should be done, and advise your manager that this is what you will do unless you hear from him with other instructions. This may at least cover you to some extent if something goes wrong.

RESPONSE 23

THE DELEGATED DIGGING

If Sharon is qualified for the project, the primary determinant of whether Kaye assigns the task to her should be her likely future involvement. If the task is to become a regular part of her job, it would make sense to actively involve her in doing this task from the first. However, if this is to be a one-time task, and if no one is more clearly qualified than anyone else, the job might as well be done by whomever can best set aside the time to perform it.

The foregoing possibility has the advantage of being easy for the supervisor. However, unless Sharon does know all of the codes and terminology, and unless she truly understands what is needed, she could be heading straight into a time-consuming failure. The second possibility has the advantage of thoroughness; with expected results clearly spelled out, a detailed procedure to follow, and a specific deadline to work toward, her chances of going astray are minimized. However, all of this takes time and effort on the part of the supervisor, and if it does turn out to be a one-time job it will have taken far longer to get the data via delegation than it would have taken Kaye to do the job himself.

The third possibility falls midway between the other two. It would likely lead to more accurate results than would the first, simply turning her loose, but it would not be nearly as time consuming as the complete delegation of the second. Also, this third approach would avoid the "overkill" of the second that would be experienced if the task did indeed turn out to be a one-time job.

Under the circumstances of the case, the most reasonable approach of those offered is the third—tell her what is wanted, recommend an approach, and turn her loose. However, to this we must add the necessity for John Kaye to stay closely in touch with the job as it progresses. Sharon should not have to call for help; the supervisor should anticipate most of her needs.

The ideal approach would be for Sharon and her supervisor to tackle this digging together. Although this data collection might become a regular part of someone's job, chances are, this will not come to pass in the exact form in which it is first encountered. The process of going through 18 months' worth of work orders could be a key part of determining exactly what is needed in the design of a preventive maintenance program.

RESPONSE 24

THE SECOND CHANCE

The situation described in this case exhibits some classic symptoms of distress caused by lack of planning and incomplete communication of objectives to the person responsible for the project. The communication of desired results, especially important in delegated projects, appears absent here. It is important to note that the assignment is a "special" work-order-analysis project and that it was "hastily assigned."

It has often been suggested that performance is generally predictable based on factors such as ability, personal motivation, and encouragement to produce. The problem in this case appears not necessarily to be with ability and motivation, but rather with encouragement—which includes proper direction and communication of the manager's expectations. It is certainly possible that the job enlargement involved in this project might be beyond Sharon's ability, but there is no evidence to suggest this may be so.

Sharon's interruptions should be viewed as calls for help as she tries to read her boss's mind, and a good manager should sense this. Too often, managers plan but then keep their plans largely or completely in their heads.

John Kaye's smartest move would be to utilize the first option: Review what Sharon has accomplished so far, show her where and how to adjust to meet the project's real objectives, and assist her in planning the remainder of the task.

Once the manager devotes the proper time to planning and conveying all appropriate information, most of the details should fall into place for the employee, and there will be fewer interruptions coming the manager's way. Doing so will also give Sharon a stronger sense of involvement, but allow John to retain ultimate control while he remains free to concentrate on other business.

RESPONSE 25

THE BUNGLED ASSIGNMENT

Delegation is a valuable tool that can maximize the performance and productivity of management personnel. Moreover, its proper practice is essential to a manager's long-term success. In substance, delegation requires the turning the authority for task performance to a subordinate who in turn is held responsible for the performance of the task.

That is probably what John Kaye *thought* he did when he asked his secretary, Sharon, to do a report for him and gave her the authority and responsibility for the report. Later he was considerably disappointed in the results. As do so many who fail at delegation, he did not delegate completely.

There is more to delegation than dropping an assignment on a subordinate's desk. Before delegating, the manager should confirm the skills, experience, and competence of the employee. If the subordinate is not familiar enough with the project content or context, more experience and training may be necessary.

The manager must also clarify expectations. He or she must explain what is acceptable in relation to quality, quantity, and time. The manager must also help the subordinate set priorities by guiding the arrangement of tasks for completion.

Once the task is assigned, the manager should become a coach. The manager becomes accessible via milestone or checkpoints, planned interactions scheduled throughout the duration of the project. If necessary the manager establishes calls for interim reports to monitor progress, coaches the subordinate, and assists with problems. If John Kaye had been more of a coach, Sharon's project might have been successful.

Delegation not only enhances management time and resources, it also provides an opportunity to encourage subordinates' potential and foster personal growth. Therefore, a dimension of humanity is evident in the concept of effective delegation. An extra bonus is the job satisfaction that accrues when subordinates make decisions and successfully meet new challenges.

RESPONSE 26

IT ISN'T IN THE JOB DESCRIPTION

One's initial reaction to the problems presented in the case might be to recommend revising that particular job description. However, it is not always possible to revise a job description simply because a manager decides to do so; in a union shop, for example, it usually requires a significant change in equipment or procedures to reopen and revise a job description.

Absent the restrictions of a union contract, supervisor Morton should certainly consider strengthening employee Thompson's job description in various ways. It should be relatively easy to add a line to the job description calling for reporting of other apparent maintenance needs encountered while working on a primary assignment. It may also be helpful for Morton to obtain Thompson's active input in the process of revising the job description.

The improved job description should also include standing instructions for the employee to follow when an assigned repair job is completed and another is not yet designated. For example, Thompson's job description could clearly indicate that he is to pursue certain known preventive maintenance activities during time open between assigned repairs.

As Thompson's job description may exhibit weaknesses, so too might there be weaknesses in the maintenance department's scheduling practices. Conscientious scheduling would not ordinarily afford the individual employee the opportunity for "prolonged breaks." Also, a work-order control system that captures elapsed time, material costs, and other information for each repair job would quickly reveal whether Thompson did in fact "usually take longer" than needed.

The matters of the job description and work scheduling and such add up to a need for Morton to provide closer supervision of Jeff Thompson. However, it was noted that much of the problem seems to lie in Jeff's attitude. Why should he have such a negative view of his responsibilities?

One can only second-guess at the possible reasons behind Jeff's attitude. However, the supervisor has one clearly positive factor to build upon—Jeff is confident in his ability to do the job. Jeff does good work and he knows it.

Supervisor Morton needs to:

- Strengthen the job description and improve his scheduling and control procedures
- Provide Thompson with closer supervision
- Stress the positive results of Thompson's efforts
- Truly get to know this employee on a one-to-one basis, making it plain that he, Morton, is interested in each employee as a whole person as well as a producer

The rest is up to Thompson. At worst, his productivity will improve, even if no attitude improvement occurs, because of closer supervision. At best, his attitude will improve over time as he is drawn into a relationship in which he and his skills are respected.

Response 27

Delayed Change of Command

The employees' view of Smitty would probably undergo considerable change over the 6 months during which there was no official manager. At the start, the employees assumed that Smitty would be appointed manager. However, because that assumption was not borne out within a reasonable period of time, some of the employees would have begun to feel that perhaps Smitty was not as strong or capable a candidate as they thought him to be, and that perhaps higher management felt there were better choices available. In short, as the weeks become months, the employees would have likely become less and less convinced that Smitty was the proper person to lead the department.

The finance director's viewpoint is extremely difficult to assess without more information. It would be especially helpful to know whether the finance director had genuine doubts about Smitty's capabilities; thought Smitty was probably "okay" but wished to test the market to make sure; felt he needed to test Smitty for a while to assure himself that Smitty was a reasonable choice; or simply procrastinated, extending to months a process that should have been accomplished in far less time.

As his position would likely deteriorate in the eyes of the department and other elements of the organization, so too would Smitty's position be likely to deteriorate in his own eyes. Assuming that he, too, believed he would move up and become manager, Smitty would probably experience growing impatience and increasing self-doubt as the weeks dragged on without a decision. Learning that candidates were being interviewed for information services manager could have been a considerable blow to whatever self-confidence he possessed. He could feel increasingly insecure in his employment with the hospital and could begin to have doubts about his future with this particular employer. Smitty could come to wonder whether this organization—and especially the finance director—held him in any appreciable regard. Certainly, Smitty could come to feel exploited in being left to handle the important elements of two positions for so long.

Finally, appointing Smitty to the position of manager after 6 months of unexplained delay does not correct the situation. Damage has been done; doubts, especially those of Smitty and the department's employees, will linger. One can almost hear some of the comments: "They finally decided to take a chance with Smitty;" "They gave it to him because they couldn't find anyone better at their price;" "I wonder what they thought was wrong with Smitty?"

If Smitty is truly good at what he does, he will succeed as manager. However, because of the manner in which his transition was handled, he will have an uphill struggle. He will have to work doubly hard to prove himself and to overcome lingering negative impressions.

Response 28

The Tight Deadline

Deadlines such as the one nurse manager Susan Wagner is facing present basic challenges in prioritizing and properly managing the time commitment to a project while allowing for the contingencies and crises that may arise in any dynamic organization. Time is ultimately the scarcest resource, and unless it is properly managed little else can be accomplished adequately. In addition to being necessary for organizational control and growth, deadlines are important means of assessing time management skills.

The problems of the assignment of tasks and the management of time are important topics in decision theory. It is always possible that overuse of deadlines breeds conscious or unconscious hostility, but nevertheless the use of deadlines is considered essential to effective management.

In making the decision about when to complete the final formulation of the overtime report or any similar task, economy of effort is an important practical consideration. You want to "get the biggest bang for the buck" relative to the major constraint, which in this case is time. Options include immediate and delayed processing. The psychological advantage of beginning the project could be enhanced through delegation of sorting and organizing processes to the secretary, Betsy Adams, who is already familiar with the process and forms. For Susan Wagner, the first option seems impractical and uneconomical, and the third option does not allow for interruptions or unplanned factors. In addition, the third option would demonstrate poor managerial skills and procrastination, thereby setting a bad example.

All factors considered, the second option seems to offer the best solution. This alternative would allow one full day to complete the assignment with an additional day (the due date) for emergencies or revisions. In addition, this option would allow the project to be completed with little interruption, which would help to ensure consistency and would enhance the sense of having finished the project.

Response 29

Ten Minutes to Spare?

Each of the three options possesses advantages and disadvantages, with the disadvantages running the gamut from merely possible to highly likely.

Option 1, putting off Mr. Wade and promising to call him in the morning, would allow you to avoid an unneeded intrusion at a busy time. However, this solution might be annoying to Wade (although he had no appointment), and it might strike him as unnecessarily delaying resolution of a genuinely small matter.

Option 2, asking for a memo so you can consider the matter later, would also allow you to delay the intrusion. On the other hand, this choice adds work for the other party and again could be an unwarranted delay in resolving a small problem.

Option 3, seeing Mr. Wade and trying to limit the discussion to 5 or 10 minutes, could potentially resolve the open issue then and there without making it part of another day's workload. However, there is a risk that the matter will prove too complicated to be resolved in 10 minutes or that the finance director, Wade, will simply tie you up for as long as he sees fit once he has his foot in the door.

Knowing no more than the case tells you about you and Mr. Wade, the cleanest, most sensible choice is the third option, meeting with Wade then and there. However, it is essential that you control the meeting. You need to make it clear that you have 10 minutes—tops—for this business, and you may need to reinforce this by getting ready to leave as your deadline approaches or politely ending the discussion when you've run out of time. As far as using your time is concerned, it may be efficient for you to deal with the problem at once and not have to face it later. However, if you allow Wade to exceed your time limit and cause you to be late for your commitment, then you have allowed someone else to dictate the use of your time.

If the "minor question" was important enough for Wade to bring to you, it probably deserves your attention. If you can resolve it within a few minutes, it will be finished; if not, then it has to become part of the next day's workload, as would be the case with any other option.

RESPONSE 30

ASSIGNMENT AND REASSIGNMENT

This is the familiar problem involving conflict over a person's ability to serve two masters with any amount of satisfaction. In this scenario, the director of nursing, Ms. Carey, violated two management principles, one more serious than the other, to achieve what she considered an effective and efficient delegation of authority and responsibility. Ms. Carey violated this in bypassing the formal chain of command and delegating assignments to an employee who was not her immediate subordinate. This type of end run around the assistant director, Ann Baker, seems unwarranted in this circumstance. At best, the action could go unnoticed; at worst, it could undermine the confidence of Carol Ames in assistant director Baker or lead to further confusion and distrust.

The second and more common violation was of the unity of command principle. This violation places the inservice director, Carol Ames, in conflict with the desires of her immediate superiors. In this position, Ms. Ames is forced to deal with potentially bruised egos of both her immediate supervisor and the director of nursing.

The delegation of functional authority to Ms. Ames for control of the nursing audit is within the realm of Ms. Carey's control. It is not a radical violation of the unity of command principle, because the higher-level orders would also apply to all subordinates of the director of nursing, including Ann Baker. Carol Ames should immediately inform Ms. Baker of the change in plans, and Carol should convey her willingness to assist with completion of the inventory and cost report immediately after fulfilling her obligations with the nursing audit.

A successful resolution to this problem will involve tact and communication as well as cooperation between the parties. The new assignments, particularly the inventory, may be sufficiently nonurgent that their delay or reassignment should cause no problems. In any event, Ms. Carey was wrong in bypassing Ann Baker to delegate this assignment. She might best try to clarify the situation in a short meeting between the parties. Carol would do well to request such a meeting.

RESPONSE 31

THE UNREQUESTED INFORMATION

As suggested by the initial option, you should indeed thank Nellie for her concern. However, asking her to report anything else she might hear is to be avoided; doing so would in effect designate Nellie as your "spy" in the group. Having a personal informant among the staff is bound to be destructive of working relationships.

The second alternative is probably the best remedy for the immediate situation. Her concern for the good of the department, if genuine, is appropriate, as is acknowledging that concern. You should certainly direct Nellie to bring you no further stories. In bringing you disturbing new and then urging your silence, Nellie has done little more for you than give you cause to worry about what may be going on in the department. In any event, there is nothing you could legitimately do anyway; it is always inappropriate to take action based on secondhand information (hearsay).

Concerning the third option, again, thank her and send her on her way. Considering what you have heard you probably cannot avoid "keeping an eye" on Marge, whether you mean to or not.

This situation will have created in you a heightened awareness of problems within your department, which should in turn lead you to step up efforts at communication within the group. Consider: probing for problems at staff meetings, holding "gripe sessions" for any who will participate, holding one-on-one meetings with your employees, offering staff a means of submitting complaints and suggestions anonymously, and whatever else might bring problems into the open.

RESPONSE 32

DID HE HAVE IT COMING?

We probably cannot answer the title question with absolute certainty, but it is reasonable to assume that Dan Smither had something coming because of his error. He did have coming some form of criticism; however, he did not deserve to be on the receiving end of Peter Jackson's emotional tirade.

Jackson's approach was anything but constructive. In a brief exchange, Smither heard that his behavior was "idiotic," that he "fiddled around" and "stalled," and that he made a "major blunder." Jackson also implied that Smither does not know his job. One need hardly wonder why Smither walked out of the office in anger.

The responsibility for this exchange rests with Jackson. It is unfortunate, however, that Smither reacted to anger with anger—understandable, but nevertheless unfortunate—because Jackson is the organizational superior. If Jackson is sufficiently crude as a manager to criticize an employee in this fashion, it is also likely that he will allow an employee's angry response to further prejudice his opinion of the employee.

One reasonable approach would start with Jackson requesting Smither's analysis of the error—what happened, why it appears to have happened, and so forth. After they have gathered as much factual information as they can, they should discuss the problem in detail to determine whether there was indeed an error on Smither's part and what steps should be taken to prevent its recurrence.

Jackson needs to be aware that criticism, to be effective, must be constructive; that is, it must embody guidance for correcting the offending behavior. And both parties—but especially Jackson, the boss—need to be aware that as anger increases in an interpersonal exchange, the potential for effective communication is diminished.

RESPONSE 33

IT'S HIS JOB, NOT MINE

Delegation is fundamental to effective management. Delegation allows employees to feel valued and that they are part of a team and gives them the opportunity to learn new skills. The department benefits overall, and managers can focus on those tasks that require special attention.

This case, however, involved assignment, not delegation, and the employee felt burdened rather than flattered by the increased responsibility. Clues should have been noted in the initial lack of enthusiasm, as well as the later procrastination and lack of enthusiasm. Miller has also noted that narrow job descriptions can be a cause of the "It's not my job" malaise. He feels that a job description should focus on the department and patient care, rather than the individual. Participative management will also be of value both in the short and long run here. If managers influence, rather than assign, employees will be committed to invest time and energy in production and performance.

To influence this employee, various "perks" might be assigned to the job. If this employee is interested in moving into management, letting the employee present the report to administration might be of personal value. Perhaps if the cover sheet for the report clearly lists the employee as author, this individual will be motivated by recognition. Giving the employee an afternoon at home to prepare the report is another strategy.

This employee may simply be unmotivated; however, if the manager employs the principles of participative management, employees will surface with an interest in furthering the goals of the department and themselves, not simply themselves.

Response 34

I Used to Run This Unit

Only time will tell whether Ms. Adams will come around and overcome her resentment of what she perceives as a demotion. If she is truly professional in outlook, she will likely come around eventually. Ms. Adams has knowledge and experience that remain valuable to the unit and the hospital, and Ms. Williams should acknowledge this and make every effort to utilize Ms. Adams's capabilities. The demotion could actually be leaving Ms. Adams in a position second only to Ms. Williams in the unit. Ms. Adams is ideally situated to undertake special assignments, serve as mentor or instructor for new LPNs and aides, and perhaps cover for Ms. Williams during occasional absences.

If time and Ms. Williams's efforts fail to soften or eliminate Ms. Adams's resentment and resistance, there may always be the possibility of transfer to some other nursing position in the organization. Or perhaps Ms. Williams will resign herself to Ms. Adam's resentful attitude as long as Ms. Adams maintains acceptable performance in her staff position. Also, Ms. Adams needs to understand that accrediting agencies and the appropriate state health department require the presence of a registered nurse in that capacity.

Two years is an overlong time to leave a person like Ms. Adams working in an "acting" capacity. In spite of a supposedly lean supply of RNs in the area, it is difficult to believe that active recruiting would have failed to find a nurse manager for all that time. The "acting" nature of the assignment should have been made extremely clear at the outset, and it should have been regularly reinforced. If in spite of all honest effort to recruit for the position it remains unfilled for a period of months, it might be wise to rotate the "acting" position through two or three individuals.

RESPONSE 35

YOUR WORD AGAINST THE BOSS'S

First, you can say that this problem should never have occurred, that the boss's behavior is inappropriate. True, the boss's behavior is highly inappropriate, but inappropriate behavior occurs at all levels, and when it is a middle or upper manager who has made the mistake, the manager's subordinates are frequently directly affected.

What you are able to do under the circumstances described in the case depends largely on your relationship with the boss. However, considering what has already taken place in the meeting, it should be reasonably clear that you should not repeat your objections then and there for two reasons: you have already been told not to pursue the topic, and speaking up again would present a direct challenge to your boss in the presence of several other people.

Your only sensible course of action lies in getting the boss alone as soon as possible after the meeting. If you are again rebuffed—even in private, even in spite of documentary evidence—then the boss is essentially out on a limb on his or her own, and you can only do the best you can do in setting the record straight informally overall and formally within your own sphere of authority.

Most importantly, resist all temptation to simply let the boss blunder along his or her own way and look foolish or even get into trouble when the record is set straight. If you are indeed correct (and it would be wise to make absolutely certain you are correct before proceeding), you will eventually be vindicated by the facts, and others who were present will know you were correct. Although you may feel the sting of what was, in effect, a public "put-down" from the boss, proving that you were right by allowing the boss to proceed in error is not to the benefit of the organization. Rather, the organization benefits most when you take steps to resolve such disagreements as quietly as possible.

Response 36

You're the Boss

Many executives consider themselves to be strong people-oriented managers who lack little or nothing when it comes to motivating staff, yet they fail to realize that being good with people also means being able to listen well. One of Ross's problems in this case may be the inability to listen well; he conveys double messages to Winslow by advising him to own a project that Winslow apparently has no control over.

If Ross is truly interested in Winslow as a person with needs to grow and take responsibility, then he must avoid the tendency to coerce him into following his way of proceeding. Instead Ross must try to convert Winslow to the new pattern of proceeding or else yield to a possibly better, even "traditional," pattern as Winslow suggests.

Human relations is one skill that can never be emphasized enough. Employees often know the solution to a problem an organization faces, but they are rarely consulted. In this circumstance, Ross depends on the technical expertise of Winslow as a healthcare finance accountant, yet Ross refuses to assist in Winslow's professional growth or use Winslow's resource capabilities effectively.

Rather than allowing Winslow to simply forge ahead on his own doing something that he obviously does not believe in, Ross should consider pulling a small group together, including Winslow, and backing up a step or two to what seems to be a charge from higher management, and exploring ways of getting the job done. In other words, if possible, go back to the stated intent of the change and involve the people who will be affected in developing the best way to get it done.

Response 37

The New Broom

Resistance to change is likely to be found in most groups of people. This is especially true in a group that has been self-reliant with little or no management for a long period of time. To be effective, change must be desired and striven for by a significant number of people in the group.

In case it is clear that a number of important changes are being attempted in a short period of time; Shari Daniels seems to perceive these problems as a personal challenge to be mastered. She must first remember that these problems took years to develop; they cannot be resolved in the space of a year. Second, she must alter the focus of the problem to place the emphasis on the group, not herself, as the key to the solution.

This group appears to have had little or no management support. Staff members have become content with managing themselves, secure in the belief that they are doing just fine because of the lack of interference from management. Shari's steamroller tactics can easily be perceived as insulting. After years of coasting, employees are now in effect being told that they have done little or nothing right. This is bound to cause resentment, which in turn leads to resistance.

Shari has engaged in a battle of wills in which there can be no winner. She would be much more effective in achieving her goals by putting her steamroller in reverse. Utilizing the weekly staff meeting as a planning session and guiding the staff toward deciding on the changes she desires would be much wiser and cause less resentment. To cite an old cliché, you can catch more flies with honey than with vinegar. Rather than forcing the staff to change to please Shari and the Joint Commission on Accreditation of Healthcare Organizations, she should strive to make the changes a matter of pride and personal choice.

Management and staff must work together to develop mutual trust and respect. When Shari begins to respect the opinions and experience of her staff, she will gain her strongest asset—a cooperative team.

Response 38

No Better Than I Used to Be?

There are a variety of possible reasons for the difference in scores between the present evaluation and previous evaluations. These include a possible difference in performance between units (for example, good pediatric nurse may not be a good cardiac nurse), a difference in performance caused by not getting along with other employees, and most likely, poor inter-rater reliability. It is not necessarily true that Sue Collins' previous evaluations were correct simply because they were higher.

Both Carrie and the institution can be faulted for not adopting a more holistic performance appraisal strategy. Carrie should have:

- Talked to Helen before the performance appraisal to determine her expectations
- Reviewed Helen's old evaluations
- Provided Helen with a means of self-evaluation before the meeting
- Anticipated and prepared for problems related to first meeting or the employee's reaction to the self-appraisal
- Provided a performance appraisal that consisted of planning for the future, not simply telling the employee that it is "close to average" or "good"

At this point, Carrie can only apply a bandage to the current appraisal. If she knows specific reasons for the lower performance, she can tell Helen what they are. If not, she is left with relatively empty statements regarding possible and unavoidable differences between raters or possible below-expected performance resulting from the newness of the unit. She should use this experience in a positive way to guide her in future performance appraisals and to recommend that the institution evaluate its own approach to performance appraisal.

RESPONSE 39

THE INCOMPATIBLE EMPLOYEES

This case presents an undesirable situation that could plague a supervisor for a long time. At its heart it is perhaps what we commonly refer to as a "personality conflict," but do not openly label it such. Calling it a personality conflict is actually rendering personality judgments of the employees, something well out of bounds for a supervisor.

As long as these people must work together and with others in the department in the normal course of business, you need to do something to try to smooth over their difficulties. In the long run, you cannot let the squabbling of two employees adversely affect the work of a dozen others.

Talk to them again, both individually and together. Look for ways of accommodating any differences in how they are supposed to relate. Try to establish some very clear ground rules as to who does what, when, why, and how, so as to minimize areas of perceived conflict. However, put them on notice that their conduct is unacceptable and changes must be made. Perhaps even considering this step as a brand-new start for both, counsel them about the need to get along on the job, and tell them the possible risks if they fail to do so.

If their technical work performance is satisfactory, let them know this. Let them know that it is generally their conduct that is in question, not their performance, but that conduct can be fully as important as performance as far as maintaining an effectively functioning unit is concerned.

As long as they both seem equally troublesome, go out of your way to ensure that you treat them absolutely equally, that neither is gaining favor with you, and that they are in fact hurting themselves.

If you have the opportunity to do so, you might try assigning them to a fairly involved joint project on which they would have to work closely with a third party (either you or a strong senior staff member). Sometimes prolonged contact will help some persons find greater tolerance for each other. However, you have to be ready to instantly pull the plug on this arrangement if necessary, because prolonged contact may actually intensify their hard feelings for each other.

Sound them out separately as to whether either would consider transferring to another department. If the interest is there in either, perhaps you can help. However, do not actively encourage one or the other to transfer; in doing so you would automatically be taking sides.

If talking appears to get you nowhere with the incompatible employees, start the formal disciplinary process. A written warning for disruptive behavior (listed under misconduct in many disciplinary processes) might well deliver the message that you were not able to plant effectively up to this point.

Response 40

Where Does the Time Go?

Kay Thatcher had no real plan for Monday. She had only an outline without an agenda for resisting others' demands or requests and no defense against her own human nature. She surely felt that she was organized; she was perhaps even *overorganized* to the extent of scheduling out all of her time, leaving little or no room for the unanticipated.

One of the most difficult parts of managing our time is recognizing that we are the biggest culprits. It is much easier to blame drop-in visitors, meetings, inadequate equipment, paperwork, phone interruptions, or crises. The real cause lies in the way we allow these interruptions, the ways in which we allow our time to be wasted. To make real progress in managing our time, we need to be prepared to change habits and be willing to make changes in the way we work each day.

A written daily plan is the most important tool in time management. Without it, our days may well become a mix of minor crises, interruptions, and frustrations; but again, that daily plan should leave time for contingencies.

Time management means performing the most important task first, and giving that task our full attention. If nothing else in our daily plan gets done, we can still feel good in having completed our top priority.

Making time work for us is a challenging task. Whether through reading, participation in seminars, workshops, or in-house training programs on time management, Kay can apply techniques such as improved planning, tactful telephone screening, effective delegation, task prioritization, and self-discipline to make a real change in her daily work life. These changes may reduce stress, improve productivity levels, hasten progress toward completing tasks and accomplishing goals, and result in a healthier balance between personal and professional lives.

Response 41

Sylvia's Choice

Unintended personal bias may have intruded in Sylvia's selection of Jane over Hilda largely because Sylvia simply liked Jane better than she liked Hilda.

Events subsequent to Jane's promotion seem to suggest that Jane may well have been the right choice. If both Jane and Hilda were equally qualified, either could probably have done the job satisfactorily; but Hilda's reaction to losing out on the position was rather unprofessional, suggesting that even if she someday entered management she may perhaps react unprofessionally on occasions when things did not go her way.

Sylvia is now faced with an employee who exhibits poor work performance and whose behavior at times border on insubordination. Even with the best of management and counseling skills, it may be too late to reverse Hilda Ross's resentment. In addition, if others in the unit also perceive Jane's selection as a result of personal bias, the morale of the entire unit could be affected.

RESPONSE 42

ULTIMATUM

Has Arthur Morris finally gotten the attention of the administrative director of radiology? We certainly hope so. It is unfortunate, however, that Morris threatened to resign to awaken the director to the presence of a problem.

What the director should do about Morris's ultimatum is exactly what the director should have done some time earlier; that is, start talking with special procedures personnel and others about workload and scheduling. That two of the three technicians have complained of inadequate staffing, and that the most senior technologist has been particularly vocal, should have suggested at least a strongly perceived problem. A perceived problem is fully as troublesome as a real one until it is addressed and either defined or defused. The administrative director has not been listening to the staff sufficiently to recognize the obvious—that there is discontent in the department involving issues of staffing and workload.

The director should not simply commit more staff to special procedures without thorough study and analysis; added staff may not be the answer. Yet it is doubtful that the problem can be defined and corrected before Morris's self-imposed deadline arrives. The best the director can do under the circumstances is acknowledge—belatedly, unfortunately—the existence of a problem and show visible signs of getting to work on it. If that is enough for Arthur Morris, he will reconsider his resignation. This would make time for which a solution might be found. However, Morris might just as readily go through with his resignation.

Indeed, the key issue in the case as presented is Arthur Morris's ultimatum. He is essentially threatening the management by telling them that if they do not do something he wants them to do, he will do something to make circumstances worse for them. This places the administrative director in a potential no-win situation for one who has just been awakened to a significant problem: The director can immediately cave in to what amounts to subordinate blackmail and add staff, thus sending a dangerous message to the rest of the organization, or take the chance of Morris actually resigning. Neither alternative is acceptable, so the director's only real choice is to acknowledge the likely existence of a staffing problem and begin at once to apply visible effort to the problem's definition and solution in a manner that, preferably, involves the special procedures staff.

Response 43

To Motivate the Unmovable

Melissa might truthfully say that "Thank you's go only so far and that's not far enough." Thank you's do go a certain positive distance in encouraging employees to perform acceptably; however, simple thanks usually fail to provide sustaining motivation.

On the other hand, Melissa cannot conclude that money always motivates because "employees talk about money so much." Although the mix of motivating forces can vary dramatically from person to person, money can indeed motivate if it is enough. (Consider whether you would step up the pace and turn out more and better work just as willingly for a 5 percent raise as you would for double your present salary.)

Admittedly, Melissa is working in a highly structured environment that limits the actions she can take on behalf of her employees. However, the restricted circumstances do not themselves prevent the supervisor from taking some positive steps with her employees.

In Melissa's circumstances it would be best to recognize the difference between the true motivators and those other factors that Frederick Herzberg referred to in his classic motivation-maintenance theory as potential dissatisfiers. These potential dissatisfiers, also frequently referred to as environmental factors, represent conditions of employment that must be continually reinforced or maintained or they will become dissatisfiers. Most often, money is in this category; periodic raises do not necessarily motivate, but their absence can breed dissatisfaction and have an adverse effect on performance.

Looking beyond the environmental factors, the potential dissatisfiers, we are eventually led to conclude that the true, lasting motivators reside in the work itself. The true motivators include the opportunity to learn and achieve, the opportunity to do interesting, challenging, and meaningful work, and the opportunity to assume responsibility and become involved in determining how the work is done.

To be able to identify the true motivators, Melissa needs to focus more on the work itself and less on the environment in which the work is performed.

RESPONSE 44

WHO'S THE BOSS?

Carrie's problem is not total quality management (TQM), but her response is typical of the true problem. TQM signals that Carrie's strengths are no longer as valuable, and she will be in less control of her work environment. To Carrie's mind, TQM has considerably reduced her status.

This is the critical time to launch a transformation from "boss" to "leader." Instead of focusing on the minutiae of management, Carrie should concentrate on the qualities needed to support her staff during this transition.

Embracing the organization's vision and imparting it to her work group, becoming a catalyst for change, and ensuring her group is getting the resources it needs to carry through its ideas, will be skills critical to her success.

Her response to "Freddie the Expert" is another indicator of Carrie's feelings. Having an assertive individual on the team can seem threatening to those reluctant to loosen controlling reins. Unless Freddie's behaviors are negatively affecting the area's work, the problem isn't Freddie.

Phrases like, "a couple of management courses" clue us that Carrie is beginning to recognize she may be working from a stagnant knowledge base. Whether she opts to take courses herself, bone up on journals, or increase participation in information-sharing professional organizations, Carrie, as leader, will earn the group's respect by updating her informational resources.

Meantime, she should focus Freddie's energy to her advantage. Giving him an analysis project or charging him with finding ways to increase the whole group's knowledge in a manner it's comfortable with are two ways she could use his "expertise" to add to the work group's efforts.

This is a critical time for Carrie. Working toward leadership status, rather than bemoaning loss of control, will serve her career best.

Response 45

But I'm Really Sick!

The personnel representative being asked for advice by supervisor Jane Babson might start by reminding Jane of something she herself said, "After all, I've got a unit to staff and whether somebody is truly ill or just faking it, the work still isn't getting done." Regardless of why any particular employee is absent on any given day, the fact remains that either the work is not getting done at all or is getting done only at the additional expense of replacement help or overtime. The key, of course, in applying the disciplinary process is consistency, in that whatever action is taken with one person for a violation of policy also must be applied with another for the same violation regardless of the supervisor's belief in possibly differing motivations or circumstances behind the behavior.

Jane needs to be dealing with both Kelly and Wilson according to the organization's policy concerning absenteeism. She cannot allow herself to "go easier" on Kelly because of apparently genuine health problems and implied threats of legal action. The disciplinary process should include a referral to an appropriate source of counseling assistance, someone in a position to help assess individuals' problems and suggest how to address them. The best such source, and certainly right in Kelly's case, is usually the employee health service. Also, appropriate counseling might be provided by an employee-relations professional, especially in cases like Wilson's that might involve mostly employee motivation and attitude.

It is extremely important for both employees to be given the full benefit of all of the organization's applicable processes. In the case of an individual such as Kelly, who may well be dealing with a chronic health problem, the solution may be found in some form of medically advisable leave, either continuous or intermittent, under the Family and Medical Leave Act. It is possible that a leave or other form of accommodation will help to both address the supervisor's staffing problem and ensure the individual's continued employment.

RESPONSE 46

ALL THAT EMPOWERMENT JAZZ

Many conflicts arise over delegation and empowerment. Before true empowerment can exist, a conducive environment must be established to facilitate what some might call "informed empowerment." We must all realize that employees cannot be expected to take on added responsibility without first being prepared. If the manager attempts to empower people before establishing the environment, this may be interpreted as "dumping."

Managers can promote a positive environment by providing a clear vision for the department or organization. This helps ensure that everyone is moving in the right direction. In time, employees will become aligned with the organization. Along with measurable goals, the vision should be established, reviewed frequently, and kept visible to all employees.

Another key element is trust. The manager must develop a trusting relationship with employees. This can be accomplished by providing open channels of communication. Shared information gives everyone the ability to play on a level field. Better decisions are made when employees hold a more global viewpoint.

People must be allowed to make mistakes. If no mistakes are made, people are not trying new and innovative approaches to their work and no growth will occur. It is not important how many mistakes are made, but what is learned from the mistake. Thomas Watson once said, "To double your success rate you must quadruple your failure rate."

Recognition is another important factor that must be linked to performance. The manager must recognize employees' successes and contributions. Simple acts such as a letter or card sent to an employee's home complimenting the positive behavior will go a long way in motivating people.

Craig Williams should advise Susan Benton to step back and begin preparing her staff for a change of culture. Empowerment will not work in just any environment.

RESPONSE 47

WHY DOESN'T ANYONE TELL ME?

Business manager Carrie Owen's frustration over the communication problem is understandable. This lack of communication prevents her from truly fulfilling her role, making it necessary to take action. Proper lines of communication should be followed, making it advisable for her to discuss her specific problem with her immediate superior, Barry. She should start by informing him of the three incidents that happened to her that week: one of her key staff members had decided not to return to work after her maternity leave, which was confirmed later that same day by the hospital's employee health service; two of her employees learned 2 days before she did about the hospital's new policy on vacation accruals; and she almost missed an important meeting, the notice of which she received later that same day.

Once she has stated her problem, she should clearly state how these occurrences made her feel and how this hampers her effectiveness. She should be assertive enough to ask for legitimate changes. Because downward communication (flow of communication from higher to lower authority) is essential in any organization for sharing new and important information, she should clearly express that she needs to be informed of meetings in a timely fashion. She must be informed firsthand of new policies to understand them, to interpret them, and to answer questions from her staff.

Because Carrie is responsible for the communication within her own unit, she should look at the patterns of communication between herself and her employees. A starting point for building upward communication (from lower to higher authority) lies in improving practices that facilitate better communication. Questioning and listening will show staff her interest in their opinions, desires, and information and that she values their input. Other practices she can use are employee meetings, open-door policies, and participation in work-related social groups.

RESPONSE 48

THE DEDICATED HIP-SHOOTER

Many people who consider this case from the assistant administrator's point of view might agree that, if such total dedication is a problem, then we all need more such problems.

Although the case situation can be tough to deal with, there are positive factors that are not encountered in many other employee problems. Specifically, Wade is totally dedicated to the organization, and he is an excellent electrician. Any solution or path to a solution should take these two facts into account and build on them as possible. Some alternative possibilities for dealing with this problem include:

- If the relative experience among the electricians permits, another of the group could possibly be designated as lead worker. Perhaps this could be sold on the basis of having Wade concentrate on that which he does best.
- It might be appropriate to abandon a departmental management structure that has led workers for each small trade group and combine the skilled trades under one or two first-line supervisors.
- Provide some highly specific management training for Wade and let him know what particular problems his "managing" (or lack of same) is causing and exactly what he can do to correct these apparent weaknesses.
- The entire electrical group—Wade, the other two electricians, and the helper—might be treated as a potentially self-directed work team and as a group could be given the challenge of improving their effectiveness through better service. This could include providing them instruction and some initial assistance in how to establish priorities.

As already suggested, any reasonable solution should attempt to capitalize on Wade's strengths. Also, because "except for Bob himself, nobody seems to know what to work on at any given time," a partial answer might lie in examining how Wade sets his own priorities and determining whether this can be applied to the others as well.

Response 49

The Paperwork Simply Isn't Important

Jean Howell's dilemma over the documentation problem presented by Julia is understandable and real. Lack of documentation keeps other staff members from forming a concise and accurate picture of the patient situation. After all, if care is not documented, it instills doubt as to whether treatment was actually performed.

Jean should start by informing Julia that she must set aside time to communicate about her documentation and you value her as an employee because of her positive results with patients and her efficient use of time. None of this, however, is reflected in her documentation. Also, it must be stressed with Julia that if lack of documentation surfaces during a state survey, the organization could be censured and fined. Concerning some patients, there could conceivably be legal problems such as malpractice lawsuits—the defense of which will depend in part on the existence of documentation.

Documentation is important to help others recognize and meet patient needs and record patient response. Documentation helps us evaluate whether procedures were performed accurately and efficiently. By documenting complete visit reports, professionals demonstrate accountability and fulfill their responsibilities in administering care to the patient. Supervisor Sharon Ward should be assertive enough to demonstrate that documentation is essential for sharing new and important information. Julia must realize that the patient record is an important tool and reference in care and treatment. All caregivers should assume this aspect of the patient care with conscientiousness. Pertinent observation of the condition of the patient, progress, and plans for the future should be made on the patient's chart by responsible practitioners who must understand that the paperwork is important.

Although Jean would surely be extremely reluctant to do so with such an otherwise great performer, as a last resort, she may have to lay out the possibility of disciplinary action. Surely this is a distasteful alternative, but missing documentation can be damaging to the organization.

RESPONSE 50

WHY SHOULD I ALWAYS GO THE EXTRA MILE?

Harry and Millie actually have similar problems concerning direct communication with their supervisors. Both need to be more proactive and anticipate what it is they want and to ask for this from their supervisors.

"Always" was a word that both Harry and Millie used to describe communication with their bosses. It should be a red flag word suggesting that neither has clearly thought through their situations. Their bosses do indeed represent different styles. Because her boss may have high control needs, Millie may need to keep her boss updated on her progress on assignments. Harry's boss, on the other hand, seems to be more laissez-faire. It appears that Harry is catching his boss in transit or between appointments. Harry should set up meeting times with his boss in advance, send memos, or leave voice mail messages stating succinctly what he needs from his boss.

Harry's problems with communication are of more concern than Millie's. When Millie offers suggestions, Harry has a rebuttal for each. If Harry truly believes his statement, "I don't think that's my place," he is perpetuating the communication problem with his boss. It is Harry's responsibility to clarify expectations because he is aware of the problem. If he is unclear about what is expected of him in terms of job performance, it will be difficult for him to be effective and productive.

Both Harry and Millie need to initiate communication but for different reasons. Millie needs to do so to offer reassurance that she understands her assignments and build her boss's confidence in her. It appears that Millie is clear about what is expected of her in terms of job assignments. For Harry, operating in the dark is a riskier situation. He should take steps to shed some light on what is expected of him.

Response 51

Don't Tell Them I Said So

Clearly, Molly, with the information she provides for "the good of the department," is doing Rita no favors. Rita can take no direct action based on hearsay, whether concerning lunch breaks, cliques, personal activities, or phone calls on work time, or even the allegations of active substance abuse. This is fundamental to disciplinary action; secondhand evidence is no evidence at all. Molly is only giving Rita cause to worry.

Rita should not necessarily discourage Molly's reports altogether. When Molly comes carrying tales, Rita should question her and attempt to learn of specifics she can follow up on. If she can use Molly's information to lead to firsthand knowledge of some infraction, Rita can then take disciplinary action.

It would of course behoove Rita to increase her awareness of what's going on in her department. She might consider:

- Increasing the frequency of department meetings
- Holding one-on-one meetings with staff members, in a few weeks working her way through the entire department
- Meeting with small groups deliberately composed, in turn, of the "ins," the "outs," and some combination of these
- Developing some new scheduling practices that have the end result of changing present assignments and altering longstanding working relationships

One of Rita's objectives in all of the foregoing should be to elicit some acknowledgment of difficulties in the department so she will have something of substance with which to deal.

Concerning the allegations of substance abuse, Rita must be especially observant when meeting privately with this individual. Should she observe any unexplainable signs or behavior, she is probably, under the policies of the organization, able to insist this person either visit Employee Health or accept referral to the Employee Assistance Program.

Many of the kinds of problems noted in the case might be avoided or at least minimized if Rita had an officially designated backup person who could serve as acting manager and look after the department in her absence. It is unfortunate if some in Rita's group require visible full-time supervision, but this may indeed be the case. Rita should examine her own behavior and decide whether anything in the way she runs the department seems to encourage laxity when she is not present.

In any case, the solutions to this department's problems—and indeed, knowledge of the true nature and extent of any problem—will depend on astute observation and improved communication.

Response 52

The Oil-and-Water Employees

It is unlikely that any action Carrie takes will change the two employees' attitudes toward one another. However, Carrie can make her expectations known and be consistent in follow-up by attempting to force change in their behavior toward one another. It is possible that Carrie's lack of action in this direction has given the employees tacit permission to continue bickering and control the group with their emotional outbursts.

Carrie may have inherited these terrible twins from a former supervisor, in which case years of positive feedback, based solely on technical skills, have reinforced their nasty interaction. It is time to make the rules clear by ensuring that job descriptions, feedback sessions, and formal performance appraisals include performance skills as well as technical productivity skills. Not addressing performance skills, such as the ability to interact to the satisfaction of clients and coworkers, signals that these issues are unimportant to the supervisor.

Carrie also needs to take a look for some underlying issues fueling the feuding. Often personality conflicts are symptoms of poor systems, resources, or leadership.

Perhaps Ellie and Nellie, for lack of a better system, have each created their own work methodologies. Individualized systems can be highly workable and might be exactly what led to the pair's good productivity reviews. Consequently, both might be wedded to individual systems that conflict with one another. A healthy systems review might be in order.

Even if the two are working on the same system but in competition for scarce resources (files, equipment, or desk space), these minor environmental aspects will strain even the cosiest coworkers. The staff relies on Carrie as group advocate to gain needed resources from the organization.

Finally, the conflicting coworkers may need an opportunity to develop interactive skills. Some internal or external training might be helpful in giving them new techniques to resolve conflict. However, training can only help employees who are willing to change. If this duo is able but unwilling to change, training is not the answer.

By making her expectations for group behavior known and reinforced, ensuring that productive easy-to-complete systems are in place and understood by all, and ensuring that the group has the resources it needs to carry through with these systems, Carrie can minimize reasons for disagreement. There is much that Carrie can do before considering disciplinary action.

Response 53

Getting Off the Fence: Jump, Fall, or Pushed?

The on-the-fence feeling is natural for a supervisor who has risen through the group he or she now supervises, and the concerns Myrna expressed are those of many up-from-the-ranks supervisors. However, what Myrna does with these concerns during her early years in supervision can have a considerable bearing on her relative success in management.

The on-the-fence feeling arises from, first, the supervisor's identification as a longstanding member of the work group who feels a commitment to the group, and, second, the knowledge of the supervisor's management responsibilities. As suggested in the case, it can seem lonely and uncomfortable on the fence. This is undoubtedly because of the supervisor's perception of conflict between his or her roles as a group member and as a member of management. However, as uneasy as the supervisor may be with that position at times, much of the supervisor's real role involves straddling the fence in terms of providing the primary link between the work group and higher management. Any first-line manager is also a worker as well, and at any time is legitimately on either side of the fence.

There are times when the supervisor must identify most closely with the work group, and there are times when the supervisor must behave primarily as a member of management. The key in determining which role to emphasize at any particular time is up to the supervisor. The greatest danger for the supervisor who is on the fence (in the sense of functioning as a member of two different groups) is being pushed or yanked off by those on one side or the other. And this can happen, for example, with a group of former peers and friends who attempt to trade unfairly on past relationships, or with a higher manager who expects the subordinate supervisor to primarily serve a "master" rather than appropriately facilitating the work of the department.

The effective supervisor straddles the fence as necessary, steps off on either side when appropriate, and avoids being pulled or pushed off by others.

RESPONSE 54

THE VOCALLY UNHAPPY CAMPER

It would be much easier to deal with Jean if her performance were substandard. Documentable performance issues are usually easier to address than issues of behavior, especially when the behavior does not involve breaches of policy. Also, issues arising from interpersonal difficulties are often tough to address without intruding into aspects of personality (perhaps labeling someone as "grouchy," "touchy," "thin-skinned," or whatever).

Some people who do not relate well interpersonally can nevertheless make a legitimate contribution if able to work in a relative vacuum. However, if continuing contact with others is necessary, then reasonable interpersonal relations with those others can be an expectation of employment.

That something must be done concerning Jean Todd is embodied in the case's opening sentence telling us the situation is "affecting the whole department's performance." Taking that as given, business office manager Carol Jamison should consider proceeding along two fronts.

She should begin to deal with Jean concerning matters of behavior in interpersonal relations within the department and utilize specific instances in which her disruptive behavior has interfered with departmental performance and caused problems requiring supervisory time and attention. This should involve not only providing Jean every reasonable opportunity to talk about what's bothering her (without prying into her personal life), but should also involve the organization's progressive disciplinary process as necessary.

Carol should refer Jean to the Employee Health Service. The professional staff of Employee Health is able to legitimately probe for individual health or personal complications that the supervisor cannot address.

Whatever path is chosen, the situation demands that something be done. A problem in an employee's personal life will forever remain none of the supervisor's business, but negative effects on departmental performance are always the supervisor's business.

RESPONSE 55

TO MANAGE THE MANAGER

It appears that by design or miscommunication, the unity of command principle is violated in this situation. Although "cross-cover" duties have merit, this technique should be used judiciously with well-defined operational guidelines. Inappropriate utilization of this staffing approach is apparently causing conflict among three "cosupervisors." It is highly likely that the subordinate employees reporting to the cosupervisors are also confused or take liberty with supervisory conflict. This may be the reason for scheduled disciplinary conferences requiring the presence of all three cosupervisors. The "cross-cover" of supervisory functions appears to not only create conflict, but resource intensive conflict resolution as well.

Nancy Wright commented that she and Mark Allen are at times "forced" to make decisions that Linda Williams neglects. The real nature of being "forced" to do someone else's work needs to be better defined or investigated. Who is doing the "forcing." Is it Jane Worth? Or is it self-imposed by the commendable, but perhaps misguided conscientiousness of Nancy and Mark?

Proper conflict resolution focuses on issues and objectives rather than personalities. Margie Olson should advise Nancy to approach this in a way that avoids leveling accusations at Linda; in this way, Nancy will also avoid offending Jane. An objective, problem-solving approach would be to ask Jane for role clarification. Perhaps the passage of time has distorted the intentions or expectations of "cross-covering" delegations of authority and resulting responsibility. Rather than complaining about a peer supervisor, Nancy might better address this situation by drawing attention to the possible employee confusion that can occur when three cosupervisors share what appears to be equal responsibility for all employees. No person can appropriately serve two masters.

Response 56

The Weekly Staff Meeting

At the weekly staff meeting and again noting that the same six or seven people are punctual, acknowledge them for their consistency. If meeting minutes are generated, list the punctual attendees by name followed by "late arrivals." Advise the remaining staff that this will be part of all future meeting minutes. Announce that all future meetings will begin at the scheduled time and that it is the responsibility of all latecomers to learn what occurred before their arrival. Follow this practice consistently for several weeks.

Select a task force of punctual employees to develop an action plan for consideration by the group. This action plan is to include what suggested action would be implemented to correct the tardiness situation, step by step. Have this task force elicit the assistance of their peers regarding effective measures to be instituted preventing tardiness in future meetings and present their findings at a staff meeting approximately 4 to 6 weeks from the date of initiation.

Before submitting the action plan, the task force is encouraged to:

- Review the effectiveness of the meeting content, ensuring that it is valuable for all staff present (if not, make recommendations for improvement).
- Review the meeting to ensure that appropriate measures are taken to keep the attendees focused and discussion flowing in an appropriate fashion (if not, make recommendations to ensure this action).
- Include a member of the human resource department to review the recommended plan before submission to the staff.

Have the task force present the action plan for discussion and final decision, then implement their plan.

One additional consideration for the manager: Before doing anything concerning staff meeting attendance, examine the necessity of a weekly meeting. Is once each week really necessary, or has it become an automatic gathering? Would a biweekly meeting make more sense? If change is in order, settle on the most apparently sensible meeting frequency and announce it to the group. Then if the chronic latecomers still continue their previous behavior, proceed as suggested.

Response 57

Where Are They When I Need Them?

It appears that Jenny Lee has not done her homework. The situation with which she is presented—the use of volunteers or unpaid personnel to help meet the needs of patients—is common in today's healthcare environment. To effectively use volunteers, you must implement systems that take into consideration the fact that they are unpaid personnel. Jenny's expectations of them seem to be the same as for her paid staff.

Jenny might consider the following plan:

1. Develop well-defined guidelines for the role and duties of the volunteers on the geriatric unit.
2. Meet with the volunteers to learn their expectations. During this meeting, let them know how important their role is and how much the patients rely on them being there.
3. Develop an orientation program to allow the volunteers to learn their role and duties. As part of this orientation, assign unit staff to work with the volunteers to help them learn about the department and facilitate communication between staff and volunteers.
4. Meet with the staff to educate them about the role of the volunteer.
5. Develop some form of ongoing recognition to show the volunteers how much their time and efforts are appreciated.
6. Provide routine feedback to the volunteers on how they are doing.
7. Continually monitor the program by seeking volunteer, employee, and patient input, and make appropriate changes as necessary.

With a little preparation and the right expectations of her unit's volunteers, Jenny should be able to implement a first-class volunteer program. She needs to remember that managing unpaid personnel is significantly different than managing paid personnel. However, one management technique that works equally as well with volunteers and paid personnel is timely, effective communication.

RESPONSE 58

THE UNNECESSARY TASK

The management of the health information management (HIM) department is responsible for the duration of the unnecessary task. The former manager, Mrs. Victor, clearly set the boundaries for the clerk's future behavior by being harshly critical of a decision the clerk made on her own in good faith. The subsequent manager, Mrs. James, perpetuated the mistake by paying insufficient attention to the employees' concerns.

The unnecessary task was perpetuated for a number of reasons. Foremost among these are the inappropriate focus of department management as suggested—the tendency to focus "upward" toward administration and the physicians rather than "downward" toward the employees and the day-to-day action—and some extremely serious communication problems. Much of a modern organization's success depends on how well communication flows upward from the employees to the management, and in this instance, the apparent barriers to upward communication in the HIM department are numerous.

One of the most valuable assets to be found among employees is the combination of common sense and courage that causes one to question the boss, selectively or constructively disobey an instruction, or, as in the case of the clerk who did the unnecessary task, make an independent decision to drop a task that "didn't make sense." An employee who exhibits this behavior will not always be right, and the manager who reacts punitively, as did Mrs. Victor, can squelch this otherwise healthy spirit. One who is harshly discouraged from behaving this way may simply shrug and go about her business the next time she sees the manager about to "shoot herself in the foot."

Covering his bases with his immediate superior, Guy Smith should of course eliminate the unnecessary task and prepare to diplomatically advise Mrs. James, on her return to work, what was done and why it was done.

Response 59

Your Wasteful Friend

This seems to be one of those classic situations in which you find yourself caught between responsibility to your employer and loyalty to a friend. As conscientious as you might be as a supervisor, you might certainly be reluctant to do anything that could be construed as "blowing the whistle" on your friend. (Although if your friend counts on you to continually overlook careless and wasteful behavior, you may see considerable truth in the old saying that begins, "With friends like this . . .").

As long as higher management is "paying no attention to what is going on in the department," you have few options other than to do your job to the best of your ability as you believe it should be done. The key here is to recognize the difference between what you can control and what you cannot control. Start with your own job description, doing everything within your responsibility in cost-conscious fashion. And keep doing it.

If there is indeed an "economic pinch" that fails to go away on its own, you can rest assured that wasteful practices will eventually come under fire. Failure to pay attention to what goes on in the department has been the downfall of many a manager. Actually, in many organizations the higher the manager is placed the more susceptible that person is to the consequences of prolonged waste and inefficiency.

It might be helpful to test higher management's attitude by submitting a comprehensive cost-control proposal for your department (describing circumstances, but naming no names) up through your normal chain of command. Management's reaction, or lack thereof, could tell you much.

However, as long as there is no one in authority to whom you believe you can take your concerns, it is perhaps best to operate defensively—doing your job to the best of your ability, documenting the significant problems you encounter, and making certain that when the inevitable correction occurs you will have done all you could do to keep yourself in the clear.

Response 60

One Boss Too Many

A great deal of time could be expended exploring possible reasons for the resistance of the manager of engineering and maintenance. Suffice it to say that this manager now has a superior, the director of environmental services, where no superior previously existed, and that this superior and the long-time manager are in constant conflict. Unfortunately, the three first-line supervisors and their staffs are adversely affected by the conflict between their managers.

A suggestion—the next time the director bypasses the manager and delivers an important instruction to the supervisors, the supervisors should stop the director, tell him what they have been experiencing, and ask for a joint meeting of the director, the manager, and the three of them. The issue of conflicting instructions—and especially of one manager's reversal of another manager's instructions, if that has indeed been happening—needs to be out in the open in front of all concerned. As long as the supervisors are bounced from director to manager and back again, they remain victims of a tug-of-war between two higher-ups.

If not blessed with an immediate meeting to iron out differences, the supervisors are left in a position of having to decide whom to obey. In the absence of any other assistance, they are probably better off paying more attention to the director, the higher of the higher-ups, than to the manager, simply because of position in the chain of command.

If every effort to correct the situation by dealing directly and jointly with the manager and the director is made and conditions fail to change, the supervisors might consider following the chain of command upward and requesting a meeting with the person to whom the director reports. This is of course a frequently risky step, and it is one that should never be taken without first making every reasonable effort to solve the problem at the level at which it occurs.

The primary responsibility for the existence of this problems lies with the director. The manager is, after all, the director's subordinate. Properly and thoroughly advised of what is occurring, the director may well address the problem before it has to go further.

RESPONSE 61

HOW TIME FLIES

Implicit in the boss's behavior is the apparent belief that his time is more important than yours, and in fact that your time is his to use as he sees fit and even his to waste as he chooses. This, unfortunately, is a circumstance frequently played out in the behavior of many managers, and it is generally behavioral, rarely articulated; only the most exploitative of bosses will openly state that the employee exists for the convenience of the boss. Quite the contrary, hardly a manager exists who does not pay some kind of lip service to the importance of the employees. However, it remains true in the long run that what a manager does sends a much clearer message than what that manager says.

What you can do to encourage your boss to show more respect for your working time will depend on how much you dare to do, which in turn depends on how well you know this manager. Dare you simply tell the boss that he or she does not seem to realize that you have plenty of work to get done and that your time is being wasted? Or that you are not going to get something important done on time because of spending an hour mostly waiting to transact a few minutes' business? An occasional boss might accept this accusation of thoughtlessness and do something about it, but many would undoubtedly react negatively.

One supervisor with whom this issue was discussed says that whenever the boss takes a call during a one-on-one meeting, dashes off a quick note on the order of "Call me when you're ready to continue" and goes back to his own office. Others who know their bosses well enough to expect this kind of behavior carry other work into the meeting to keep themselves productively occupied during the manager's digressions.

You might also use the boss's behavior as a reminder of what not to do in your relationship with your own employees. Even if you are not conscious of doing so, you are constantly learning more about management, forming impressions, and absorbing practices and techniques from the managers you are exposed to daily, and especially the one manager to whom you report. In a very real sense, these managers are your role models. Have the good sense to be ever critical of your role models, always learning from their behavior what you should do—and what you should not do—in your relationship with your employees. You owe it to your employees to treat them the way you would like to be treated yourself.

RESPONSE 62

YOUR UNHAPPY DUTY

Because the staff has already had a visit from the CEO and heard firsthand the expectations of them, there is not a great deal you need to do to get the word across to your employees. It could be helpful, however, to get the staff together early the following morning and discuss the situation. In doing so, you should get their reading on what they heard and make certain that all of you are in agreement as to the nature of the CEO's edicts, namely, the prohibitions against eating in the department and having a coffeepot in the department. Of less immediate concern is the "no boisterous laughter" demand; this is too highly subjective to be a realistic guideline for behavior. It might be best interpreted as caution against a level of noise in the department—laughter or otherwise—that could be heard in the public corridor.

Because you were not able to talk the CEO out of his lunch and coffeepot mandates, you had best reinforce these in the department. You may not agree with his demands and you may not be happy about reinforcing them, but you may well be in a position of having to do what you are told or look for another job.

An important precaution is in order in this case: Avoid the tendency to simply side with the department, adding your own complaints about the boss's strictness to your own, and essentially say, "Hey, don't blame me—I didn't agree with this, but I've got to do as I'm told." All too often, first-line supervisors will redirect the blame for unpopular decisions to higher management, behaving in a manner that says, "This wasn't my idea; 'they' made me do it." Fortunately, in this instance the employees received most of the bad stuff firsthand, so they are less likely to place much blame on the supervisor.

The group's morale is certainly adversely affected, perhaps significantly. What you can do under the circumstances is to continue to be the kind of supervisor you have been up until this worrisome turn of events. You need to modify your behavior only to the extent necessary to enforce the lunch and coffeepot edicts, and you can surely do so in a much more acceptable manner than did the CEO. Your staff will likely understand that you have no choice concerning these changes, but except for observing these two new rules you can probably run your department much the same way as you did before the CEO's visit. Other than your continued humane supervision, what is most needed for restoring staff morale is the passage of sufficient time to blunt the effects of the unpleasant incident.

RESPONSE 63

THE INDEPENDENT EMPLOYEE

Jim Wood and Bob Trent each own a share of the blame for the situation that has developed between them as supervisor and employee, and between employee Bob Trent and his work. Most of the blame, however, resides with the supervisor. Like many other supervisors who have employees who seem difficult to direct, Jim Wood is more adept at complaining about Trent and feeling frustration when Trent goes astray than he is at providing the kind of guidance Trent may need to get him on track and keep him there.

We could reasonably suspect that Jim Wood might be dealing with Trent the same way he deals with other employees. However, what works with some will not always work with others.

Wood seems to believe that "delegating" consists of little more than handing out an assignment. Part of the delegation process that he might not have to give much attention at such times is the employee's knowledge of what is to be done; Wood seems to know that Trent can do the work, so that's not a concern. Proper delegation, however, includes follow up as well. And "follow up" is decidedly not waiting until after the deadline has passed to ask about the job.

One of the most frequently repeated pieces of advice given to first-line supervisors is know your employees. Jim Wood should know his employees well enough to know who he can turn loose with minimal direction and who he has to follow up with regularly.

Concerning future assignments given to Bob Trent, Jim Wood should:

- Be specific about when to do the job, not "today or tomorrow," as in the case, but something like "today," "this morning," or perhaps even "right now."
- Set a definite deadline that's a bit tighter than the "real" deadline, keeping enough time in reserve for response if the job does not get done.
- Follow up, follow up, follow up—early in the job to ensure it is started, during the job to ensure it is being done, at the deadline to ensure it has been done and done correctly.

It may seem—especially to Jim Wood—that the supervisor should not have to expend such time and energy staying right on top of Bob Trent's activities to the extent suggested. However, this kind of close follow up, accompanying extremely specific instructions, may be exactly what is required to modify Trent's behavior to the requirements of the position.

Response 64

Here We Go Again

It is probably not a far stretch of the imagination to suggest that morale among the four senior business office employees would not be especially high. Having been passed over twice—even for a position that perhaps none of them would have readily accepted under the circumstances—sends the kind of message employees do not like to hear. It is one thing for them to have turned it down when it was offered; one can do this with dignity. However, to be bypassed, especially amid mixed messages ("You've come along very well and we'll consider you next time," then, in effect, "It's now the next time and we don't even think enough of you to ask you"), is readily perceived as demeaning and belittling.

The business office staff would not represent one of the happier, more productive departments. The entire business office would likely be distrustful of the organization's top management, and especially of the finance director. The four senior employees would be likely to distrust the finance director and have little respect for that individual's capabilities as a manager. Also, these four employees, having twice seen outsiders fill the next position up in what they perceive as their promotional path, may come to view their present position as a "dead end."

As a result of the attitude toward the organization's upper management, the business office may well become—if it is not already—a magnet for the problems that often accompany morale difficulties (sagging productivity, increasing error rates, increasing turnover, and such).

The apparent wage and salary inequity may or may not be justifiable; we do not have sufficient information about the pay structure. However, it is fairly common for the ranges of senior nonmanagerial workers to overlap the ranges of supervisors, so the pay of the four senior employees could already be in the supervisory pay range. Nevertheless, it is also fairly common—and only reasonable—to provide at least a modest increase in pay for taking on the responsibilities of supervision.

RESPONSE 65

THE FORCEFUL ORGANIZER

If you recognize the apparent organizer as an employee, you need to immediately intrude and ask him to return to his own work area. You may need to remind him that he cannot organize on working time, neither his nor other employees' working time. (An internal organizer has the right to solicit interest in a union on his own time—such as lunch time and recognized break times—but cannot solicit people who are not likewise on their own time.) If you get an argument or encounter resistance, call the individual's supervisor or hospital security.

If certain the man is not a hospital employee, ask him to leave the premises at once and immediately call hospital security. Stay on the scene until the organizer is gone or security arrives; it is important that the employee, who is apparently being badgered, not be left alone with the outsider.

Addressing the third question, regardless of whether you do or do not recognize the apparent organizer as an employee, your very first action should be to break into the conversation. At the very least you are able to ascertain that the housekeeper, trapped in a corner by the man, gives every appearance of being distressed by the circumstances. As a member of management you have a responsibility to all employees to provide them with an environment free from pressure and harassment. You need take immediate steps to free the employee to go about her normal business.

RESPONSE 66

THE REQUESTED FAVOR

Denying the request avoids upsetting the status quo. With no change to Mrs. Allen's hours, there is then no risk that others will be asking for the same consideration, and no risk of thoughts or grumbles among the staff about "favoritism" for Mrs. Allen.

However, simply denying the request out of hand—although probably consistent with some published policy or guideline—could make things difficult for Mrs. Allen. Perhaps Mrs. Allen would leave if she could not be accommodated, and you might not wish to risk losing a good nurse (assuming, of course, that she is a good nurse).

Granting the request is likely to keep Mrs. Allen happy, and you would not risk losing her. However, doing so could bring upon you the aforementioned charges of "favoritism" unless you were prepared to do the same for any other staff who make the same request. Also, depending on Mrs. Allen's role in the unit, granting her request might cause difficulty with the shift reporting that takes place during the critical overlap period between shifts.

Granting the request on a temporary basis possesses most of the pluses and minuses enumerated in the preceding. In doing so, however, you can provide Mrs. Allen with a temporary solution while she seeks a permanent arrangement, and you can keep most other criticisms at bay with the temporary nature of the request (as long as "temporary" does not become "indefinitely").

It might be appropriate to extend Mrs. Allen some temporary relief, perhaps 2 to 4 weeks, letting her know that this probably cannot be permanent and that she had best make another arrangement. The most straightforward reasons you could give her are your belief that you must provide consistent treatment for all employees who are similarly situated, and the fact that it is the needs of the unit and its patients that govern staffing and schedules, not the needs of the individual employee.

RESPONSE 67

BOSS? WHO NEEDS ONE?

In beginning to deal with Kay Morgan, do not assume that—and especially do not behave as though—her "seemingly quiet and stern manner" actually indicates resentment and thus resistance. You need to experience significant exposure to her before beginning to assess her behavior relative to your presence.

Initially, and making little of the fact that the reception area is now part of your responsibility, approach her as someone who has a need to learn as much as possible about how her job is run. Chances are, she has a fair amount of useful knowledge to impart. You might be able to see immediately how many tasks could be done better, but she is in the best position to have the most accurate information about how the details of her job are performed. Although a manager may be able to see the need for improvements in a macro sense, it is invariably true that no one knows the inner working details of a job better than the person who does that job every day.

Kay Morgan could indeed be resistant to change, well entrenched in ways of doing things that she developed herself. This potential resistance suggests that you need to become less of a threat to her. Assure her that she is needed and that her job is as secure as any other position (providing, of course, that this is true). You can also explain that the administrator, whom she considered her only "boss," has experienced expanding responsibilities such that each of his direct-reporting employees could no longer receive the attention they deserved. You have been assigned her area because you can give it more attention than the administrator is able to provide.

In short, be open, friendly, and nonthreatening. Respect her knowledge and experience, learn from her, and make her feel as secure in her position as possible.

RESPONSE 68

CHOICES

Everything you know about the first candidate is forbidden information; age, marital status, and children are all out of bounds for use in making hiring decisions. For the second candidate, again age and marital situation are forbidden information. The length of time she has been out of work is not forbidden but is probably irrelevant. You have no forbidden information about the third candidate.

We are not allowed to solicit that which has been called "forbidden information" because the use of any such information in making hiring decisions is contrary to civil rights legislation. If we request such information and the ultimate decision is challenged, it may well be assumed that the decision was discriminatory.

A potential problem in hiring the first candidate resides in the statistically verifiable claim that single mothers generate higher rates of absenteeism. Also, it is often assumed that when someone's family includes a disabled individual, as with the second candidate, the employee's attendance suffers and attendant benefits costs—health insurance and such—are higher. Also concerning the second candidate, the hiring supervisor is often left with an uneasy feeling—usually completely unwarranted, but nevertheless there—when a candidate has been unemployed for a lengthy period. Concerning the third candidate, if you hire this one you may be open to charges of favoritism. And looking at this third candidate from a selfish viewpoint, you know that she is going to be trying to transfer to the "department of her choice" so you will probably have to recruit all over again.

You would be most likely—and completely legally and safely—rule out all three candidates if none of them met all of the job requirements contained in the job description. The single best reason for taking one candidate over another is that the person selected is the best qualified for the job.

Response 69

Shortage of Help

This case can be responded to relatively easily and briefly—you are probably best off telling the applicant about the every-other-weekend scheduling policy and taking your chances with her reaction.

That you face this situation at all suggests the open position was not thoroughly communicated in your advertisement, job posting, or whatever was used. Weekend rotation should have been known to the applicant before she made her decision to apply. You really need to tell her that every-other-weekend is an expectation.

Until you address the issue directly you will not know for certain how she will react. For all you know she may be familiar with your practices, but is simply trying you out to see whether she can obtain exactly the schedule she prefers. Also, it is possible that one weekend off out of two might be acceptable to her.

Resist the temptation to take her for weekday evenings only and fill the weekends with part-time or casual help. Regardless of how much of this latter kind of help you employ, the fact that this person would be working weekdays only still means that those who rotate will do more weekend work than they would if she rotated as well. Making an exception of her can cause problems with the rest of your staff.

If she refuses the job as it is offered, the worst you will be facing is continued recruitment to fill the position or perhaps continued overtime or agency nurse cost for a time.

RESPONSE 70

WHO ANSWERS TO WHOM?

Ideally, the incident occurring between Tom Mooney and the head nurse of the medical/surgical unit should be handled by Ross and the nurse together. However, if they cannot agree at their level this may have to go to the next highest level of management. (This should not occur, but it often does—there are few legitimate reasons for involving higher management in such a dispute. When resolution has to be sought at that level it usually means that one or both of the dispute's participants are being stubborn or inflexible.)

Ross and the nurse need to take steps to ensure that neither Mooney nor any other housekeeping employee is put in such a position again. It is grossly unfair to Mooney to be placed such that one manager is countermanding the instructions he has gotten from another manager.

Mooney must ultimately respond to Ross's authority. Ross is Mooney's boss—that is the chain of command. However, perhaps Mooney's basic work assignment needs to be modified to include providing certain kinds of assistance when necessary. In some hospitals, in fact, there are housekeeping staff permanently assigned to each unit under nursing unit management.

Mooney could have perhaps defused the conflict by helping out as requested and then advising Ross later and asking for help with future such requests. Also, the head nurse would have been far more likely to have gotten Mooney's willing assistance had she not approached him in such authoritarian fashion.

Response 71

When Do You Stop Being General?

After having addressed the error problems with the department at two successive group meetings, you should no longer continue to deal with the group at large in an attempt to improve the quality of output. You can, of course, and probably should, feature some kind of a quality update at every monthly staff meeting. As a group, your people need to know how they are doing in terms of overall quality. However, you will have no appreciable long-run effect on the quality level of those making most of the errors by keeping your criticism general.

It is not a matter of making your criticism "increasingly specific" that is required to address this problem. It must be made specific, period, with each individual who is exhibiting quality problems. If you do not have individual quality monitoring in place, this means that you must establish it and pursue it for a sufficient length of time to be able to identify the error rates for all of your transcriptionists individually.

The approach you should take is one suggesting performance improvement, not disciplinary action. Performance improvement usually involves counseling, perhaps corrective instruction, and plenty of conscientious follow-up. More often than not this approach works to correct the situation.

As suggested, you may wish to keep the entire group up to date on the quality situation in general. However, the troublesome employees' quality problems should be addressed individually, one-on-one, with specific data.

RESPONSE 72

AN ACT OF NEGLIGENCE

You should separate Jenny from the rest of the group and deliver the reprimand in private. It is an absolutely fundamental requirement for delivering criticism or conducting disciplinary action that such discussions always occur one-on-one in private. The other employees who were present are certainly bright enough to realize that Jenny did something that earned criticism; but nevertheless, in fairness to Jenny, they need not be witness to her reprimand.

Also, you need not deliberately stage Jenny's reprimand so that it can be a "warning to the others." Another fundamental requirement of fair and effective disciplinary action is that we should never make an example of anyone.

You can improve upon the rather simply stated option by getting Jenny alone and first asking her what happened. Simply because you believe you clearly saw what occurred in a way that left little room for doubt still does not mean that you have full knowledge of the situation. Overall, you should be trying to make your contact with Jenny more of a lesson than a reprimand.

Response 73

It Wasn't My Decision

Even if the solution developed by Sampson and his two colleagues was the most reasonable answer available, there remains plenty of legitimate reason for resistance from the two supervisors who were expected to carry it out. They are not in a position to feel any sense of ownership in the solution, and because they did not participate in the process, they are certainly not guaranteed to see the result as "the most reasonable answer available."

None of us is likely to react completely favorable to the "directive" from Sampson. Consider the position "we" as in as the absentees; we see the result as the classic reaction to just about anyone's absence from just about any meeting or other working gathering—those who aren't there get the assignments piled on.

The perception of anyone outside of the decision-making threesome—remembering that perception is reality to the perceiver—is likely to be that Sampson and company railroaded the decision through to their own advantage. Anyone in the position of one of the two people left out of the process should ask for another meeting. Sampson and company should participate in another meeting, this time of all five, and work toward a solution that all five can accept.

Response 74

The Dodger

If Jane deals firmly with Alice's behavior, she may rapidly put herself in the position of having to terminate Alice, or perhaps she may nudge Alice into quitting rather than facing disciplinary action. In either case Jane loses Alice's services at a time when she can ill afford to lose any staff. On the other hand, if Jane ignores Alice's behavior indefinitely, the scheduling difficulties caused by Alice's unreliability will likely continue. Also, and Jane may well not pick up on this until nearly too late, Alice's behavior may have been noticed by others who are feeling increasingly frustrated because of what they perceive Alice is "getting away with."

Of course, Jane should discuss the attendance problem with Alice. However, she should do so within the context of a "clean slate." Jane should freely admit that she had not picked up on Alice's attendance problem when she should have. She should review what she has found with Alice, indicating that if she had been aware of the pattern as it emerged, disciplinary action would have occurred already.

Jane should clearly spell out the conditions of the new start, indicating what is expected of Alice in terms of attendance, and how many absences in what period of time, or what sort of amount or patterning of absences, will trigger disciplinary action.

Finally, Jane should make it a practice to consciously monitor attendance, not just Alice's, but all others as well.

Response 75

Yours, Mine, and Hours

What you should be doing the first free moment after hearing out your employees is to take the story to your immediate manager. In considering this particular predicament, you should have plenty of help untangling the situation. At the heart of the problem is a hospital-wide issue: Is the basic workweek 37.5 hours or 40 hours? Is the workweek different for different departments?

The case description reads as though the majority of the staff in the department strongly favor the 37.5-hour week and consider it a condition of their employment, except, of course, for the two new people hired into the 40-hour week. However, in its unwritten state the 37.5-hour week is not enforceable.

The assistant director you hired might be an exempt employee and considered a member of management. If this is the case, the expectation of exempt—or salaried—employees is usually 40 hours a week or whatever the organizational standard is, regardless of how many hours are worked by the nonexempt—that is, hourly—employees.

The new transcriptionist might present a problem if working 40 hours alongside people working 37.5 hours. However, if these employees are all hourly, as is likely, the person working 40 hours earns 2.5 hours more pay in a week.

Your department could perhaps operate a 37.5-hour week for its hourly employees, but chances are, administration would prefer a standard workweek, either 37.5 hours or 40 hours, but not a mixture of these, throughout the hospital. Regardless, this is one case for which you can safely say the answer must come primarily from others—administration, human resources, and perhaps finance.

RESPONSE 76

AN EXPENSIVE GAME

The case suggests that there are probably not quite enough nurse anesthetists in the region to comfortably fill all ten hospitals' needs. If the supply were adequate, much of Dr. Gable's argument would vanish because the hospitals would be less likely to be "competing" for staff.

Whether the interorganizational "bumping" of pay rates is or is not "professional" behavior will likely be a matter of opinion, depending on individual perspective. The costs of various kinds of labor will fluctuate with supply and demand. One might be tempted to regard the playing-off of hospitals against each other as anything but professional, but in a shortage situation employers will in fact "bid" against each other for help. When this occurs, we might well consider the pressure exerted by those in short supply as one legitimate element of market force.

If the area's ten hospitals decide to get together and establish "fair and consistent pay rates" for nurse anesthetists, they would be in violation of antitrust statutes. To establish pay rates cooperatively between and among employers is a form of price fixing, so this is illegal and thus unacceptable as a potential approach to the nurse anesthetists' pay problem.

There is no simple solution to the nurse anesthetist pay problem. Dr. Gable may well be manipulated into advocating for the nurse anesthetists and exaggerating the so-called shortage, but there is no way to know for certain until additional staff are lured away by offers of higher pay. There is in this situation but one near-certainty: Salary-bumping between and among employers in the area will do nothing to alleviate the area's limited supply; rather, all it will accomplish is increasing the cost of this particular skill for all local employers.

Response 77

The Reclassification Request

The major problem in the request is one of proper communication. Through his comments about "magic" and the "so-called system," Dr. Smithers is suggesting that he is not a proponent of the formal reevaluation method. Lori has been aware that Pat has been at the top of his pay scale and the laboratory has lost good people because of money. Yet, instead of being proactive in initiating the request, she waited until her director is acting irrationally. Carl has already demonstrated that Pat is the highest paid hematology supervisor in the region, but this was apparently never shared with the laboratory managers. In this era of strong competition for clinical employees, department managers and human resource personnel must work closely together to have a process to continually look at appropriate pay scales.

Adequate time needs to be given for conducting a thorough examination, which considers factors for hospital-specific variations, rather than being pressured into a change because of one valued employee. If Carl's analysis does reaffirm that the position should not be upgraded, this needs to be properly communicated back to the department, but also to the top-level administrators with the supporting documentation clearly presented. This will make any complaints as to the upgrade denial impotent.

To strengthen the enforcement of his recommendation and prevent this situation from reoccurring, Carl needs to conduct management training to go over the salary review process. Carl seems to have a good handle on how to proceed, but this information has not been transmitted to the department managers. Many times, departments that are highly functional, such as human resources, consider themselves as the "experts" and withhold information as a method of exerting control. A broader, system-wide perspective needs to be considered that includes a more participative approach to personnel management.

RESPONSE 78

SEEKING THE LIMITS

A common approach available for clarifying the limits of your authority involves testing your boundaries by cautiously making decisions that fall in that gray area of doubt concerning how far you can go. In even the best of circumstances, boundary testing takes courage and self-confidence, and apparently working for Jackson is anything but the best of circumstances. Jackson's perception of your limits is flexible to the extent of the quality of the outcomes of your decisions; that is, he seems not to care if you overstep your authority as long as the results are satisfactory. And you have experienced his reaction when the results are *not* satisfactory. So the present limits of your authority, if there are indeed any, are flexible according to circumstances.

First, determine whether there is a job description for your position. If so, review what it says, if anything, about the authority of your position, and plan on requesting a meeting with Jackson to strengthen the job description and seek agreement on what it should say concerning how far you can go. In preparing for this meeting, draft an updated version of the job description reflecting the position as you envision it. Let Jackson know that you are aware of the demands on his time and that you would like to be as supportive of him as you can, and to do so you need well-defined limits governing what you can and cannot do. Bring up the recent instances described in the case as examples showing that you need more specific decision-making guidance.

You may be unsuccessful in your efforts to get Jackson to clarify the limits of your authority. If so, as long as you report to this individual, you will most likely approach questionable decision situations cautiously, perhaps taking small chances while avoiding significant risks, and attempt to default potentially troublesome issues to Jackson himself. It is unfortunate that Jackson's style and approach place his subordinate managers in a position of having to manage defensively, but this condition is a sad reality encountered in some working relationships.

Response 79

A Peer Problem

In addressing the problem she is experiencing with Carl Stratton, Sally Lowe might consider the following approaches:

1. Speak directly with Stratton, telling him of her observations and concerns and asking him to be more attentive to his responsibilities.
2. Talk with others of the staff, PAs and nurses and others as necessary, to determine the extent to which Stratton might be just "her problem," or whether there are similar concerns among others who have simply not yet spoken to any of them.
3. Speak directly with the emergency department director, Dr. Markis, about her concerns with Stratton's behavior and performance.

People who are consistently not pulling their own weight in a group situation, as may be the case with Carl Stratton, eventually come under criticism by a number of group members. It may be that Sally, because she is apparently the person who works most closely with Stratton most of the time, is simply the first person to feel the strain apparently created by Stratton's behavior. However, whatever Sally chooses to do, she will have to reveal her dissatisfaction and concern to Stratton himself, thus potentially alienating Stratton.

Sally should probably begin by speaking to Stratton alone and airing her concerns. However, she would best do so by framing her remarks in a way that reflects her concern for the department and its overall effectiveness in serving its patients. That is, she should take the broader view encompassing the department as a team rather than the narrow view that might sound like personal complaining on her part. It may help for her to remind Stratton that they are both supposedly professionals working within a group of professionals, and that how any one of them is viewed by others can be a reflection on the entire group. She should also consider asking Stratton whether all is right with him; that is, giving him the chance to reveal whether there is any problem that might be affecting his performance.

Speaking with others of the group becomes riskier for Sally because no matter how well she approaches it, her efforts will likely be seen by Stratton as complaining about him to the rest of the department. On the positive side, doing so will likely set some of the others thinking about their own experiences with Stratton and will probably sensitize them to the situation such that they will be more tuned in to Stratton's behavior. If enough of the staff have genuine concerns about Stratton, peer pressure may eventually place him in a "shape up or ship out" position.

Sally might be able to accomplish something by speaking directly with Dr. Markis, but doing so as her first choice would be almost certain to alienate Stratton and possibly certain others of the staff. The crew of the emergency department might consist mostly of professionals, but even professionals will often take a dim view of someone who is perceived as tattling on one of their number.

Although problems with Carl Stratton persist, Sally should attempt to do her best under the circumstances but should also remain well aware of the ways in which Stratton's behavior could be affecting her performance. For example, if Sally were to be criticized for not completing a particular task in timely fashion her response might be that she had to first redo an important task that had been done improperly. She need not even name Stratton for it to become evident before long that it is his lack of real effort that is causing extra work for Sally—and for others.

In a group that is expected to function as a team, any team member not pulling his or her weight will be noticeable. Because of her position relative to Stratton, Sally may simply be the first to notice his behavior. Eventually, most of the group will notice and the leader will notice and something will be done about the substandard contributor.

Response 80

The Orphan Supplies

Jerry has obviously opened the door to a significant problem that could have serious implications for the central supply group, the purchasing department, and any others who are involved in requesting, ordering, and stocking such material. Also, in addition to making the hospital vulnerable in the event of a safety inspection, this condition would not be looked upon favorably during an accreditation survey. One might wonder how the corridor stock condition managed to exist for any length of time without drawing strong criticism; perhaps the basement level was seldom visited by outsiders.

Either the hospital's systems for requesting, ordering, receiving, and stocking material were weak and outmoded, or these systems were only partially utilized as intended. It would seem that the latter was more likely the case because of missing signatures and missing receiving copies.

In addition, someone in administration, finance, or both could be justifiably upset over the amount of money tied up in idle and perhaps useless stock.

It sounds as though the two groups that might be most responsible for the overstock—central supply and purchasing—are both actively avoiding any possibility of responsibility for the condition. Although active exercise of authority does not seem to enter into problem, certainly failure to fulfill certain responsibilities plays a strong role in the state of affairs that Jerry found.

For materials that may be grossly overstocked, such as the item of which a 10-year supply was on hand, it might be possible to recover some of their value by working an arrangement with the original vendor or other using organizations. Circumstances also suggest that this hospital's purchasing system should be closely examined, with the possibility of complete overhaul occurring in the near future. There must be a rational approach in place for responding to purchase request, determining how much to stock and when to reorder, and generally keeping track of all material coming into the hospital and going out to using departments.

RESPONSE 81

THE EMPLOYEE WHO IS ALWAYS RIGHT

When Wilma said, "You always turn things around so that you look innocent or correct," she generalized; she was not addressing a specific instance. A wise individual once said, *All generalizations are dangerous, including this one.* Rarely, if ever, can a generalization be successfully defended. Also, Wilma used absolute terminology, specifically "always." Words such as "always" and "never" leave no room for exceptions; they describe an all-or-nothing situation that simply does not apply in interpersonal communication.

In this specific situation, the only way that Wilma can begin to get at the cause of the misunderstanding and accomplish anything constructive is to bring the three of them together: Wilma, Janice, and Dr. Gordon. However, if Wilma cannot achieve this meeting—after all, she cannot order Dr. Gordon to participate—she would do best to avoid writing a "disciplinary dialogue" on Janice; doing so would amount to taking disciplinary action based on hearsay.

In her future dealings with "the employee who is always right," Wilma must:

- Address only specifics and avoid generalizations.
- Not "save up" criticisms, but rather deal with a specific situation immediately after its occurrence.
- Make notes of every counseling-type contact she has with Janice.
- Make certain that she is absolutely correct concerning the matter at hand.
- Rely on firsthand knowledge only, avoiding criticizing or disciplining based on hearsay.

RESPONSE 82

THE DRILL SERGEANT

Concerning her staff, it was stated that Dianne had "known most of these people for several years." This in itself should be a clue to some possible weaknesses in Dianne's management style. If she enjoyed a truly open communicating relationship with her employees, complaints about Eve would probably have been reaching her all along. This suggests that Dianne should work more on communication. However, she at least related well enough to her people to receive apparently honest answers about Eve's performance when she asked.

It states that Dianne "knew nothing about how Eve was functioning as weekend charge because she had never seen Eve in action in that capacity." This highlights another potential weakness in Dianne's style. As manager, Dianne bears some responsibility for what goes on in the unit at all times and certainly bears responsibility for the performance of a charge nurse that she, Dianne, put in place. A conscientious manager in Dianne's position would casually "drop in" while Eve was in charge and check on how things were going. Dianne made the same mistake that many, managers and others alike, regularly make: They implicitly assume that all is well because they hear nothing to the contrary.

Dianne needs to assess the litany of complaints she has received and condense them to a few important and pertinent problems in preparation for speaking with Eve. It is within Dianne's authority to lay out some of what she has heard for discussion with Eve, and do so without naming names. Much of what Dianne has heard is legitimate feedback on Eve's performance and should be discussed with Eve. And Dianne needs to be timely about this; it is not appropriate for her to wait until performance evaluation time. Dianne cannot legitimately take any kind of disciplinary action at this stage because everything she has is secondhand information; however, feedback from customers (and employees are indeed internal customers), always secondhand in nature, cannot be ignored.

It is more than likely that Eve had never received any sort of training about supervising people, and apparently Dianne put Eve in this position with little thought about having one enter supervision—and a weekend charge position is indeed supervision, although of entry level—with no more preparation than conferral of a title.

Dianne needs to lay out the apparent problem for Eve, acknowledge Eve's capabilities as a nurse, review the apparent shortcomings indicated by Eve's behavior in the charge position, tell Eve what needs to change, provide Eve with appropriate training or guidance in supervision, and, if Eve elects to remain a charge person, monitor Eve's performance through regular visits and discussions.

Response 83

The Tyrant

Office manager Wende Carlson finds herself in the position of a great many managerial, administrative, and support personnel in health care organizations: They work in conjunction with physicians who, although not in positions of authority in the chain of command, may wield implied or assumed authority stemming from or growing out of automatic organizational deference to physicians in general. In other words, many physicians who have no managerial standing in the organization can get away with "managing" because of the importance that attaches to the role of physician.

Wende certainly needs to discuss the incident with Sue, the apparent victim of Dr. Greer's outburst. This discussion should take place in private after Sue has calmed down enough to deal with her feelings and her reaction to the incident, perhaps 2 or 3 days after the problem occurred. Wende should give Sue the opportunity to tell what happened in her own words and at her own pace, preferably without interruption except perhaps to request clarification of something said.

Even conceding Sue's booking error as a genuine mistake, it's still relatively safe to say that Dr. Greer was way out of line in the way he addressed the error with Sue. He called her names, he threatened her employment, and not only did he criticize in anger, which is rarely if ever acceptable, he delivered his criticism in public, which is never appropriate. It is bad enough for the doctor to berate one employee in the presence of others, and inexcusable for him to do so in the presence of patients.

What Wende can do and how she should do it will depend largely on the strength of the management in her chain of command. She could of course ask Dr. Greer for some time to discuss the incident, and do so when tempers are even and rational discussion is possible. If the incident occurred under truly stressful conditions it might perhaps be readily resolved when the pressure is off. Should she encounter resistance from Dr. Greer she may have to address the issue with her organizational superior. Wende may find that she has appropriate backing when needed, or she may find—unfortunately—that her boss is fearful of "taking on" a physician.

It has been suggested that this is probably not the only time Dr. Greer has teed off on an employee; recall the reference to him being "a bear most of the time." If working conditions become increasingly stressful because of this person's behavior, some employees may quit rather than continue to face the doctor's temper. Should Sue decide to resign, she—and anyone else who leaves for similar reasons—should be encouraged to give Human Resources some frank and honest answers in the exit interview. Management deserves to know why employees leave their jobs whether or not they make specific use of this information.

Response 84

The Busy Boss Delegates

The first two paragraphs of the case description that suggest Tom Netter's espoused belief "in active delegation of authority and active participative management" was probably little more than lip service. The seeds for resistance to his delegation were planted earlier in his apparent unwillingness to delegate anything of substance. He was on something of a prolonged ego trip in being identified "so strongly with so many important functions."

Tom Netter's primary failing in his working relationship with his subordinate managers—or at least a significant failing—was his apparent neglect of the necessity to develop subordinates. The manner in which he ultimately "delegated" made it plain that he was peeling off and dumping on his subordinates those responsibilities that he least wanted to be bothered with. This is not delegation; it is simply dumping—and any reasonably intelligent subordinate can readily tell the difference. Any time the perception is that the boss is "delegating" by attempting to shed the apparently undesirable tasks and sticking employees with them, the delegation is destined to cause resentment and resistance.

Tom Netter has a great deal of ground to make up with his subordinate managers before he can effectively delegate to them. Rather than simply handing off the unwanted tasks, he needs to make up his mind to delegate tasks that can be seen as learning and growth opportunities. Whenever delegation is contemplated, the employee to whom the task is given has every right to ask, perhaps not in so many words but in effect, "What's in it for me?" To overcome his subordinate managers' resistance—a chore that could consume a long period of time—Netter needs to delegate thoroughly and highly selectively, taking considerable time to instruct and motivate the employee, and be certain he is delegating something of significance and not something that will immediately be seen as "something I'm stuck with because Tom doesn't like doing it."

RESPONSE 85

THE MANAGEMENT EXPERT

If Walt does indeed act as though he has all the answers, a few good doses of reality could go a long way toward tempering his attitude. Although Walt's behavior change is obviously related to his recent educational experiences, he is nevertheless coming across as the typical know-it-all who plagues many managers. The surest way to deal with this or any know-it-all is to place him in a position in which his beliefs or ideas are tested in practice.

First, however, and already mentioned in the case description but of sufficient importance to repeat, Walt needs to understand that all criticism, whether of George or anyone else, must always be delivered privately, one-on-one. Whenever criticism is applicable to a single party, it is never appropriate to criticize that party in front of others. (This is so fundamental to interpersonal relationships that George may be tempted to suggest that Walt must not have yet heard that advice in his school program.)

When Walt advances an idea for doing something differently than it is being done, George might try putting the task in Walt's hands if circumstances permit. Perhaps Walt is approaching a state of obnoxiousness, rendering George chronically annoyed. If George can overcome his annoyance long enough to do some thoughtful delegating, he can be placing Walt in a put-up-or-shut-up position. There is no better way to deal with the know-it-all than to let him implement his idea in his own way. If it fails to work, perhaps the know-it-all has learned something. If it works, perhaps the manager has learned something.

On the positive side, Walt, a good technical performer, is interested and enthusiastic. If George can help Walt learn what often occurs when theory meets practice, Walt could further develop as a productive employee with potential for advancement.

As concerns Walt's posture on some of the larger issues, for instance the organization's budgeting approach and performance appraisal process, Walt has to understand that these are processes for which so-called experts go in different directions. For example, from one teacher Walt may hear that anniversary-date appraisal is the only way to go; from another, he may learn that all-at-once appraisal is best. As to how such processes are addressed in this particular organization, it would perhaps help if Walt could meet informally with certain executives (finance director, human resource manager, etc.) to discuss why these are done as they are.

Overall, if George can suppress his annoyance with Walt and avoid feeling threatened by him, he can help Walt become all the more valuable to the organization.

RESPONSE 86

NO LONGER PULLING HER WEIGHT

Mary is correct in believing she cannot let matters remain the way they are because doing so could hurt the entire unit. Other employees may be sympathetic toward Eleanor, but that sympathy will begin to weaken when others start feeling increased pressure because of this person who cannot keep up with the unit's demands. Eleanor is apparently considered a "nice" person by the others, and Mary has probably already discovered that it is more difficult to deal with a problem employee who is pleasant and agreeable than one who is unpleasant and disagreeable.

All likely options should begin with Mary having a serious talk with Eleanor, putting the situation before her firmly but kindly: You have been unable to keep up with the increasing demands of the unit, and your inability to do so is placing extra burdens on the remainder of the staff. Something appears to be wrong, and we would like to make it possible for you to learn what the matter is and do something about it.

After acknowledging the presence of a problem, Mary could address Eleanor's problem by:

- Suggesting that Eleanor seek transfer to another, less demanding unit
- Offering Eleanor an assessment by Employee Health to determine what sort of work—her present job or any other—she could capably perform
- Suggesting that Eleanor seek help through the Employee Assistance Program (EAP) in addressing any problem that might exist

Nice person or otherwise, Eleanor should be expected to keep up with the demands of whatever job she holds. Eleanor's problem may be related to age; some peoples' physical capacities decline more rapidly than others' as they age. Or perhaps Eleanor is experiencing some health problem or personal difficulty of which Mary and others in the unit are unaware. In dealing with Eleanor, it is important that Mary remember to avoid asking Eleanor about her personal problems, if any. Eleanor may tell Mary whatever she wishes to tell her voluntarily, but as manager Mary should always avoid questioning an employee about personal matters. Mary, or any manager similarly situated, may—and should—refer an employee to a source of help (such as Employee health, EAP, etc.) but should never ask about the employee's problems and never presume to give the employee advice (even if the employee asks for advice on a personal matter).

Mary might diplomatically suggest that Eleanor consider transfer if she felt she might cope better in another assignment, but that is as far as Mary should go.

All employees may reasonably be expected to meet the demands of their positions. Regardless of an employee's age or other status, what counts in the end is the person's ability to meet the demands of the job; and because Eleanor seems no longer able to do so, some action needs to be taken.

Response 87

She's Having a Rough Time

In this particular situation there may well be no single course of action available that does not have significant obstacles associated with it.

Janet Carling certainly seems aware that differential treatment—treating one employee differently from others based on that one person's particular circumstances—is inappropriate in the work place. Janet, and perhaps some of the other employees in the department as well, may be inclined to allow Dale Hamlin considerable slack because they like her and know that she has a legitimate chronic health problem. However, such treatment, no matter how well intended, can in fact be discriminatory.

The organization offers paid time off, such as sick time, vacation, and perhaps personal time; therefore, there are undoubtedly policies in place governing the use of these benefits. It is likely that there is also a policy addressing absenteeism. As difficult as it may be for Janet to do so, she is obligated to treat Dale, with her legitimate problem, the same way she would treat another chronic absentee who was thought to be working the system for maximum time off. Janet clearly feels the need to do something because Dale's behavior is noticeably affecting the other employees.

Janet has already outlined the alternatives that would ordinarily be most workable in this kind of a situation; that is, change Dale's hours or possibly make her part-time instead of full-time. Letting Dale continue indefinitely taking unpaid time off is not appropriate because it shifts the burden of completing her work onto the few others in the department.

Note, however, two potentially significant problems that could make it next to impossible for Janet to act reasonably: The character of higher management (recall the reference to *Mister Indecision*), and the likelihood that Mr. Miller is "pulling rank" on behalf of a relative. This implied behavior of Miller's is of course inappropriate, but as the old anonymous saying goes, *The boss ain't always right—but the boss is always the boss.*

Probably the best direct action that Janet can take without openly defying her immediate superior is to factually report to Mr. Miller every legitimate problem or delay resulting from Dale's situation and ask for direction. Other than that, she would be well advised to take her dilemma to the appropriate person in the human resources department.

Response 88

Discharge for Cause

It appears evident from the first two paragraphs of the case that the employees of Benton Memorial Hospital were subjected to a dramatic change of leadership style with the replacement of an easygoing, low-key chief executive by one who is fast-paced, brusque, and intimidating. Therefore, it is reasonable to suppose that Mrs. Jackson and other managers might be apprehensive about dealing with the new chief executive. Mrs. Jackson may have felt she had good reason to fear Mr. Short's wrath, especially if she had already seen other managers adversely affected by this "new broom."

Mrs. Jackson's primary error, of course, was her failure to admit up front that policy and procedure had not been followed in approving overtime. There could have been a good chance that she might have escaped with no more than a reprimand and an admonition to follow proper practices in the future. However, in choosing to deny any wrongdoing and cover her tracks after the fact, she committed infractions that could well cost anyone their employment.

She was initially untruthful in claiming she had misplaced the logs, and it is unlikely that claiming she "saw no good reason why he should need them" would have dissuaded Mr. Short.

Mrs. Jackson's after-the-fact creation of the overtime logs, definitely poor judgment on her part, constituted a clear case of falsification of information, a serious infraction in most organizations and one consistently addressed in policy.

Clara Jackson was again untruthful when she denied creating the logs, and it is not likely that her subsequent admission of doing so could have erased the impact of the lie. Her admitted fear of relating the truth would not be likely to go far on her behalf in establishing a reasonable defense of her actions.

Also, Mrs. Jackson's direct appeal to hospital trustees, a route often attempted in smaller communities in which everyone knows everyone else, would do nothing to endear her to management. (Any member of a board of trustees who attempts to intercede on behalf of an employee is out of line as a trustee by becoming involved in operational issues.)

It is most likely that the discharge of Mrs. Jackson would be upheld on the bases of violation of policy (by failing to follow the overtime authorization procedure) and falsification of records (by creating the overtime logs after the fact).

RESPONSE 89

THE "DEMANDING" MANAGER

Alan has of course encountered significant resistance to change, deep-seated resistance stemming from his efforts to alter a pattern of behavior not only tolerated by his predecessor but actually instilled and encouraged by the retiring Fred. The problem most likely became a problem because of Fred and his management style and approach. Although we are not told how long Fred was in charge of this group, the situation suggests that he was in place more than long enough to have hired all of the present staff and to have himself "set the pace" for the group. Fred apparently used the "difficult nature of much of the work" to rationalize a slow and supposedly careful approach to the work.

Fred let the employees "work independently at their own pace," utilizing a hands-off style that many technical and professional employees naturally prefer. However, Fred seems to have avoided communicating any real concerns about productivity. We may have cause to wonder why "relations with the line departments . . . were generally good" if there was "always a considerable backlog of repairs and calibration work." It is likely that Fred was well liked beyond the borders of his department; one can bet that Fred would have been encouraged to behave differently if the line departments constantly complained about slow service. The department may well have consisted of "a cohesive group of people with high morale and upbeat attitudes" because Fred was a friendly individual who demanded little of employees and generally let them have their own way. Fred had essentially conditioned the employees to accept their continuing low level of output as the norm.

It was fully appropriate for Alan to get involved in personally working together with someone in the group on the more challenging repair jobs; doing so could demonstrate that greater productivity was within their reach. However, his individual productivity reports may have been introduced too soon or perhaps called for too much detail. Alan should certainly have first expressed his observations to the staff and opened up a dialogue on productivity before starting to track individual productivity.

If he has not already done so, Alan needs to ensure that his immediate superior is up to date on the situation in biomedical engineering. A pair of simultaneous resignations would no doubt raise some questions in administration and human resources because it amounts to one third of Alan's staff walking out. Alan needs to convince his boss that he is right in trying to improve productivity, and then proceed cautiously with every reasonable effort to involve his employees in determining what should change and by how much. It could take Alan many months to cement a good working relationship with his employees.

Also, if Alan is correct about industry standards of productivity, departing employees who may be hired into another organization's biomedical engineering department will quickly learn that more is expected of them than they have been accustomed to doing.

RESPONSE 90

THE UNCOOPERATIVE COLLEAGUE

Melinda's advice to Irene might legitimately begin with the suggestion that Irene start over again in trying to talk with Tami. This time, however, Irene should go armed with a written list of specifics. This is not to say that Irene should bombard Tami with all of her gripes large and small at one time; rather, Irene's list of specifics should consist of the three or four most glaring problems, those with potential quality implications; for example, packs assembled incorrectly, work left half done, sterility requirements ignored, etc.

If talking specifics with Tami does no good, Irene should report this back to Melinda and talk about what to do next. Melinda may agree that it is time for Irene to discuss the situation with her manager, the person who is also most likely Tami's manager as well. In talking with her manager, Irene needs to be calm and rational and not simply dump all of her complaints on her boss. Irene should attempt to get her manager sufficiently interested in her situation to make some personal observations, including dropping in unannounced on Tami's shift. However, Irene must proceed cautiously; the manager *should* be paying sufficient attention to all of his or her subordinate supervisors, but this may not be the case. All too often, a second-shift group in a service area does not receive sufficient management attention.

It almost always makes one uneasy to go "telling tales" on a colleague, so Irene should first make every reasonable effort to deal with Tami directly before going to their manager. In the process of meeting with her manager, Irene might suggest the use of a log in which various problems and conditions can be described by any supervisor for consideration of the following shift.

Response 91

The Informant

In frustration, Estelle might wish that the "informant" would never bring her any information at all. This assumes that Estelle is aware that it is likely that she cannot directly use anything Edwina brings to her, for two reasons: first, repeating what Edwina said could put this valuable volunteer at odds with some staff members and create dissension within the group; and second, an inviolable rule of discipline, action must never be taken based on secondhand information, that is, hearsay.

Most managers whose departments that make use of volunteers would regard a steady, reliable, hard-working volunteer as an asset to be nurtured. Therefore, Estelle will most likely want to keep Edwina in place and so may do nothing to upset her, such as flatly telling her to say no more about what she observes.

This could be one of those occasional situations that the manager might best quietly tolerate or address only peripherally and extremely diplomatically. Consider the "scary part" as stated by Estelle, *"—every time I've been able to check out something she's told me, it turns out that she's absolutely correct."*

Estelle should listen carefully to what Edwina has to say and try to differentiate between what is substantive and what seems to be gossip. Perhaps she can gently discourage the gossip; surely most thoughtful supervisors have had experience in squelching rumors—the substantive information she should keep to herself. It will be sufficient that what she has heard will raise her awareness of certain potential problems, and she will be all the more attuned to what is occurring and will experience some of it firsthand.

In brief, Estelle should continue to listen to Edwina, discourage gossip and rumor, and remain tuned to potentially legitimate observations.

Response 92

Managing the Drama Queen

Although we can understand her frustrations, Janice's casual reference to Helen as the "drama queen" is a personality judgment that amounts to name calling, never part of a constructive approach in employee relations.

Based on just the information given in the case, we can only guess at the reasons for Helen's behavior. Anyone who has managed people knows that there can be vast differences in attitude and behavior in even a small group. Whether or not we know "why" a person acts or reacts in a particular manner, we still have to deal with the individual and address the behavior. Helen may simply be a sensitive individual whose lifelong reaction to criticism has involved resentment, defensiveness, and perceived injury. Or perhaps Helen is the occasional employee who has been so conditioned by unpleasant relations with previous managers that her every reaction to criticism is negative.

Unfortunately, some managers who are ill at ease addressing employees' emotional reactions compensate by diluting their criticism to the point of ineffectiveness or avoiding criticizing altogether. However, rarely does a problem that's unaddressed go away of its own accord, and more often than not it worsens as time goes by. So ignoring or soft-pedaling deserved criticism is never appropriate.

In dealing with Helen, Janice must initially ensure that any criticism she delivers is truly constructive; that is, it should always include suggestions for correction or improvement. Also, it is evident in the case information that Janice is well aware of the need to always address criticism with an employee one-on-one, in private. In dealing with someone who appears as sensitive to criticism and prone to defensiveness as Helen, Janice should take great pains to be factual, specific, and totally objective in both the rendering of the problem and what must be done to correct the situation. Janice must stick to facts—never, as most managers are aware, relying on hearsay—and proceed diplomatically; and proceed she must, without being put off by frowns, anger, defensiveness, or tears.

Our best advice for Janice in dealing with Helen is to be certain she is always focused on the problem, not on the person. She must look at the results of behavior— "This is what was incorrect" —and never attempt to second-guess the cause of the behavior that led to the results; for example, "You're stubborn and careless." Name calling and personality judgments are never appropriate.

RESPONSE 93

THE HOLIDAY SWITCH

One in Dana Daniels' position might consider advising Carrie that although this appears to be an obvious planned occurrence, two infractions do not constitute enough of a pattern to assume that Sue is pursuing this practice deliberately. This especially holds true if the nurse manager can recall only one other occurrence. Many people want to be with their families on holidays and some are inclined to claim illness on these days. Sue may not have been sick, but there is no way of knowing for certain.

Carrie should consider holding an informal counseling session with Sue. Without making accusations, Carrie should advise Sue of the inconvenience created when she fails to honor her revised schedule in full. Depending on the state of Sue's overall attendance record, Carrie might need to suggest that chronic or consistent absence can become cause for disciplinary action. Yet Carrie cannot take any action against Sue at this time; she must take Sue's claim of "illness" at face value and move on.

Carrie might also try to stimulate interest in revisiting the organizational policy that allows taking the alternate day off *before* the actual holiday. If the alternate day must be taken *after* the holiday, this closes what some employees may see as a loophole in the organization's attendance policy. Such a policy change might be seriously considered if the "holiday switch" problem seems to arise with noticeable regularity.

Response 94

The Elusive Employee

In some organized activities, and especially in certain areas of health care, it is not unusual for some employees who work evenings, nights, or split shifts to be off on their own for extended periods. Such employees are admittedly often more difficult to supervise. However, given the nature of some healthcare organizations, particularly hospitals, these different shift assignments are essentially necessary. Therefore it falls to the immediate supervisor to determine how to oversee such employees.

Claiming that Dan "seems to be" getting the work done but that it is "hard to tell because I just don't see him" may suggest that Dan is indeed elusive, and it can also suggest that perhaps Vera has not done all that she should be doing as supervisor. It is not enough to make a couple of attempts to telephone Dan from home; Vera should make an effort to occasionally "drop in" during Dan's shift to see how he is doing. As long as Dan is technically Vera's employee, Vera bears a measure of responsibility for Dan's performance.

As to whether Dan is actually responding to stat calls when he says he is, the truth could be established if he was required to maintain an activity log that provides a record of such calls and the times they were received.

There are two ways available for Vera to stay more closely in touch with Dan's activities. One is the provision of more direct supervision by Vera herself. This may consist of occasional unscheduled visits by Vera, her implementation of the aforementioned activity log, and—quite important—crystal clear productivity expectations communicated to Dan. The other way is one approach often taken under such circumstances: The individual who works the off-shift without benefit of immediate supervision is required to report to whoever is in charge of the "house" at that time, in this instance, perhaps the night nursing supervisor. If Vera does indeed see Dan for only about 10 percent of the shift, Dan should be required to answer to someone else during the other 90 percent. With this more complete coverage, Vera and the night nursing supervisor may be able to keep better tracks of the "elusive" one and also collaborate on a reasonable performance evaluation.

RESPONSE 95

THIS PLACE OWES ME

Human resources representative Ellen Francis would most likely be advising Darlene to effectively start over in dealing with Jennifer Wilson, especially if there is nothing contrary in Jennifer's personnel file. We are told that there have been no disciplinary actions, and if informal counseling sessions are documented at all, such notes will likely reside in Darlene's personal files. Therefore, if there is no record of any difficulties or any attempts at correction, for all practical—and legal—purposes, she has never done anything wrong. If something is not on paper, it is regarded as never having occurred.

It should be obvious that Darlene could have avoided or at least minimized the present problem by using the organization's progressive discipline policy, which usually begins with counseling, to address chronic absenteeism or sick time abuse when Jennifer's conduct first reached the problem threshold; and of course Darlene should be applying such policies equally to all other employees who exhibit behavior similar to Jennifer's. It would also be helpful if Darlene were able to implement a rotational scheme for covering vacations or illnesses or assigning overtime.

Needed policies are primarily those that address employee counseling and progressive discipline, especially as concerns attendance.

The problem Jennifer presents is one of attitude as much as behavior; and it is a fundamental premise of discipline that one cannot discipline for "attitude," but must focus on behavior. The organization "owes" Jennifer certain considerations that have been extended as part of the employment relationship, but Jennifer owes the organization reasonable job performance and adherence to rules and regulations. Should Jennifer be treated more favorably than other employees who do the same work simply because she has worked there longer? Perhaps in some small ways like observing seniority in vacation scheduling or such, but not to the extent of exempting her from rules and regulations that others must observe.

Response 96

He Didn't Work Out

This is one of those instances in which we might see considerable truth in the adage, *The boss isn't always right—but the boss is always the boss.* Certainly, Jackson dodged responsibility by ordering Young to get rid of Kelly, although one might try to build an argument to the contrary because Kelly was indeed Young's employee. Still, Jackson chose to exercise the authority of his position in the hiring process, reasoning that Young, being new to management and never having interviewed and hired, needed to learn about the employee selection process. When Kelly did not work out and had to be released, Jackson behaved as though there was nothing to be learned about terminating an employee so Young could handle the task. However, most everyone who has hired and fired will concede that although interviewing and hiring require a certain amount of insight and caution, firing someone is much more troublesome to the person who has to do the firing. Jackson deferred the unpleasant task to Young.

The most obvious alternative approach would be for Jackson and Young together to explain to Kelly why it was felt that he could not continue in the job. After all, they interviewed him together, so why not terminate him together?

This incident would probably make Young wary and cautious in his future dealings with his manager. Jackson seems not to hesitate to exercise the authority of his position but he is apparently inclined to back away from responsibility when matters do not go his way. It is fundamental to management that with acceptance of authority comes an equal measure of responsibility. In avoiding responsibility, Jackson is avoiding some of the less pleasant or less favored parts of the management role. This represents a weakness that could at times make life trying for Young in answering to Jackson. If Young is intelligent and conscientious, he will soon learn to regard some elements of Jackson's behavior as lessons in how not to manage.

RESPONSE 97

TAKE YOUR CHOICE

There is only one reasonable choice that is consistent with the fundamentals of management and the rules of proper delegation, whether ad hoc or formal, through the creation of an organizational hierarchy, and that is the first choice: You step into the job with the full authority and responsibility of the position as experienced by your predecessor. It is absolutely fundamental in any management position or delegated activity that the authority to decide and act and the responsibility for doing so exist in equivalent amounts.

Concerning the second choice, assuming the full authority of the position but with somewhat reduced responsibility, might be appealing to you, but it would be bad for the organization. Under this, you could often act or decide at will and not have to answer for results.

The third choice, having equal responsibility and authority but at a lesser level than your predecessor, would actually weaken the position to the extent of reducing its effectiveness.

The final choice, assuming the full responsibility of the position but exercising less authority than your predecessor, is a poor choice for the organization and the worst possible choice for you. This choice would leave you responsible for results over which you had no authority, effectively holding you responsible for actions in which you have no voice.

Response 98

Why Should I?

"Because I said so, that's why!" is of course not a legitimate response, and it is not surprising that it can increase hostility in the party to whom it is spoken. It might spur the individual to action, but compliance will be unwilling at best. A reasonable response to her question might be, "Because this has to be done, and it falls within your capability."

Take a close look at the individual's job description; you may be able to point to that often used but frequently forgotten clause that in one fashion or another calls for the performance of "all other tasks as directed by supervision." If no such clause is present, revise the job description to include it. A reasonable job description for a technical or professional worker cannot possibly include everything the individual might legitimately be called upon to do, so a catch-all requirement is fully appropriate. If the job description must in fact be revised, invite the employee to participate in the revision. However, whether she does or does not choose to participate, do not give up the addition of the catch-all requirement. If her job description is one of a kind, you might consider making it extremely detailed, although this is more of a stop-gap measure than a solution.

If she continues to balk, politely suggest that her behavior is approaching insubordination, which it will in fact become if she directly refuses to comply.

There is one set of circumstances under which she might legitimately refuse to do something not listed in her job description: If she belongs to a union that has in its contract a strict requirement to adhere to the contents of job descriptions.

Response 99

The Drop-in Visitor

Many supervisors seem to feel they are being rude if they do not welcome drop-in visitors, be they sales representatives or fellow supervisors or others. However, it is the visitors who are being rude or at least presumptuous by dropping in unannounced and expecting the normally busy supervisor to drop all else and make time for them.

Some organizations do not allow sales persons to go directly to department supervisors and managers but rather require them to go through the purchasing department. However, many sales representatives seem to believe they are more likely to meet with a favorable response from individual managers, so some often try to bypass purchasing.

The first suggestion to offer Janet and other supervisors who are similarly situated is to require sales persons to visit purchasing, or, if going through purchasing is not a requirement, to call the department secretary in advance and make an appointment. Supervisors do not have to feel they must make time for any outsider who drops in without an appointment.

Other supervisors will often drop in to socialize or perhaps address a small item of business, the discussion of which wanders off into social conversation. However, you do not need to let others waste your time. It is always possible to limit the time that others tie you up with nonessentials, and to do so with tact and diplomacy.

Returning to consideration of Janet's problem, she could have not agreed to see the drop-in sales representative. She was certainly in a position to honestly state that she was trying to finish something important before going to a meeting in 1 hour.

Your time can be consumed by your employees, other employees, other supervisors, vendors and other outsiders, and higher management. Without being abrupt and without ignoring anyone, you can generally control the extent to which others consume your time. The one exception to this, or at least the direction from which demands on your time are hardest to regulate, is higher management. It is often extremely difficult to control the extent to which your immediate superior wastes your time. That, however, is a completely different problem.

RESPONSE 100

PROMOTION

This case represents circumstances in which numerous workers find themselves upon promotion to supervision: being placed in a position of authority over persons with whom they have worked for a prolonged period of time and with whom they have perhaps even socialized as friends.

Some of the advantages you find in your new position are obvious: You know the department and its tasks, you know how this department relates to the rest of the organization, you know the hospital's management structure, and you know the employees as individuals. These are all advantages that would not be available to a new supervisor coming from outside the organization.

The disadvantages of you new position are obvious as well: You must now direct the activities of, give orders and instructions to, and perhaps even discipline, former coworkers, acquaintances, and friends. Some resentment over your appointment is to be expected; it is likely that one or two of the other employees would like to have received the promotion.

If you do your job as you should, it will not be necessary to consciously "pull away" from these people with whom you have worked for so long. The job will do that for you; there will be expectations of you that will necessarily pull you partially away to the extent of making you part of a management group as well as part of the department.

As far as your relationships with former coworkers are concerned, the most important term to apply is *consistency*. You should consider it essential to be constantly aware of the need to treat everyone in the department equally, apply all policies consistently to all individuals in all cases, cultivate a one-to-one relationship with every employee, and avoid all appearances of favoritism. It can become extremely troublesome if one or more of your "friends" expects or demands favored treatment. If this occurs, it is time for you to reexamine individual relationships: A true friend will understand your position and not presume upon your friendship.

Part IV

Variations and Conclusions

VARIATIONS ON THE CASE STUDY METHOD

Role-Plays

A large number of work situations, including many that lend themselves to use as case studies, can be adapted to role-playing situations in which individuals assume certain positions and act out a problem and attempt to find a mutually agreeable solution. The following is an example of a potential case (not from the 100 presented in this book) adapted to a role-playing exercise.

"It's a Policy" *The setting is an 82-bed hospital located in a small city.*

One day, an employee of the maintenance department asked his manager, Mr. Mann, for an hour or two off in which to take care of some personal business. Mann agreed, and asked the employee to stop at the garden equipment shop and buy several lawnmower parts the department needed.

While transacting business in a local bank, the employee was seen by Mr. Carter who supervised both personnel and payroll for the hospital and was in the bank on hospital business. Carter asked the employee what he was doing there and was told the visit was personal.

Upon returning to the hospital, Carter examined the employee's time card. The man had not punched out to indicate when he had left the hospital. Carter noted the time the employee returned, and after the normal working day he marked the card to indicate an absence of 2 hours on personal business. Carter advised the administrator, Mrs. Arnold, of what he had done, citing a longstanding policy (in their dusty and infrequently used policy and procedure manual) requiring an employee to punch out when leaving the premises on personal business. Mrs. Arnold agreed with Carter's action.

Carter advised Mann of the action and stated that the employee would not be paid for the 2 hours he was gone.

Mann was angry. He said he had told the employee not to punch out because he had asked him to pick up some parts on his trip. Carter replied that Mann had no business doing what he had done and that it was his—Mann's—poor management that caused the employee's loss.

Mann appealed to Mrs. Arnold to reopen the matter based on his claim that there was an important side to the story that she had not yet heard. Arnold agreed to hear both managers state their positions.

The Role Positions *Mann: You feel strongly that the employee should be paid for the 2 hours. You led him to believe he would be paid, and you also feel that in spite of the time spent on personal business, it was time well used because it saved you a trip out of the hospital.*

Carter: You believe in the policy, and you feel that the action sanctioned by Mann was contrary to the policy.

Arnold: Listen thoroughly to both Mann's and Carter's statements of position. Work with them in an attempt to develop a mutually acceptable solution to the present problem and to also provide a way to prevent the problem from recurring.

Any "solution" to the foregoing may well hinge upon whoever best states his position, as well as on how the administrator relates individually to both Mann and Carter and how she interprets the policy and its value herself. About the only near certainty that can be predicted is a decision to revisit the "dusty and infrequently used policy and procedure manual" for possible revision and updating.

Role-playing exercises can be of considerable help in zeroing in on the key difficulties in a given situation and providing experience in hammering out solutions that require some measure of compromise.

Group Responses to Questions

A frequently helpful group activity involves a number of managers—for example, the attendees at a management development session—providing their individual responses to a question, with these responses then woven into a comprehensive response. Usually provided by instructor or discussion leader, a comprehensive response merges the individual responses, weeds out the inevitable duplications, and sets forth a range of reasonable approaches to the problem presented by the question.

Each question, so employed, is initially asked by a working first-line or middle manager, so each represents a problem actually experienced by a manager on the job. Responses are not the answers of a single person, and they are not simply textbook answers. In every instance, the response is developed from suggestions offered by the peers of the manager who raised the question. This is a collaborative approach to management development: the real questions of working managers answered through the pooling of the knowledge and experience of other working managers.

The following is a brief question and the resulting range of potential solutions.

"How can I convincingly tell an employee who is 'never wrong' that she is, in fact, undeniably wrong?"

First, it is advisable to question the question itself. The employee may give the impression of forever claiming to be right, and this impression may be properly perceived by the manager, but the phrase "never wrong" is likely to be an unwarranted generalization. For that matter, "never" and "always" are risky words to use either in active interpersonal communication or when describing the acts or attitudes of people.

The employee who projects the impression of never being wrong could be self-assured to the extent of overconfidence. This employee may have a strong self-opinion and may take considerable pride in being right. This person may even be aware of truly being wrong, but may be prevented by pride from any admission of wrongdoing.

The manager should try to deal with the person in a way that avoids destroying the individual's confidence. It is invariably best to focus initially on a specific error or problem rather than dealing with generalities. That is, the manager's approach should never be, "You're making too many mistakes." Rather, the approach should be more on the order of, "Here's a specific error that we need to talk about." The manager needs to determine why the employee was wrong and help that person decide what can be done to correct the situation.

As a manager who must deal with such an employee, make certain you do your homework first. Determine beyond any reasonable doubt that the employee is, in fact, wrong and that you have the correct answer. Be certain that you have proof. In all personnel matters, you should avoid acting on hearsay or secondhand information. This is especially important with the employee who would appear to never be wrong; this person usually requires absolute proof of wrongdoing and will take no one else's word for it.

Back up your criticisms and comments with facts, proven and documented when possible. Factual information so presented is difficult to dispute. When necessary, use specific institutional policies and procedures when they apply. Policies and procedures must have been established in advance and should constitute agreed-upon guidelines for behavior. If you have no absolute proof of wrongdoing in the form of factual information, then attempt to reason with the employee to bring about an understanding of the apparent error.

In dealing with the employee, provide a nonthreatening atmosphere in which you may converse in private, one-on-one. The person who insists on always being right may show obvious rigidity, inflexibility, and resistance to change, and should be dealt with diplomatically. However, the person's tendencies may simply display a basic inability to see more than one side of a question or more than one possible answer.

In dealing with the employee who is never wrong, consider the following:

- *Open on a positive note.* Do not begin by tossing the error back in the employee's face. Rather, begin by emphasizing the individual's positive attributes (good employee, hard worker, always punctual, etc.) and dispense some reasonable praise before attempting to zero in on what may appear to be an inability to take criticism. As in many activities consisting of multiple steps, rarely has everything been done wrong; point out the correct elements of the employee's approach. You should be interested in conveying the belief that you are not "out to get" the employee. You want to convince the person that accomplishing the work of the department is a cooperative undertaking in which everyone must take part.
- *Be tactful and understanding.* Nobody can expect to be 100 percent right 100 percent of the time. In dealing with the individual who has difficulty admitting fault, you may have to be gentle and tactful to avoid affecting the individual's confidence or avoid a defensive reaction. Also, you need to let the person know that if there are personal problems affecting his or her work, you are available to listen if that is the employee's wish. Do not bring up past mistakes, but concentrate on dealing with only one current problem.
- *Stress mutual understanding and cooperation.* Convey your belief in the value of collaborating on ideas and bringing misunderstandings out into the open so they may be dealt with by all concerned. Perhaps the current solution to the problem of the moment would be of value to a number of people in the work group. Make it plain that you are looking for some common ground on which

the two of you can agree and for a chance that both of you will eventually see the situation in the same general way. Strive for compromise, recognizing that it may be necessary for each of you to give something to obtain something in return.

- *Listen carefully.* Listen to all of the employee's views and the reasons for doing what was done. Remember that in the mind of the employee, no mistake was made and no wrong was done. Should you find it necessary to draw conclusions and relate them to the employee, ask for the person's impressions of your conclusions. Be sure to question what you do not understand, listen carefully, and probe for reasons conveyed in what the employee is saying.
- *Use facts and examples.* If you must plainly point out that the employee has been wrong, get all of your facts, put them in order, and logically demonstrate what went wrong and how it should be corrected. If the problem involves job performance and there are established standards for the job, compare the actual results with the standards and explain why the difference is unacceptable. Noting that nobody is right all of the time, do not be reluctant to provide examples from your own experience. Use specific examples, and draw parallels using your performance and the performance of others to provide insight. Ask direct questions and listen carefully to the responses.
- *Participate in problem solving.* Unless there are only two possible resolutions to a situation (and rarely are there only two alternatives), you may be able to get the employee to understand that there may be multiple solutions that work, but only one or two that are acceptable for various reasons. You may be able to point out that the employee's approach is acceptable under certain circumstances, but for specific reasons a particular answer is most appropriate. Offer alternatives—again, the notion of compromise—when that is possible, and never just say that the employee is wrong and let it go at that without explaining why and what the correct approach should have been. Of course if there *are* only two possibilities, then it may have to come down to saying, "One of us is wrong." However, if it is indeed the employee who is wrong, your use of managerial authority to dictate what is right should be the last resort.
- *Communicate openly.* Attempt to be supportive. Exercise empathy, imagining yourself in the employee's place. Explore any possibilities for misinterpretation or misunderstanding in the employee's work instructions. While doing so, be alert for signs that indicate defensiveness on the part of the employee or suggest a shutdown of communication. Do not argue with the employee and do not try too hard to rationalize or defend the position you see as the right one. A view that is truly correct will usually survive attack without requiring active defense. Always leave room for discussion, keeping in mind that you are aiming for a point at which you can say, "Now we both understand." Although it may seem to be your intention, you are not actively looking for the chance to say, "Now you see it my way."
- *Follow up.* In dealing with the employee who is never wrong, you will probably accomplish little in only one interchange. You may have to exercise

patience and go through the process multiple times, focusing each time on a new specific problem, to stand any chance of changing the employee's work habits and attitude. Recognize, however, that as manager you may eventually have to insist on things being done in the way you believe is correct. Also, as follow-up, retain some documentation of your contacts for a while. It may not be necessary to enter the documentation in the employee's personnel file—unless circumstances have reached a state in which formal corrective action is necessary—but you should be able, for both your sake and the employee's, to produce a record of discussions that have taken place.

Is there quite a lot to consider in the foregoing? Certainly, but not all of the advice provided will apply in every situation. So much was said by the managers who responded to the question that the reader may be left thinking that an inordinate amount of time and effort would have to be devoted to every employee who behaves in that particular manner. Not so; there are many factors that enter into a manager's relationship with each individual employee, and it is the whole person and that individual's overall cooperativeness and productivity that will dictate the amount of attention the manager must invest in the relationship.

WHAT YOU CAN GAIN THROUGH THE CASE STUDY METHOD

Practice, Practice

The conscientious use of case studies and similar activities provides practice in analyzing problems and making decisions. Certainly a case is not the "real world," so true decision-making pressures and emotional involvement in the decision situation are missing (although adding a time constraint can contribute a certain amount of pressure, as experienced, for example, by students who are given a specific block of time to complete an examination). Yet there is a plus side to even these apparent shortcomings of the case method: One can practice decision-making techniques without the risk of damage occurring through an occasional "wrong" decision.

Because a real world decision includes personal involvement, potential consequences, and often the pressure of time, a case study cannot simulate all of the moves required in making and implementing a decision. However, a case study allows you to go through some of the necessary moves and thus more closely parallels reality than does a simple recounting of rules or principles. In one especially important way, decision making is like many other human endeavors: The more you practice, the more proficient you become.

A New Problem-Solving Outlook

Although a case is not reality, it nevertheless demonstrates the complexity of the real decision-making environment. Addressing a case requires you to retreat from theory and other abstractions and face the uncertainties of the real world. Through the case study method you learn to make necessary simplifications, to cut through a maze of apparent facts and information and create a working order that you can deal with in a practical way.

No single case ever supplies "all of the facts." In dealing with a case, just as in pondering many real-life situations, it is always possible to ask "What if . . . ?" Rarely does a manager have "all of the facts" in any but the simplest of situations.

Trying to decide without full knowledge of a situation is often frustrating, but this is an inseparable part of the manager's task. If there were fewer such frustrations, there would likely be fewer difficult decisions to make, and if there were fewer decisions to make, there would most likely be fewer managers required to make them.

In spite of the shortcomings of the case study method, however, conscientiously working your way through a number of case studies can leave you with a new outlook on problem solving. This new outlook may well include your recognition of the need to:

- Thoroughly evaluate all available information and arrange bits of information in some logical order.
- Arrange your information into meaningful patterns or decision alternatives.
- Evaluate each alternate according to the objectives to be served by the decision; and make a choice.

Rarely is there a single "right" solution to a given case. More often than not it is even difficult to say whether one particular answer is better than another. In this respect, however, the case study method supports reality: In real-world situations, what is "right" is usually relative to the conditions of the moment and the needs of the people involved.

The use of the case study method also reminds us of the true role of rules, principles, and theories. We quickly discover that rules, principles, and theories are but the tools we work with, and not the ends we are trying to serve. We learn to arrange information so we can use our tools as they are needed, rather than attempt to organize our case analyses around the tools. In other words, we learn that theory *serves* practice—it does not *dictate* practice.

To help you decide for yourself whether you are getting something from the case study method, try to asses your "answer" to each case you complete according to the following questions:

- Do my recommendations show that I fully understand the issues involved in the case?
- Given the absence of unforeseen circumstances, could my recommendations realistically solve the problem? That is, is what I decided workable given the circumstances?
- Do my recommendations appear to be as fair as possible to all parties involved in the problem?

- Do my recommendations support the goals of the organization rather than the goals of some specific person or group?
- If this were not an exercise but rather a real problem, could I live with my recommendation?

A Broadened View

The advantages of the case study method are never more apparent than when cases are considered by a group of persons working together. The multiple inputs provided by group activity serve as a strong stimulus to creativity. Ideas lead to more ideas; another person may offer an idea that had not occurred to you, and this in turn can lead you to think of something that neither of you had mentioned. Ideas—implications, possibilities, variations, what have you—build upon other ideas, and often the thought that leads to a sound solution springs from discussion of peripheral issues or matters of yet-to-be-recognized importance. Much of the time, group consideration of a case reveals more potentially productive alternatives than one person would have generated alone.

Also, different persons viewing the same case will bring different viewpoints to bear. Each of us possesses a unique viewpoint; the sum of our own attitudes, experiences, knowledge, and background. We are inclined to view the same problem in different ways; we will see some factors as more important than others because of the way we are put together.

Consider, for example, a problem concerning a request for more housekeeping personnel arising during a period when finances are severely constrained. To the finance director the dollar problems may loom as the most significant issue in the overall problem. However, the housekeeping manager, struggling with an overworked and understaffed crew, is likely to see understaffing as the critical issue. Even without professional involvement in the problem, any two managers from different disciplines may well view matters differently. The same hypothetical problem—the housekeeping staffing situation—may be viewed in two completely different ways by, say, a registered nurse and a laboratory technologist.

Differing views come from different orientations. You alone stand in a unique spot in the organization, so no one else views all things quite the same way you do. No department exists in isolation from all others in the delivery of health care, and there are few kinds of problems that do not cross departmental lines, so the views of a number of people of varying backgrounds usually contribute to the development of more numerous and comprehensive alternatives.

Group participation in case study activity also points up the need for compromise in problem solving. Again reminded that few activities and few problems in a healthcare organization are isolated from each other, any decision rendered usually has to accommodate more than one particular interest. We find that our need becomes not that of developing the "best" solution, one that may be "best" logically and economically, although it may serve the desires of but one interested party, but rather developing a solution that is fair and workable overall, one that serves the objectives of the organization rather than the desires of an individual.

THE BENEFITS OF THE CASE STUDY METHOD

In summary, the case study method of learning provides the following:

- Practice in idea generation and creative problem solving
- Familiarization with logical problem-solving processes
- Broadened perspective, owing to the sharing of ideas and viewpoints with others
- Encouragement in developing the habit of approaching problems analytically
- Some limited "practice" in solving problems and making decisions

As noted elsewhere in this book, the case study approach is only one of several methods available for presenting management development material. No manager's continuing education should rely 100 percent on the case method; many necessities—specific rules, principles, and techniques, for instance—are best acquired by other means. However, the case method has characteristics that make it worth consideration as a significant part of a manager's continuing education: It calls for the active involvement of the manager in the learning process, and it significantly narrows the gap between theory and practice.

COLLECTING YOUR OWN CASES

Material Is Where You Find It

One excellent source of material for original cases is your own experience. Many items suitable for case presentation can be found in experiences you have had in your present position and jobs you have held in the past.

Hardly a day goes by in which each working manager could not point to at least one or two instances that could be written up as cases. Such events involve all of us day in and day out. However, most potential cases slide by us unrecognized; only the truly troublesome matters remain clearly in mind after the fact. Of course the big problems, those we remember clearly, make excellent cases, but so do many of the lesser matters we regularly deal with and forget.

If you want to collect case material, your conscious decision to do so will probably remind you to remain alert for opportunities. When something happens that may later make a useful case, make note of it, briefly but in sufficient detail to allow you to recall the incident when you need to do so.

Even a relatively new manager's brief experience, say 3 or 4 months, can furnish many useful cases. None of these cases may be truly original as far as the issues they involve are concerned, but each is likely to have unique implications.

Remaining with your experience for a moment, another excellent source of case material—quite likely the best available source—is your mistakes, those perhaps painful occasions when you "learned the hard way." If you made a mistake, recognized that you erred, and benefitted from the experience, then it is likely that you have the issues clearly in mind. It is also likely that you know something about the cause of the error, why the mistake was indeed a mistake.

You may also find case material in your observations of the actions of other people, people you have worked for, those who have reported to you, and others whose working lives have touched yours. You can use secondhand information as well, stories of the experiences of other managers.

You can also fabricate cases completely from scratch. Start with a basic question, especially one on the order of "What should I do *if* . . . ?" and build a brief tale that describes the problem acted out rather than expressed as a question. Many of the questions a manager might raise in the course of a day can be used in this fashion. In fact, a few of the cases presented in this book were generated in this fashion. If a manager asks, for example, "What can I do with an ordinarily good employee who will not take orders from one particular head nurse?" you can surely make up a two- or three-paragraph "short story" featuring an employee's unwillingness to respond to a supervisor's orders.

Fact in Fictional Form

When writing up cases based on actual events, be sure to fictionalize your material. Write in such a way that no actual person can be identified. Do not name specific organizations known to you—especially your own organization—and never describe an actual organization, department, or other setting so accurately that the people involved can be identified without being named. Make up names for your characters, and you should indeed consider them to be characters, just as though you were writing fiction.

Invent names for institutions, and consider altering institutional characteristics such as size, affiliation, and elements of organizational structure to further obscure the source of your material.

If an actual happening you would like to use as a case proves to be unique, so odd, unusual, or dramatic that the participants could still be identified no matter how they were disguised, then forget it. It is better to let an even excellent example go unused than to run the risk of invading someone's privacy.

For each case you write you should be able to pose the central issue, the main problem or topic of the case, in the form of a relatively concise question. For example, the question "How can I get an employee to do a particular task when this person thinks I should really be doing it myself?" advances the central issue of Case 33, "It's His Job, Not Mine." Having thus clearly identified the central issue, proceed to weave your fictional tale to show the development of the problem in a brief scene (as opposed to simply restating the question).

The following are a few more samples of the kinds of questions that lend themselves to the creation of cases:

- "How should I handle an employee who becomes disturbed and resentful when reprimanded?"
- "What should I do with an employee who continues to repeat mistakes after having been spoken to about them several times?"

- "What can I do with an employee who I know can do better but refuses to try?"
- "How should I deal with an employee who behaves flippantly over an error that is potentially quite serious?"
- "How can I get higher management to follow through on problems that desperately need attention?"
- "How can I keep myself from being trapped in the middle when dealing with two different bosses?"

The supply of questions that lend themselves to the development of case studies is essentially endless. In addition to capturing questions that occur to you personally, you need only to listen to employees, managers, customers, visitors, and others. Everyone has questions from time to time, and many questions, properly simplified, can become cases.

Keeping It Simple

Simplify your material, sticking to just those things you need to develop the issue at the heart of the case appropriately. In none but the most elementary of management problems can we hope to capture all of the available information; in most instances we cannot do so without generating cases that are far too long and complicated for practical use. This is especially true of problems concerning people. There are many sides to most people problems, and much of the available information is subjective.

Sticking to the central issue, provide a few pertinent facts. Also, if you believe it would be helpful—as it usually is in cases involving people problems—insert a few words of observation or insight relative to a person's characteristics or manner of behavior. A bit of character description can provide the user of the case with some insight into the kinds of human relations problems that might be involved.

In general, the depth of information used in a case should be such that the reader can clearly identify the central issue and deal with that issue while filling in minor information gaps with reasonable assumptions.

The first case or two that you write may perhaps take more time than you believe the process is worth. You may find, however, that writing cases is much like using cases—and in fact much like making decisions—in that your performance improves with practice. The more you do, the better you become at doing it.

INDEX